THE ELECTIONS OF 2004

Edited by
Michael Nelson
Rhodes College

A Division of Congressional Quarterly Inc.
Washington, D.C.

CQ Press
1255 22nd Street, N.W., Suite 400
Washington, D.C. 20037

202-729-1900; toll-free: 1-866-4CQ-PRESS (1-866-427-7737)

www.cqpress.com

Cover design by McGaughy Design, Centreville, Virginia

Printed and bound in the United States of America

09 08 07 06 05 5 4 3 2 1

♾ The paper used in this publication exceeds the requirements of the American National Standard for Information Sciences—Permanence of Paper for Printed Library Materials, ANSI Z39.48-1992.

LIBRARY OF CONGRESS CATALOGING-IN-PUBLICATION DATA

The elections of 2004 / edited by Michael Nelson.
p. cm.
Includes bibliographical references.
ISBN 1-56802-834-2 (pbk. : alk. paper)
1. Presidents—United States—Election—2004. 2. United States. Congress—Elections, 2004. 3. Elections—United States. 4. United States—Politics and government—2001- I. Nelson, Michael.
II. Title.

JK5262004 .E64 2005
324.973'0931—dc22

2005002867

To my mother and the memory of my father,
who quickened my interest in politics and supported me in my study of it

Contents

- Chapter 3: Gerald M. Pomper describes and analyzes what happened in the general election campaign and why; he also suggests ways to improve the electoral process.
- Chapter 4: Nicole Mellow interprets voting behavior in the 2004 elections and finds that Bush and the Republicans appealed to voters' desire for security more successfully than did Kerry and the Democrats.
- Chapter 5: Matthew Robert Kerbel critically appraises the role of the media in the elections, devoting special care to the growing importance of the Internet.
- Chapter 6: Marian Currinder reviews and analyzes the role of money in the 2004 elections, the first ones to be held since the passage of the Bipartisan Campaign Reform Act of 2002.
- Chapter 7: Paul J. Quirk and Sean C. Matheson weigh the presidential election of 2004 against three criteria that are important for successful presidential governance: the winning candidate's qualifications, commitments, and support.
- Chapter 8: Gary C. Jacobson explains the results of the 2004 congressional elections in terms of the growing ideological polarization of the parties.
- Chapter 9: Wilson Carey McWilliams interprets the meaning of the elections in the broad context of national politics and culture.

Many thanks go to these contributors, some of whom—Jacobson, Kerbel, and Quirk and Matheson—are familiar names from earlier books in this series, and others who are new members of the team—Burden, Currinder, McWilliams, Mellow, and Pomper. Pomper and McWilliams' own books on elections have been justly praised for more than a quarter century, and I am pleased beyond measure to welcome them to this collection.

Thanks also to the outstanding editorial, production, and sales teams at CQ Press for the assurance, skill, and helpfulness with which they treated this book: Brenda Carter, Colleen Ganey, Nancy Geltman, James Headley, Charisse Kiino, Gwenda Larsen, Sabra Bissette Ledent, and Robin Surratt. Aware of the quadrennial burdens that the writing and editing of these books impose on family life, I thank Linda, my wife, and Michael and Sam, our sons, for being patient, loving, and supportive.

Michael Nelson
January 2005

Contributors

About the Editor

Michael Nelson is professor of political science at Rhodes College. More than forty of his articles have been anthologized in works of political science, history, and English composition, and he has won national writing awards for articles on music and baseball. His recent books include *Governing Gambling: Politics and Policy in State, Tribe, and Nation* (with John Lyman Mason, 2001); *The Evolving Presidency: Addresses, Cases, Essays, Letters, Reports, Resolutions, Transcripts, and Other Landmark Documents, 1787–2004* (2nd ed., 2004); and *The Presidency and the Political System* (8th ed., 2005).

About the Contributors

Barry C. Burden is associate professor of government at Harvard University. His research on U.S. politics emphasizes electoral politics and representation. He has written about partisanship and split-ticket voting, minor-party campaigns, public attitudes toward political leaders, congressional politics, candidate strategies, and voter turnout. He is coauthor with David C. Kimball of *Why Americans Split Their Tickets: Campaigns, Competition, and Divided Government* (2002) and editor of *Uncertainty in American Politics* (2003). Burden has also published articles in the *American Political Science Review, American Journal of Political Science, British Journal of Political Science, Legislative Studies Quarterly, Political Science Quarterly, Electoral Studies,* and elsewhere.

Marian Currinder is assistant professor of political science at the College of Charleston. Her research focuses on Congress and institutional change, congressional party organizations, and campaign finance. Her work has been published in *Legislative Studies Quarterly* and *State and Local Government Review.* She was a 2003–2004 APSA congressional fellow.

Gary C. Jacobson is professor of political science at the University of California, San Diego, where he has taught since 1979. He previously taught at Trinity College, the University of California at Riverside, Yale University, and Stanford University. Jacobson specializes in the study of U.S. elections, parties, interest groups, and Congress. He is the author of *Money in Congressional Elections, The Politics of Congressional Elections* (6th ed., 2004), and *The Electoral Origins of Divided Government: Competition in U.S.*

House Elections, 1946–1988 (1990). He is coauthor with Samuel Kernell of *Strategy and Choice in Congressional Elections* (2nd ed., 1983) and *The Logic of American Politics* (3rd ed., 2006). Jacobson is a fellow of the American Academy of Arts and Sciences.

Matthew Robert Kerbel is professor of political science at Villanova University, where he specializes in media politics. He is the author of four books and numerous articles about the media, campaigns, and the presidency, including *If It Bleeds, It Leads: An Anatomy of Television News* (2000), *Remote and Controlled: Media Politics in a Cynical Age* (2nd ed., 1999), and *Edited for Television: CNN, ABC, and American Presidential Elections* (2nd ed., 1998). His interest in media politics derives from his previous work as a television news writer for public broadcasting in New York and as a radio news reporter.

Sean C. Matheson is assistant professor of political science and international relations at Knox College. A contributor to *The Elections of 1996* and *The Elections of 2000,* his research is divided between presidential impeachment and post-genocide reconstruction, particularly in Rwanda. He is currently completing a manuscript comparing the impeachment efforts and proceedings of Andrew Johnson, Richard Nixon, and Bill Clinton.

Wilson Carey McWilliams is professor of political science at Rutgers University. He is the author of *The Idea of Fraternity in America* (1973) and *Beyond the Politics of Disappointment? American Elections, 1980–1998* (1999). He is a frequent contributor to *Commonweal* and other journals of opinion.

Nicole Mellow is assistant professor of political science at Williams College, where she teaches classes on U.S. political development, the presidency, political parties, and social change. She has published articles on gender and politics and on education policy. She is currently completing the provisionally titled *Unfinished Nation: Regional Coalitions and Party Conflict in Postwar America,* which examines regional sources of partisanship.

Gerald M. Pomper is the Board of Governors Professor of Political Science (emeritus) at the Eagleton Institute of Politics at Rutgers University. He also held visiting professorships at Tel-Aviv, Oxford, Northeastern, and Australian National Universities. He was the editor and coauthor of a quadrennial series on national elections from 1976 to 2000, the last of which was *The Election of 2000.* His latest book is *Ordinary Heroes and American Democracy* (2004), which was nominated for the Pulitzer Prize.

Paul J. Quirk holds the Phil Lind Chair in U.S. Politics and Representation at the University of British Columbia. He has published widely on the presidency, Congress, public opinion, and public policymaking. He received the 2003 Aaron Wildavsky Enduring Contribution Award of the Public Policy Section of the American Political Science Association. He is currently coediting *Congress and the American Democracy: Institutions and Performance* and is coauthor of *Deliberative Choices: Debating Public Policy in Congress.*

1

The Setting: George W. Bush, Majority President

Michael Nelson

What does it mean to claim, as the title of this chapter does, that George W. Bush is a majority president? In the narrow sense, it means that he won more than half the electoral votes in the 2004 presidential election: 286 for Bush, 251 for his Democratic opponent, Sen. John F. Kerry of Massachusetts.[1] Bush also won a majority of the national popular vote: 62.0 million (50.8 percent) to Kerry's 59.0 million (48.3 percent), the first time in sixteen years that any candidate for president has secured a popular majority.[2] Equally important, the president's party retained control of both houses of Congress, increasing the size of the Republican majority by three in the House of Representatives and four in the Senate. The across-the-board victory earned by the president and his party is what allowed Vice President Richard B. Cheney to declare after the election that Bush had run "forthrightly on a clear agenda for the nation's future, and the nation responded by giving him a mandate." [3] Bush expressed the same sentiment in different words. "I earned capital in the campaign, political capital," he declared in a postelection news conference, "and now I intend to spend it." The president then added, "I've got the will of the people at my back . . . , and that's what I intend to tell the Congress." [4]

Bush is the fifth president to be elected to a second term in the post–World War II era. Each of his victorious predecessors—Dwight D. Eisenhower (1956), Richard Nixon (1972), Ronald Reagan (1984), and Bill Clinton (1996)—was reelected by a much larger margin than Bush. But in every case, theirs were "lonely landslides" in which the president did well but his party's congressional candidates did not. In no instance did the president's party do what Bush and the Republicans did in 2004: gain additional seats in both the House and the Senate while securing reelection for the president. Nor did Eisenhower, Nixon, Reagan, or Clinton begin his second term as the head of a united party government—that is, one in which the same party controls not just the White House but also both houses of Congress.

Eisenhower, who liked working with the Democrats' centrist congressional leaders more than with his own party's conservative leadership, was actually pleased when the Republicans lost one seat in the Senate and another in the House in 1956, preserving the Republicans' minority status in Congress even as he was winning 57.4 percent of the popular vote and 86.1 percent of the electoral vote.[5] Nixon, Reagan, and Clinton wished their parties' congressional candidates well but did little else. Each of them was preoccupied with maximizing the size of his own victory, which meant neglecting the rest of the ticket.[6] Although Nixon won 60.7 percent of the popular vote and 96.7 percent of the electoral vote in 1972, his party lost two seats in the Senate. Reagan's personal victory in 1984 was equally grand (58.8 percent of the popular vote and 97.6 percent of the electoral vote), but the Republicans again lost two Senate seats. Clinton's 49.2 percent of the popular vote and 69.3 percent of the electoral vote were impressive tallies in the three-candidate election of 1996, but the Democratic ranks in Congress were reduced by two in the Senate.

Bush approached the elections of 2004 in an entirely different way. "Don't give me a lonely victory," he reportedly told his political strategists. "I don't want what Nixon had. I don't want what Reagan had." According to one Bush aide, "He was explicit that he doesn't want to win with 55 percent and have a 51–49 Senate. He wants to expand the governing coalition." [7] The fruits of Bush's efforts were apparent on election day, when the Republicans secured a 55–44 Republican majority in the Senate and a 232–202 majority in the House, the largest number of Republican House members elected since 1946.[8]

By any standard, the elections of 2004 made George W. Bush a majority president in the narrow sense—that is, as the head of a united party government for at least the first two years of his second term. But there is another, more important sense in which Bush can also be described as a majority president: he is the leader, as well as one of the builders, of the nation's new majority party.

This is a controversial claim. As Nicole Mellow observes in Chapter 4, political scientists and journalists have grown comfortable with the idea that although the New Deal Democratic majority forged in the 1930s has atrophied in recent decades, nothing has risen to replace it. The United States, many believe, no longer has a majority party. Instead, it has "dealigned" (that is, become a country in which political parties do not matter very much) or deadlocked, becoming a "49–49" country in which the parties matter a great deal but are evenly matched. But the elections of 2004 prompt a reconsideration of this belief. Since 1968, Republican nominees have won seven of ten presidential elections, cumulatively amassing 3,381 electoral votes (62.8 percent) to the Democrats' 1,949 (36.2 percent).[9] Neither of the two Democrats to be elected president in this period, Bill Clinton of Arkansas and Jimmy Carter of Georgia, exceeded the 50.8 percent of the national popular vote that Bush won in 2004 in any of their elections. Carter, who received 50.1 percent in 1976, is the only Democrat since Lyndon B. Johnson in 1964 to win a popular vote majority.

Johnson, like Carter and Clinton, was a southerner; indeed, the only Democrat to be elected president in the past half century who was not from the South was John F. Kennedy of Massachusetts in 1960. Yet the talent pool of Democratic southerners from which the party can draw its future presidential nominees has steadily shrunk. By 2005, only four of the region's eleven governors and four of its twenty-two senators were Democrats—historic lows for the party that, as recently as 1960, consistently won every southern gubernatorial and senatorial election, almost without exception. In 1976, when Carter was elected president, the Democratic Party could choose among fifteen southern Democrats in the Senate and eight Democratic governors when nominating its candidate for president. In 1992 fifteen Democratic senators were from the South, and Clinton was one of seven southern Democratic governors.

The new Republican majority extends to Congress as well as the presidency. The party's victories in the 2004 congressional contests marked the sixth consecutive election in which the Republicans won control of both the House and the Senate. In 1946 and 1952, the only other congressional elections since the 1920s in which the Republicans were victorious, they lost their majority just two years later. By contrast, the Republican takeover that took place in 1994 has lasted for more than a decade. As for the third branch of the federal government, the judiciary, it also has become a Republican bastion. Control of the presidency and the Senate has enabled the Republicans to choose a large majority of judges at all levels of the federal court system. Since 1968, Republican presidents have made nine of eleven Supreme Court appointments (81.8 percent), 218 of 335 federal appeals court appointments (65.1 percent), and 834 of 1,342 district court appointments (62.1 percent).[10] More often than not, these judges have interpreted the Constitution in the way the presidents who chose them intended.[11]

At the state level, Republicans have enjoyed a majority of governorships since 1994 (twenty-eight of the fifty governors are Republicans as a result of the 2004 elections), and in 2002, for the first time in the post–*Baker v. Carr* era of "one person, one vote" legislative apportionment,[12] they attained a majority of state legislators. Among voters, by 2003 registered Republicans outnumbered registered Democrats in the states that allow party registration.[13] A December 2004 Gallup poll showed Republicans leading Democrats by 37 percent to 32 percent when voters were asked if they identify with a party,[14] constituting "the most Republican electorate America has had since random-sample polling was invented" in the 1930s.[15] Because the share of the electorate that votes Republican typically exceeds the share of Republican self-identifiers by several percentage points, Republicans now outnumber Democrats among regular voters. The dramatic surge in voter turnout from Bush's first election to his second—from 54.3 percent of eligible voters in 2000 to 60.7 percent in 2004[16]—helped him secure 11.5 million additional votes, the largest increase ever in popular votes for a presidential candidate from one election to the next. Surges in voter turnout, such as those that occurred in 1860 and during the 1930s, often mark the appearance of a new majority party.[17]

The emergence of a Republican majority has understandably been difficult to recognize.[18] In contrast to previous majority coalitions, such as the Civil War Republicans and the New Deal Democrats, the new Republican majority is small rather than large. Geographically, Republican strength is grounded in the twenty-nine states that Bush carried in both 2000 and 2004 (now commonly known, thanks to the television networks' election night maps, as the "red states"). These states constitute all or most of every region of the country except the Northeast, the Pacific coast, and the upper Midwest. Underscoring the broad-based nature of the Republican victory in 2004, every House and Senate seat that the Republicans took from the Democrats was in a state carried by Bush. Three-fourths of the senators from the red states are Republicans, as are two-thirds of the representatives.[19] Nineteen of the twenty-nine red state governors are also Republicans.

Demographically, the Republican majority rests mainly on a foundation of white men and married women who live in suburban or rural communities. In addition, Bush's sustained efforts to win support from Hispanic and elderly voters were rewarded with strong showings in 2004. Ideologically, Republicans tend to be philosophically conservative on most issues of culture, economics, and national security. In religious faith and practice, they are, for the most part, church-going Christians. In socioeconomic terms, the Republicans have what John Judis and colleagues describe as a "Brooks Brothers and Wal-Mart" coalition, including majorities of both those white voters who report incomes of $50,000 or more and those who lack a college degree.[20]

To say that the Republican majority is small is not to say that it is fragile. As Gary C. Jacobson shows in Chapter 8, the United States has entered into an era of polarized politics in which conservative voters, activists, and candidates have clustered in the Republican Party and liberal voters, activists, and candidates in the Democratic Party much more consistently than in the past. As recently as the 1970s, the GOP had a significant liberal wing and the Democrats included a substantial number of conservatives. Seeing no dramatic difference between the parties, many voters were inclined to split their tickets in each election and to change their loyalties from one election to the next. But as the parties became more polarized through the 1980s and 1990s, these voters increasingly chose sides and their loyalties hardened. Going into the 2004 elections, the Republicans' majority in the House was small but solid—so solid, Jacobson reports, that the Democrats had no realistic chance to win the modest number of additional seats they needed to take control.[21] In Senate elections, Republicans enjoy a different advantage. The constitutional mandate that every state, regardless of population, be represented equally in the Senate benefits the party that dominates the most states, which in recent years has been the GOP.

The new Republican majority did not come about through a dramatic realigning election, such as the 1860 contest between Abraham Lincoln and Stephen A. Douglas that helped to make the Republicans the nation's majority party for many years or the 1932 election in which Franklin D. Roosevelt's landslide victory over Herbert Hoover ushered in the recent era of Democratic dominance.[22] Instead, there has been a "rolling" (or to use the term preferred by political scientists, a "secular") realignment,[23] tied mostly to the gradual transformation of the conservative South from a pillar of the Democratic coalition to a mainstay of the Republican majority and, in response, the transformation of the liberal Northeast from the most Republican to the most Democratic region of the country.[24]

Because the South is larger and has been growing rapidly in population and the Northeast is smaller and in relative decline, the parties' exchange of regional bases has benefited the Republicans.[25] Sweeping the South's 153 electoral votes now puts the Republican presidential nominee well over halfway to victory, an advantage that was not enjoyed by Democratic candidates when the South was solidly Democratic but had only 120–125 electoral votes.[26] Remarkably, even though John Kerry named a southerner, Sen. John Edwards of North Carolina, as his vice-presidential running mate in 2004, the Democrats saw so little opportunity for victory in the South that they made no serious effort to win even Edwards's home state. As in 2000, Bush carried about 80 percent of counties in the South, the first candidate to win more than 1,000 southern counties in consecutive elections since FDR.[27]

Viewed this way, the narrow Republican victories in 2000 and 2004 speak more impressively about the GOP's majority status than it may seem on first inspection. To be sure, Bush's margins in both 2000 and 2004 were slight. (Famously, he received a half million fewer popular votes in 2000 than his Democratic opponent, Vice President Al Gore.) But they came in the face of short-term political conditions that, absent an enduring Republican majority in the country, probably would have cost Bush both elections. In 2000 a prosperous nation at peace chose Bush over the vice president of the popular two-term Democratic administration. Four years later, a majority of voters said they were either "angry" or "dissatisfied" with the Bush administration, thought the condition of the economy was "not good" or "poor," and believed that the war Bush launched against Iraq in 2003 had failed to make the United States "more secure." [28] They reelected Bush anyway. Put another way, an electorate that told pollsters the country was moving in the "right direction" after eight years of Democratic rule elected a Republican president in 2000, and an electorate that thought the country was on the "wrong track" after four years of Republican rule reelected him in 2004.[29]

Some have argued that Bush's reelection was an artifact of the public's gratitude for his leadership in the aftermath of the September 11, 2001, terrorist attacks on the United States and, therefore, is of little lasting political significance. In truth, far from being a passing effect of 9/11, the durability of the Republican majority is attested by its continuity. With one exception, every state that Bush carried in 2000 supported him again in 2004.[30] As Alan Abramowitz reports, "By far the strongest predictor of George W. Bush's vote in 2004 was his vote in 2000"—even though the issues that dominated the two elections shifted radically from domestic policy in 2000 to war and terrorism in 2004.[31] And, as often has been the case historically, in 2004 the nation's minority party fought the election on issues defined by the majority party. Kerry ran less as the champion of a Democratic agenda than as the anti-Bush, promising mainly to pursue Bush's war on terror more effectively and to make Bush's tax cuts fairer. Bush ran as himself, defending his conservative Republican record and promising more of the same. As Gerald Pomper points out in Chapter 3, on election day the great majority of Bush's votes came from people who said they were for him, while nearly half of Kerry's votes came from people who said they were against Bush.

The relative success of third parties in several recent presidential elections and, equally important, their failure in 2004 offer another indication that a realignment has been under way. Historically, realignments like the ones that occurred in the 1860s and 1930s have been preceded by periods of rising support for third parties, which end once the realignment is complete.[32] For example, the 1910s and 1920s saw a flurry of strong third party activity,[33] but in the nine elections that took place from 1932 to 1964, when the New Deal Democratic majority was strong, the average share of the national popular vote received by all third party candidates was only 1.6 percent per election. The average share third parties received in the nine elections from 1968 to 2000, however, was 6.7 percent, four times as large. This average was swelled by the candidacies of George C. Wallace in 1968 and H. Ross Perot in 1992 and 1996. By 2004, most Wallace and Perot voters had migrated to the GOP.[34] Between them, Bush and Kerry received 99.1 percent of the national popular vote in the 2004 election, and third party candidates only 0.9 percent.

How the Republican Majority Emerged

How has the rolling (or secular) realignment that has slowly brought about a narrow but enduring Republican majority in national politics evolved over the years?

In some ways, the story begins in 1948, even though the Democratic majority that Roosevelt built in the 1930s was then in the midst of winning its fifth consecutive presidential election. FDR's New Deal coalition was a complex assemblage, constituted differently in different parts of the country. In the North, it rested on the support of groups that Roosevelt had helped to attract into the Democratic fold: blue-collar workers, especially members of labor unions; Catholic and Jewish voters, many of them with strong ethnic loyalties; ideological liberals; and African Americans. Support from these groups had been essential in toppling the Republican majority that prevailed from the 1860s to the 1920s—a majority that had been especially strong in the Northeast.

The southern part of the New Deal coalition—essentially, every white voter in a region where, in most counties, only whites could vote—was one that Roosevelt inherited. The South had been solidly Democratic since the

Civil War and Reconstruction era, when southern whites developed a strong antipathy toward the occupying Republicans and their agenda of civil rights for the newly freed slaves. During the many years that the South was a Democratic bastion, Republicans had to win about two-thirds of House and Senate seats outside the South in order to control Congress.

Despite the New Deal Democrats' majority status, a fault line ran through their coalition: the interests of blacks and southern whites were clearly not harmonious. As long as African Americans did not press a civil rights agenda on the federal government, this fault line remained latent and, therefore, politically insignificant. But in the aftermath of World War II, returning black veterans who had fought against racism and tyranny abroad increasingly demanded federal protection for their civil rights at home. Northern liberals and union leaders supported these demands. Forced against his will to choose between the northern and southern wings of his party, President Harry S. Truman reluctantly accepted a strong civil rights plank in the 1948 Democratic platform. He won the election, but only at the price of a crack appearing in the solidly Democratic South. Although Roosevelt had carried every southern state in all four of his elections, in 1948 four of the five Deep South states—Alabama, Louisiana, Mississippi, and South Carolina—cast their electoral votes for Democratic governor Strom Thurmond of South Carolina, the third party nominee of the angry southern Democrats who had walked out of their party's pro–civil rights convention.

All of these Deep South states returned to the Democratic fold in the 1952 and 1956 presidential elections, when the party muted its commitment to civil rights. But a new crack then appeared in the Solid South, this one along economic lines. The Republican candidate in both elections, Dwight Eisenhower, did well in the six states of the Peripheral South, where racial issues mattered somewhat less and, as metropolitan areas began to grow rapidly after World War II, the GOP's pro-business economic and defense policies mattered more. Eisenhower carried Florida, Tennessee, Texas, and Virginia both times he ran. Of the eleven southern states, therefore, all but two, Arkansas and North Carolina, had now left the Democratic fold at least once in a postwar presidential election.

The Republican breakthroughs in the South proved to be enduring. In 1960 the GOP presidential candidate, Vice President Richard Nixon, lost the election but carried three Peripheral South states: Florida, Tennessee, and Virginia. Four years later, Sen. Barry Goldwater of Arizona, an opponent of strong federal civil rights legislation, won all five Deep South states: Alabama, Georgia, Louisiana, Mississippi, and South Carolina. (The only other state Goldwater carried in losing overwhelmingly to President Lyndon Johnson was Arizona.) Starting with Goldwater, Republican nominees have outpolled their Democratic opponents among southern white voters in every presidential election since 1964.[35]

The 1968 election took place in a changed political environment. Because of the Civil Rights Act of 1964 and the Voting Rights Act of 1965, both of them championed by Democratic presidents,[36] African Americans in the South were newly enfranchised and enjoyed federal protection against many forms of racial discrimination. In response, a strong southern Democratic opponent of civil rights, former Alabama governor George Wallace, bid for the support of southern whites and northern blue-collar workers who felt threatened by these and a host of other recent developments—"ghetto riots, campus riots, street crime, anti–Vietnam [War] marches, poor people's marches, drugs, pornography, welfarism, rising taxes, all with a common theme: the breakdown of family and social discipline, of order, of concepts of duty, of respect for law, of public and private morality." [37] Between them, the Republican Nixon, who carried most of the Peripheral South, and the third party candidate Wallace, who nearly swept the Deep South, dominated the region. Vice President Hubert H. Humphrey carried only Texas—the poorest showing in the South for any Democratic presidential candidate since Reconstruction. In the rest of the country, Nixon and Wallace cut into Humphrey's support among culturally conservative Catholic, ethnic, and blue-collar voters, who, like white southerners, had been mainstays of the New Deal Democratic coalition but who also felt threatened by racial and social disorder.

During his first term as president, Nixon labored to bring the 13.5 percent of voters who had supported Wallace—about half of them in the South and about half in the North—into his 1972 reelection coalition. Nixon's efforts to use issues such as law and order and opposition to school bussing to graft white Catholic and working-class Democrats onto the traditional middle-class Republican base were rewarded on election day. Nixon swept the South, carrying every state in the region with majorities ranging from 65.3 percent to 78.2 percent. With the support of 52 percent of Catholic voters and 54 percent of union members and their spouses, he swept the rest of the country as well, losing only Massachusetts and the District of Columbia to his Democratic opponent, Sen. George S. McGovern of South Dakota.

The success of Republican presidential candidates in the South began to be echoed in other southern elections.[38] As Earl Black and Merle Black observe, "Modern Republicanism came to the South from the top down." [39] The infusion of millions of loyally Democratic African American voters into the southern electorate in the late 1960s made the party more liberal and drove many conservative whites into the Republican Party. Subsequently, the GOP's economic, social, and national security conservatism replaced racial issues as the party's main lure. The number of Republican senators in the twenty-two-member southern delegation rose from none as late as 1960 to three in 1966, seven in 1972, eleven in 1982, thirteen in 1994, and eighteen in 2004. Similar gains occurred in southern elections to the House of Representatives, where the Republican ranks grew from 7 percent of southern members in 1960 to 22 percent in 1966, 29 percent in 1982, 51 percent in 1994, and 63 percent in 2004. In time, Republicans began to compete successfully for state offices in the South, such as governor and legislator. The number of Republican governors in the eleven southern states increased from none in 1960 to seven in 2004. Republicans controlled none of the twenty-two southern state legislative houses as recently as the late 1960s; they now control eleven. As in the voting for president, the Republicans' gains in congressional and state elections generally came first in the Peripheral South and then in the Deep South.

The Republican growth that has taken place since the 1980s among erstwhile white Democrats in the South and in other regions owes much to Ronald Reagan. Nixon's scandal-spawned resignation in 1974 and the Democrats' nomination of a southern moderate, Jimmy Carter, for president in 1976 had slowed the GOP's progress. Carter, the former governor of Georgia, was able to carry ten southern states on the basis of regional pride; as a born-again Southern Baptist, he also won the support of most evangelical Christian voters. But, forced to the left as president by his liberal party in Congress, Carter alienated his home region and many of his coreligionists. White evangelicals, who had not been especially active in politics during most of the twentieth century, were roused to organized opposition by a Carter administration proposal to withdraw tax-exempt status from the mostly white Christian schools to which many of them sent their children.[40] In addition, for the first time in history, evangelical Protestants put aside their long-standing suspicion of the Vatican and forged an alliance with conservative Catholics to fight against abortion, which the Supreme Court had legalized, with strong Democratic approval, in 1973. Other voters were drawn to a different grass-roots conservative cause: cutting taxes. In June 1978, Californians overwhelmingly adopted Proposition 13, a dramatic property tax reduction measure that conservative activists had placed on their state's ballot by petition. Similar measures quickly appeared on sixteen other state ballots that November, and twelve were approved. In Washington, Rep. Jack Kemp of New York and Sen. William Roth of Delaware rallied their Republican colleagues behind a proposal to reduce federal income taxes by 30 percent.

Reagan capitalized on all of these developments, as well as on a stagnant economy and a decline in American power abroad, when he ran against Carter in 1980. To spur economic growth, Reagan supported the Kemp-Roth tax cuts, which appealed not just to well-to-do Republicans but also to many blue-collar workers, who increasingly had come to believe that, instead of benefiting from most federal social programs, they were footing the bill for welfare recipients who did not want to work. Reagan also called for economic deregulation, a cause that united large corporations with small businesses. In the past, labor unions would have persuaded their members that Reagan's policies, however appealing they might sound, were not in workers' interests and ought to be opposed. But unions, which had represented about 40 percent of the American workforce in 1950, represented only 20 percent in 1980, with further declines (to 13 percent by 2004) in store.[41]

Reagan's appeal to the voters went beyond economic conservatism. To restore America's position in the world, he promised dramatic increases in defense spending and a more assertive posture toward the Soviet Union in the ongoing cold war. Many southerners, whose regional economy relied in part on military bases and defense contractors, and many northern ethnic voters, whose ancestral homelands in Central and Eastern Europe had been occupied by the Soviets since World War II, embraced his positions. Reagan's strong rhetoric opposing abortion and upholding traditional values appealed to many Christian voters across denominational lines. These policies and others, including his opposition to gun control, helped Reagan to open a "gender gap" in which the Republicans increased their support among men without losing ground among women.[42] In all, Democratic pollster Stanley Greenberg concedes, Reagan's "interwoven ideas proved relevant and expansive enough to convince a growing majority of Catholic working-class voters in the North, virtually all white people in the South, but particularly the Evangelicals, small and big businessmen, and the most economically privileged that there was both advantage and hope in the Reagan Revolution." [43]

Reagan not only won by a landslide in 1980, securing the largest electoral vote majority in history against an incumbent president, but he also had long coattails in the congressional elections.[44] This was no accident: he and several hundred Republican candidates for Congress had gathered in Washington during the campaign to publicly pledge their mutual commitment to the GOP's conservative platform. Once in office, they were able to enact much of Reagan's agenda, especially in the areas of economic and national security policy. In strictly partisan terms, however, despite Reagan's easy reelection in 1984 and the election of his vice president, George Bush, to succeed him in 1988, the Republicans could claim only to have drawn even with the Democrats. Although Bush won the presidential contest handily, the GOP lost ground in the 1988 elections for the House, the Senate, the state legislatures, and the state governorships—the first time this had ever happened in a national election. Congress remained strongly Democratic, and Bush was defeated for reelection in 1992 by Bill Clinton, the governor of Arkansas.

Bush's defeat had seemed almost unimaginable from the vantage point of 1991. His administration had marked the collapse of the Soviet Union in 1990 and, soon afterward, had rapidly rolled back an Iraqi invasion of Kuwait in the first Gulf War. For a time, Bush's approval rating among voters approached 90 percent. Ironically, however, these foreign policy triumphs contributed to his undoing. As Mellow points out in Chapter 4, in the cold war era national security issues had constituted the Republicans' most consistent area of political strength. But the victories in the cold war and the Persian Gulf dramatically reduced the salience of these issues to voters, freeing them in the 1992 election to vent their disappointment with an economy that seemed to be performing poorly.[45]

Clinton's victory cheered the Democrats temporarily, but it turned out to be the exception that demonstrated the rule—namely, that the Republican march toward majority status was still under way. His 43.2 percent of the national popular vote was no greater than the average percentage earned by Democratic nominees in the previous six presidential elections, of which they had lost five. It was enough to defeat Bush, but it left 18.9 percent—the share won by third party candidate Ross Perot, a wealthy businessman—up for grabs. In the 1994 midterm elections, Perot voters, many of them working-class white men who were unhappy with Clinton's decision to yoke his presidency to the Democratic Party's liberal congressional leaders and its core feminist, minority, and anti-gun constituency groups, broke strongly in favor of Republican candidates for Congress. Their support enabled the GOP to win a sweeping victory and take control of both the House and Senate after forty years of Democratic domination. For the first time since 1872, the Republicans won a majority of seats in both the South and the rest of the country. In state elections, the number of Republican governors rose from nineteen to thirty, including George W. Bush, the newly elected governor of Texas. Clinton successfully adjusted to the results by moving toward the political center, declaring in his 1996 State of the Union address that "the era of big government is over." [46] But the chief political legacy of his presidency was losing Congress to the Republicans and never winning it back. Despite being reelected in 1996, Clinton governed with a Republican Congress for the final six of his eight years as president. In 2000 his vice president, Al Gore, was defeated by Governor Bush.

George W. Bush and the New Republican Majority

From the start of Bush's first term as president, he was a party builder. After two important milestones in the term—the first when he was declared the winner of the bitterly contested election of 2000, and the second the September 11 terrorist attacks—Bush was counseled by many political pundits (and Democrats) to govern in a broadly bipartisan manner. Both times, however, he refused to do so, choosing instead to pursue a conservative Republican agenda of dramatically cutting taxes, toughening national educational standards, involving faith-based organizations in the administration of federal social programs, promoting oil production in the Alaskan wilderness, restricting certain forms of abortion, opposing gay marriage, limiting embryonic stem cell research, banning human cloning, developing a national missile defense system, implementing business-friendly regulatory policies, withdrawing from controversial environmental and military treaties, and, after 9/11, launching a "war on terror" that included invasions of Afghanistan and Iraq. To be sure, Bush adopted some policies traditionally supported by liberal Democrats, including expanded farm subsidies, increased tariffs on steel imports, demographically diverse appointments to his staff and cabinet, and a new prescription drug benefit for Medicare recipients. In making these exceptions, however, Bush's purpose was to increase support for the GOP in particular regions of the country (specifically, the farm belt and the steel-reliant states of Ohio, Pennsylvania, and West Virginia) or among specific groups of voters, especially senior citizens and Hispanics.

In preparing for the 2002 midterm elections, Bush recruited strong Republican challengers to oppose incumbent Democratic senators, raised $141 million for his party by making dozens of appearances at fund-raising events, and campaigned ardently for Republican candidates throughout the country. The risk Bush ran was daunting. No Republican president had ever seen his party gain seats in Congress in a midterm election, and not since 1882 had any president's party taken control of the Senate away from the other party at midterm. Yet Bush bid to do both on behalf of his fellow Republicans. In addition, Bush knew that political campaigning typically reduces the president's approval rating because it brings his partisanship into sharp relief. But he regarded that as a price worth paying in order to help the GOP. In all, Bush threw himself into the midterm election on behalf of his party earlier and more energetically than any president in history.

The results of the 2002 elections vindicated Bush's decision to become actively involved in the campaign. The Republicans not only gained six seats in the House, doubling the size of their majority in that chamber, but also added the two seats they needed to take control of the Senate. For the first time since 1954, the president and a majority of members in both houses of Congress were Republicans. Political analysts were quick to describe the historic nature of the GOP victory. Not only did it mark the first time since voters, rather than state legislatures, were empowered to elect senators that the president's party had regained control of the Senate at midterm,[47] but it also was the first election since 1934 in which the president's party gained seats in both houses of Congress in a first-term midterm election. At the state level, 2002 was the first midterm election in which the president's party made gains in the state legislatures. Republicans added about 200 seats instead of losing 350, the average loss at midterm. For the first time since 1952, Republicans outnumbered Democrats in the nation's statehouses.

Analysts were quick to credit Bush with his party's success. An election eve CBS News poll indicated that 50 percent of the voters were basing their decision on their opinion of the president—many more than the 34 percent who had done so in 1990 or the 37 percent who had done so in 1998. Of these 50 percent, 31 percent were pro-Bush and only 19 percent opposed him.[48]

Soon after the 2002 results were in, Bush began to focus on 2004. He had reason to be concerned. As Andrew Busch points out, every previous victor of a disputed election—John Quincy Adams in 1824, Rutherford B. Hayes in 1876, and Benjamin Harrison in 1888—had failed to secure a second term.[49] But Bush instructed his political strategists to plan and execute a campaign that not only would reelect him but also would make the Republican Party "stronger, broader, and better." [50] No president has ever had a more united party on which to build. As Jacobson shows in Chapter 8, Bush consistently enjoyed the highest approval ratings from the voters of his party of any president in the history of polling; even when his overall approval rating hovered around 50 percent, it exceeded 90 percent among Republicans.[51]

Intense partisan support also marked his relationship with the Republican majority in Congress. According to Harold F. Bass, throughout Bush's first term his "party support average [in Congress] was unparalleled" among presidents, earning him a 92 percent party support score in the Senate and an 84 percent party support score in the House.[52] In seeking the GOP nomination for a second term, Bush faced neither an opponent (as Johnson, Nixon, Ford, Carter, and Bush's father did) nor rumors of an opponent (as Clinton did) at any time.

As both the dramatic increase in the president's national popular vote from 2000 to 2004 and the length of his coattails in the 2004 congressional elections indicate, Bush and his campaign team developed and executed a remarkably successful political strategy to secure the across-the-board Republican victory he sought.[53] Just as important to Bush and his party's success as their campaign strategy, however, were the public policies Bush pursued as president.

In foreign policy, Bush's declaration of a prolonged "war on terror" assured that, as was the case during the cold war but not afterward, voters would remain continually attentive to national security issues, traditionally the area of greatest Republican strength. When the first president Bush defeated Iraq in the first Gulf War, he portrayed it as an isolated event. When the second president Bush defeated Iraq in the second Gulf War, he described it as merely one campaign in an ongoing struggle that, like the four decades-long cold war, had no clear end in sight. In characterizing America's foes in the war on terror as the "axis of evil," Bush even evoked Reagan's cold war description of the Soviet Union as the "evil empire."

In domestic policy, Bush was intent on creating new bastions of strength for the GOP with an "ownership society" agenda. During his first term, low mortgage rates enabled more Americans than ever before to own homes, many of them in new subdivisions in the rapidly growing "exurbs," farther out from the city core than the traditional suburbs. On election day 2004, Bush reaped a bonanza of support: voters in ninety-seven of the nation's one hundred fastest-growing counties chose him over Kerry, providing the president with nearly half of his national popular vote majority.[54] During his second term, Bush hopes to increase ownership of stocks and bonds by creating tax-free investment accounts and by reforming Social Security to allow workers to direct a share of their retirement contributions into individual investment accounts. In doing so, he plans to take advantage of the fact that at every level of income, "direct investors"—that is, those who own stock in companies—are more likely to vote Republican than those who are not.[55]

Bush's strongly pro-business tax and regulatory policies energized both large and small companies to support the GOP more ardently in 2004 than ever before, both with campaign contributions and through efforts to rally their employees.[56] He completed the transformation that Republican congressional leaders began after they took control of the House and Senate in 1994, pressuring business groups to stop funding incumbent candidates of both parties and instead to align themselves consistently with the GOP.[57] Having secured his party's financial base, Bush hopes during his second term to weaken one of the Democratic Party's main sources of campaign contributions. His tort reform proposal would cap the size of awards in civil lawsuits, thereby reducing both the income of trial lawyers and, more to the point, their ability to pump large amounts of money into Democratic coffers.

Finally, Bush has successfully identified himself and his party as the chief defenders of traditional social values, both by what he upholds (religious faith, flag-waving patriotism, marriage between a man and a woman, restrictions on abortion, the rights of gun owners) and what he opposes (gay marriage, sexual permissiveness, gun control). According to the Democrat Greenberg, "[Republicans] don't say, 'Vote for us because we're making progress.' They say, 'Vote for our worldview.' "[58] Therein lies a source of enduring Republican strength and, in some cases, of new Republican appeal, especially to socially conservative, pro-military Hispanics.[59] Voters who support a party because they share its values are much less likely to abandon it than voters whose support is based on how well things are going in the economy or the world. Remarkably, Bush handily defeated Kerry, the first Catholic candidate for president since Kennedy in 1960, among Catholic voters.

All of the trends that prepared the way for the new Republican majority to emerge in 2004, and all of George W. Bush's efforts to secure it for the future, have been vital to the GOP's success. Republicans will not win every election in the years to come. They may not even win in 2008. Presidents' second terms almost always have been less successful than their first terms,[60] and winning three elections in a row is notoriously difficult for any party. But the foundation on which the Republican majority stands places it in a strong position to win considerably more elections than it loses. The GOP has become the default setting in American politics.

Notes

1. The votes do not add up to 538, because a Minnesota elector who was pledged to support Kerry voted instead for Sen. John Edwards of North Carolina, Kerry's running mate.
2. United States Elections Project, "Voter Turnout," http://elections.gmu.edu/voter_turnout.htm.
3. Adam Nagourney, "After Kerry Concedes, Bush Cites 'A Duty to Serve All Americans,' " *New York Times,* November 4, 2004.
4. Mike Allen, "Confident Bush Vows to Move Aggressively," *Washington Post,* November 5, 2004, A1.
5. Michael Barone, *Our Country: The Shaping of America from Roosevelt to Reagan* (New York: Free Press, 1990), 280–284.
6. Reagan's indifference to his party's congressional candidates is noted in Erwin C. Hargrove and Michael Nelson, "The Presidency: Reagan and the Cycle of Politics and Policy," in *The Elections of 1984,* ed. Michael Nelson (Washington, D.C.: CQ Press, 1985), 189–213. Clinton's indifference is chronicled in Michael Nelson, "Turbulence and Tranquility in Contemporary American Politics," in *The Elections of 1996,* ed. Michael Nelson (Washington, D.C.: CQ Press, 1997), 44–80.

7. Dan Balz, "GOP Aims for Dominance in '04 Race," *Washington Post,* June 22, 2003; Dan Balz and Mike Allen, "Four More Years Attributed to Rove's Strategy," *Washington Post,* November 7, 2004.
8. In addition, one self-declared independent serves in the House and one in the Senate. Both independent members caucus with the Democrats.
9. Third party candidates, notably George C. Wallace in 1968, received the other 1.0 percent.
10. Calculated from data provided by the Federal Judicial Center (www.fjc.gov).
11. Cass Sunstein and David Schkade, "A Bench Tilting Right," *Washington Post,* October 30, 2004.
12. *Baker v. Carr* (369 U.S. 186 [1962]) ushered in the modern era of state legislatures by in effect requiring that all of a state's legislative districts be equal in population.
13. John Micklethwaite and Adrian Wooldridge, *The Right Nation: Conservative Power in America* (New York: Penguin Press, 2004), 231.
14. Harold F. Bass, "George W. Bush, Presidential Party Leadership Extraordinaire?" *The Forum* 2, no. 4 (2004), www.beprss.com/vol2/iss4/art6/.
15. Michael Barone, "Reshaping the Electorate," *U.S. News and World Report,* November 29, 2004, 32.
16. United States Elections Project, "Voter Turnout."
17. See, for example, V. O. Key Jr., "A Theory of Critical Elections," *Journal of Politics* 17 (1955): 3–18; and Walter Dean Burnham, *Critical Elections and the Mainsprings of American Politics* (New York: Norton, 1970), 7–8.
18. For a prescient early view, see Kevin P. Phillips, *The Emerging Republican Majority* (New Rochelle, N.Y.: Arlington House, 1969).
19. Specifically, forty-four of the fifty-eight senators who represent these states are Republicans, as are 143 of the 218 representatives.
20. National Election Poll exit survey data, www.cnn.com/ELECTION/2004/pages/results,states/US/P/00/epolls.0.html (accessed November 3, 2004). From 2000 to 2004, Bush made large gains among Hispanics (+7 percentage points), voters sixty years and older (+6), and voters who did not graduate from high school (+10). The "Brooks Brothers and Wal-Mart" quotation is from John B. Judis, Rey Teixeira, and Marisa Katz, "30 Years' War," *New Republic,* November 15, 2004.
21. Democrats only needed to gain thirteen seats to win control of the House.
22. Even David Mayhew, a strenuous critic of realignment theory, urges acceptance of a "stripped-down version" that "keeps[s] using the term *realignment* to characterize the two genuine outlier eras of American political history—the 1860s and 1930s." Mayhew, *Electoral Realignment: A Critique of an American Genre* (New Haven, Conn.: Yale University Press, 2002), 162.
23. "Rolling realignment" is the term used by chief George W. Bush political strategist Karl Rove. According to political scientist V. O. Key Jr., a "secular realignment . . . may be regarded as a movement of the members of a population category from party to party that extends over several presidential elections." Key, "Secular Realignment and the Party System," *Journal of Politics* 21 (May 1959), 199.
24. Against FDR, Herbert C. Hoover carried only five states in 1932 and Alfred M. Landon carried only two in 1936: all were in the Northeast. The Northeast was the only region of the country that Thomas E. Dewey won against Harry S. Truman in 1948. By contrast, Kerry carried every northeastern state in 2004, and Gore carried all but New Hampshire in 2000. In this chapter, the South is defined as the eleven states of the old Confederacy and the Northeast as the ten New England and Middle Atlantic states.
25. In the most recent census, the South's population grew 19 percent from 1990 to 2000, nearly double the 11 percent increase in the rest of the country. Earl Black

and Merle Black, *The Rise of Southern Republicans* (Cambridge, Mass.: Harvard University Press, 2002), 4.

26. When FDR swept the South in the 1930s, for example, he received only 121 of the 266 electoral votes he needed to be elected. By contrast, the Northeast then had 139 electoral votes, but now has only 104.
27. Ronald Brownstein, "GOP Has Lock on South, and Democrats Can't Find Key," *Los Angeles Times*, December 15, 2004.
28. National Election Poll exit survey.
29. "Real Clear Politics Poll Averages: Right Direction-Wrong Track/Direction of Country," http://realclearpolitics.com/Presidential_04/direction_of_country.html.
30. New Hampshire supported Bush in 2000 but not in 2004. More than offsetting this loss, however, two larger states that Bush lost in 2000, Iowa and New Mexico, supported him in 2004.
31. Alan Abramowitz, "Terrorism, Gay Marriage, and Incumbency: Explaining the Republican Victory in the 2004 Presidential Election," *The Forum* 2, no. 4 (2004), www.bepress.com/vol2/iss4/art3/.
32. James L. Sundquist, *Dynamics of the Party System: Alignment and Realignment of Political Parties in the United States*, rev. ed. (Washington, D.C.: Brookings, 1983), 312–313.
33. Most prominently, Theodore Roosevelt won 27.4 percent of the national popular vote and eighty-eight electoral votes in 1912 as the nominee of the Progressive Party; Eugene V. Debs won 6.0 percent of the popular vote as the Socialist candidate in 1912; and Robert M. La Follette won 16.6 percent of the popular vote and thirteen electoral votes as the Progressive nominee in 1924.
34. Stanley B. Greenberg, *The Two Americas: Our Current Political Deadlock and How to Break It* (New York: St. Martin's Press, 2004), 288.
35. Black and Black, *Rise of Southern Republicans*, 4.
36. John Kennedy introduced the Civil Rights Act in 1963, and, after he was assassinated, his successor to the presidency, Lyndon Johnson, oversaw its enactment by Congress the next year. In 1965 Johnson introduced and persuaded Congress to pass the Voting Rights Act.
37. Sundquist, *Dynamics of the Party System*, 383.
38. The post–World War II transformations in southern politics are chronicled in Earl Black and Merle Black, *The Vital South: How Presidents Are Elected* (Cambridge, Mass.: Harvard University Press, 1993); and Black and Black, *Rise of Southern Republicans*.
39. Black and Black, *Rise of Southern Republicans*, 256.
40. Godfrey Hodgson, *The World Turned Right Side Up: A History of the Conservative Ascendancy in America* (Boston: Houghton Mifflin, 1996).
41. U.S. Bureau of the Census, *Statistical Abstract of the United States: 2003* (Washington, D.C.: U.S. Department of Commerce, 2003), 432; and Steven Greenhouse, "Membership in Unions Drops Again," *New York Times*, January 28, 2005.
42. The gender gap was initially regarded as a movement of women into the Democratic Party. But subsequent research has shown that since the 1950s the Republicans have gained support among men without losing support among women. See, for example, Karen M. Kaufmann and John R. Petrocik, "The Changing Politics of American Men: Understanding the Sources of the Gender Gap," *American Journal of Political Science* 43 (July 1999): 864–887; and Daniel Wirls, "Voting Behavior: The Balance of Power in American Politics," in *The Elections of 2000*, ed. Michael Nelson (Washington, D.C.: CQ Press, 2001), 93–108.
43. Greenberg, *Two Americas*, 53.
44. Reagan's 489–49 electoral vote victory against Carter in 1980 surpassed even FDR's defeat of Hoover in 1932. The GOP also gained thirty-three seats in the

House and twelve in the Senate, enough to take control of that body for the first time since 1952.

45. Only 8 percent of voters in 1992 identified foreign policy as an important consideration in deciding whom to support, and 87 percent of them voted for Bush. Michael Nelson, "The Presidency: Clinton and the Cycle of Politics and Policy," in *The Elections of 1992,* ed. Michael Nelson (Washington, D.C.: CQ Press, 1993), 125–152.
46. "Bill Clinton's Third State of the Union Address (1996)," in *The Evolving Presidency: Addresses, Cases, Essays, Letters, Reports, Resolutions, Transcripts, and Other Landmark Documents, 1787–2004,* ed. Michael Nelson (Washington: CQ Press, 2004), 255–258.
47. The Seventeenth Amendment to the Constitution changed the method of election in 1913.
48. Adam Nagourney and Janet Elder, "In Poll, Americans Say Both Parties Lack Vision," *New York Times,* November 3, 2002. An election eve Gallup poll reported that 53 percent would be using their vote "in order to send a message that you support [or oppose] George W. Bush." Of these, 35 percent said they would vote to support him, and 18 percent said they would vote to express their opposition. In 1998, the last election in which the president's party gained seats, the split was 23 percent to 23 percent among the 46 percent who said they were using their vote to express their attitude toward President Clinton. David W. Moore and Jeffrey M. Jones, "Late Shift toward Republicans in Congressional Vote," Gallup Organization, November 4, 2002.
49. Andrew E. Busch, "Rolling Realignment," *Claremont Review of Books* 5, no. 1 (Winter 2004), http://claremont.org/writings/crb/winter2004/busch.html.
50. Balz and Allen, "Four More Years Attributed to Rove's Strategy."
51. Bush also suffered the lowest approval rating of any president among voters in the opposition party.
52. Bass, "George W. Bush, Presidential Party Leader Extraordinaire?" By "party support average" Bass means the party support score for the president that has been calculated annually by Congressional Quarterly since 1952.
53. See, for example, Thomas B. Edsall and James V. Grimaldi, "On Nov. 2, GOP Got More Bang for Its Billion, Analysis Shows," *Washington Post,* December 30, 2004.
54. Ronald Brownstein and Richard Rainey, "GOP Plants Flag on New Voting Frontier," *Los Angeles Times,* November 22, 2004.
55. Claudia Deane and Dan Balz, "GOP Puts Stock in 'Investor Class,' " *Washington Post,* October 27, 2003.
56. Tom Hamburger, "Business Groups Invested in Races, Now Wait for Return," *Los Angeles Times,* November 8, 2004.
57. Thomas B. Edsall, "Study: Corporate PACs Favor GOP," *Washington Post,* November 25, 2004.
58. Mike Allen, " 'Fired Up' Kerry Returning to Senate," *Washington Post,* November 9, 2004.
59. Kirk Johnson, "The Electorate: Hispanic Voters Declared Their Independence," *New York Times,* November 9, 2004.
60. Michael Nelson, "The Perils of Second-Term Presidents," in *The Elections of 1996,* ed. Michael Nelson (Washington, D.C.: CQ Press, 1997), 1–13.

2

The Nominations: Technology, Money, and Transferable Momentum

Barry C. Burden

In contrast to previous elections, money and momentum turned out to be imperfect predictors of who would win the Democratic nomination for president in 2004. The candidate with advantages in both of these domains—Howard Dean—failed to win a single contest outside of his home state. The 2004 Democratic nomination was unusual precisely because, although Dean ultimately failed as a candidate, the influence of his campaign continued after his withdrawal from the race. He introduced a host of new campaign techniques, elevated criticism of Bush, and improved the Democrats' chances for recapturing the White House. By making his party viable, Dean inadvertently transferred the momentum he acquired to Kerry.

Presidential selection necessarily begins with the nominating process. This process starts early, often a year before the first votes are cast and a full two years before the general election. The early months define the field of candidates in each party, which in turn defines the terms for winnowing to two nominees. Looked at in that way, nothing about 2004 was particularly unusual. Yet in other ways the 2004 nominations were anything but ordinary.

All of the candidates seeking the Democratic nomination tried to distinguish themselves, each suggesting that he or she both was faithful to party values and could beat George W. Bush in the fall. Once the official nominating events began, the field quickly shrank as candidates abandoned their campaigns. The factors that allowed John Kerry to sew up the nomination turned out to be critical in the general election as well.

Historical Context

Although presidential nominations tend to be governed by a set of regularities, every cycle brings new phenomena that do not fit the academic models. The peculiarities of 2004 can only be understood in the larger context of nominations in general. What did scholars say about nominations before 2004? I highlight four widely held beliefs:

1. *Delegates matter.* The presidential nominating process underwent major reform in the early 1970s that placed particular weight on delegate

accumulation. The reforms came in response to the 1968 Democratic convention, where Hubert Humphrey was nominated despite not having run in a single primary. Humphrey was essentially selected by state party leaders in the face of strong opposition to his candidacy by many rank-and-file Democrats. After Humphrey narrowly lost to Richard Nixon, the Democratic Party was in disarray and vowed to improve the nominating process by democratizing delegate selection. The McGovern-Fraser Commission adopted a proposal to require nominees to win delegates in open contests, using proportional allocation of delegates to candidates. As a consequence, primaries became increasingly popular mechanisms for choosing delegates. Republicans soon mimicked the Democrats' change. Since 1972 it has been delegates, not state party bosses, who have chosen the parties' nominees.

2. *The earliest events matter most.* The first two nominating events—the Iowa caucuses and the New Hampshire primary—matter more than all the other state nominating events combined. Depending on how news stories are counted, somewhere between a quarter and three-quarters of media coverage of the nomination process is devoted to just these two states.[1] Rarely has a candidate been nominated without winning at least one of these events.[2] Sometimes a dark horse candidate can emerge from the pack with a surprise victory, as Jimmy Carter did in Iowa in 1976. The lengthy "invisible primary" of speculation, fund raising, and courting supporters during the year before the election builds in anticipation of these two events.[3] As a result, early fund-raising and poll standings are good predictors of how candidates will perform when the voting starts.[4] Typically several candidates will abandon the race after failing in Iowa or New Hampshire. Republican Phil Gramm aborted his 1996 campaign after a dismal finish in Iowa. Others who fail to win Iowa or New Hampshire might carry on for a bit longer, but it is these earliest nominating events that do the most to winnow the field of candidates to two or three.

3. *Winnowing happens quickly.* Because of the fast pace of events, the difficulty of sustaining organizations in many states, and fund-raising demands, the number of presidential contenders shrinks rapidly. After the first nominating events, party activists maneuver furiously to decide whom they will support, and more voters become engaged in the process. Success on the campaign trail translates into further success, while losses beget further losses. This dynamic creates rapid spirals upward or downward for particular candidates.[5]

4. *Party elites play a substantial role in selecting the nominee.* Even though primaries and caucuses select delegates, party leaders still serve an important function. The national and state party committees organize the primary and caucus calendar. In addition, party officials provide financial and other forms of support to favored candidates or try to dissuade those they would prefer not to run. They can also alter the delegate count. Starting in 1984 the Democrats added "superdelegates" to the process. These party leaders and elected officials may pledge themselves to any candidate running for president, regardless of the primary or caucus vote in their states. They give

a powerful signal to rank-and-file voters when they coalesce around one or two candidates.[6]

The Environment in 2004

Every nominating season brings new challenges for voters, candidates, and parties to navigate. From one election to another, some states will change the dates or rules of their nominating events. The national parties may modify the ways that delegates are selected, as they did in 1972 and 1984. These matters are at least under party control. But many other forces influence the nominations without party elites having much say. Real-world events sometimes shape the context for party nominations in a grander fashion than any modest changes in rules can.

The most important aspect of a party nomination battle is whether an incumbent is running for reelection. This includes not just literal cases, such as President Ronald Reagan's quest for renomination in 1984, but also vice-presidential heirs to the nomination, such as George H. W. Bush in 1988. The main difference between the Democratic and Republican nominating contests in 2004 was incumbency. President Bush was certain to seek reelection and the Republican Party was happy to nominate him without much dissent. The Democrats' clearest heir to the nomination, former vice president (and 2000 presidential popular vote winner) Al Gore, decided that he would not be a candidate. To fill the vacuum, ten Democratic contenders joined the fray. They spent the better part of a year and many millions of dollars competing with one another, while Bush and the Republicans had the luxury of raising money and thinking ahead to the general election.

In addition to this asymmetry, the electoral environment had three new features in 2004. First, this was the first presidential election held under the Bipartisan Campaign Reform Act (BCRA) of 2001. Also known as "McCain-Feingold," the BCRA eliminated previously unlimited "soft money" contributions to parties, increased the maximum "hard money" amounts that could be contributed to candidates, and imposed restrictions on the actions of independent political groups near election day. Observers widely believed that the BCRA would favor the Republicans because the GOP already held an advantage in hard money contributions and Democratic labor unions would face new limits on their activities. Bush had proved himself a formidable fund-raiser in 2000 and apparently would have an even greater advantage in 2004, as an incumbent seeking reelection under new laws more favorable to his party.

As with most campaign reform efforts, however, the BCRA had some unintended consequences. A loophole in the law allowed a new kind of group to emerge. Named after the provision of the Internal Revenue Service code that defines them, 527s are tax exempt and may spend unlimited amounts of money on voter mobilization and issue ads. Democrats and liberals took early advantage of this new outlet early in the 2004 cycle. Conservative groups would respond in kind later in the campaign.

Second, the 2004 contest was the first national campaign following the terrorist attacks of September 11, 2001, in New York and Washington, D.C. Domestic terrorism was a new issue for most Americans, and foreign policy would likely play a bigger role than it had in most previous campaigns. To compete with Bush, Democrats might be expected to seek a candidate with military experience or intelligence credentials to boost their credibility on security issues.

Third, the front-loading of primaries to earlier and earlier dates continued in 2004, as it had ever since the democratization of the nominating process thirty years earlier, but especially since 1988.[7] It seemed obvious that front-loading would cause the invisible primary to begin earlier and thus would accelerate the winnowing of the field. Indeed, Democratic National Committee (DNC) chair Terry McAuliffe pushed for front-loading as a way to settle the party's nomination sooner. Identifying the nominee quickly, he thought, would position the party to unify against Bush.

The Calendar

The 2004 calendar of caucuses and primaries had some expected and unexpected consequences. As expected, front-loading forced the entire process to begin earlier. Candidates began forming exploratory committees, raising money, and testing the political waters more than two years before the general election. Former governor Howard Dean filed a Statement of Organization with the Federal Election Commission (FEC) in May 2002. Sen. Joseph Lieberman made the first official entry into the race in January 2003. With Iowa not holding its caucuses until January 19, 2004, this was a full year before the first event involving voters.

In 2000 the Democrats had instituted a moratorium on state nominating events for a full month after the late-January New Hampshire primary. By five weeks afterward only 1 percent of delegates had been selected. In 2004 the moratorium was lifted, and states quickly moved their dates closer to the date of the New Hampshire primary. Almost a quarter of delegates were chosen in the same five weeks this time around.[8] This acceleration continued a longer-term movement toward front-loading that was only briefly interrupted in 2000. In 1972 only 17 percent of delegates had been chosen by the first Tuesday in April. By 1984 the proportion had risen to 52 percent. In 2004, 80 percent of Democratic delegates were allocated by the first of April.

At the same time, the strong trend toward primaries in the wake of the McGovern-Fraser reforms has halted, if not reversed course. The return to caucuses has consequences for the kind of candidates who will succeed. Because caucuses feature more limited participation and require more effort, they favor organization, structure, and insider support. Primaries—especially those of the "open" variety that allow crossover voting by voters of the other party—elicit broader participation and favor broad-based appeal.

As Figure 2-1 demonstrates, the 2004 cycle showed real movement away from primaries and toward caucuses. Only thirty-five states scheduled presidential primaries, the lowest number in two decades. In addition, five of the thirty-five states with Republican primaries canceled them, mostly as a cost-saving measure.[9] Without a serious race for the Republican nomination, holding a primary would be a waste of time and money for cash-strapped state governments. By the time most states voted, the Democratic nomination already would be settled, as well. Although primaries are funded publicly by the states, caucuses are funded privately by the parties that hold them.

The primary and caucus calendar is too compressed for most candidates to devote resources to every state where a contest occurs. In the past some candidates decided to skip some states, concentrating their efforts in a smaller number of venues. Republican John McCain, for example, skipped Iowa in 2000. The strategy worked in that McCain earned a small vote in Iowa (thus beating expectations) and won in New Hampshire (beating expectations once again). In 2004 Lieberman did the same thing, only to fail in both states.

The Democratic Field

The pool of 2004 Democratic contenders conformed quite well to the historical pattern, as the data in Table 2-1 suggest. Although the field of ten candidates was a bit larger than usual, it resembled earlier fields in terms of the candidates' backgrounds. Seven candidates were considered top tier by the political community and thus deemed worthy of heavy media scrutiny.

Figure 2-1 Use of Presidential Primaries, 1960–2004

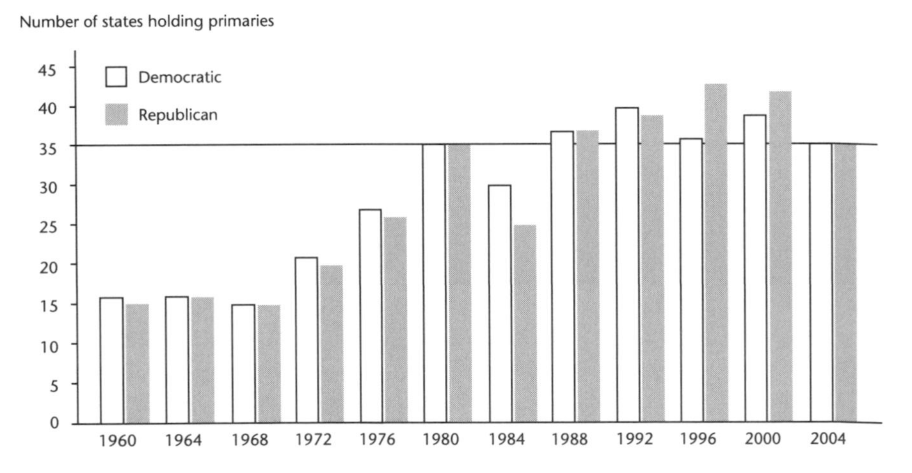

Sources: Number of states using primaries to select convention delegates for 1960–2000 taken from Harold W. Stanley and Richard G. Niemi, *Vital Statistics on American Politics, 2003–2004* (Washington, D.C.: CQ Press, 2004), 66. Information on 2004 compiled by the author. The figure counts as primary states the five states that canceled Republican primaries in 2004.

Table 2-1 The Democratic Contenders

Candidate	2003 announcement date	Immediate background
First tier		
Wesley Clark	Sept. 17	Four-star Army general until 2000
Howard Dean	June 23	Vermont governor 1991–2003
John Edwards	Sept. 16	Trial lawyer; North Carolina senator 1999–2005
Richard Gephardt	Feb. 19	Missouri congressman since 1977
Bob Graham	May 6	Florida governor 1979–1987; senator 1987–2005
John Kerry	Sept. 2	Massachusetts senator since 1985
Joseph Lieberman	Jan. 13	Connecticut senator since 1989; 2000 vice presidential candidate
Second tier		
Dennis Kucinich	Oct. 13	Ohio congressman since 1997
Carol Moseley Braun	Sept. 22	Illinois senator 1993–1999; ambassador to New Zealand 1999–2001
Al Sharpton	April 23	New York minister; civil rights activist

The three second-tier candidates were notable, however, in that they included the only two black candidates in the field and the only woman.

The 2004 field displayed some interesting parallels with those of 1988 and 1992, the two previous elections in which no Democratic president or vice president was seeking the nomination. The "seven dwarfs," as the 1988 Democrats were called, included several senators, such as Al Gore and Sam Nunn, but also a black civil rights activist with no elected experience (Jesse Jackson) and a northeastern governor (Michael Dukakis). As in 1992, the Democrats in 2004 were choosing a nominee to challenge an incumbent Republican named Bush in a weak economy and after a military conflict in the Middle East. But in 1992 foreign policy had largely receded from the voters' agenda by the time the Democratic contest got under way. Only one candidate—Sen. Robert Kerrey of Nebraska—had serious military credentials, and the eventual nominee was a southern governor, Bill Clinton, with no military record or foreign policy credentials. In this respect, the post–9/11 environment of 2004 was dramatically different. Although another small-state governor grabbed the lead for a while, Democratic voters eventually turned to a more "electable" candidate who had served with honor in Vietnam.

Four of the seven top-tier Democrats in 2004 came from the U.S. Senate. The Senate has frequently been described as the "presidential incubator" and "mother of presidents." Aside from the vice presidency, it is the highest elective office in the land. John Edwards, Bob Graham, John Kerry, and Joseph Lieberman not only had varying amounts of Senate experience but were sitting senators throughout the nomination period. As Table 2-2 shows, senators frequently seek the presidency. Roughly one-third of all presidential contenders from 1960 to 2004 were senators, far more than held any other

Table 2-2 Backgrounds of Presidential Candidates, 1960–2004

Last office held	% of contenders	% of nominees	Nomination success rate	% of primary vote
President	5.1	28	0.88	69.3
Vice president	6.4	28	0.7	36.2
Governor	21.8	20	0.15	14.3
Senator	36.5	24	0.11	9.6
Representative	10.9	0	0	4.3
Sitting senators	33.3	24	0.14	9.5
Former senators	9	24	0.43	24.8
Never in Senate	57.7	52	0.14	14.8

Source: Data updated by the author from Barry C. Burden, "United States Senators as Presidential Candidates," *Political Science Quarterly* 117 (Spring 2002): 81–102.

Note: Nomination success rate = nominees/contenders.

office.[10] Yet senators do not perform especially well as presidential candidates. In part, they are less calculating than other politicians in seeking the presidency, less adept at assessing and taking advantage of the "political opportunity structure." [11] Although they are 36.5 percent of contenders, senators are only a quarter of nominees. And only one in ten senators who seeks a nomination wins it.

This is not the whole picture. Presidents seeking reelection and vice presidents seeking the mantle do quite well, and many of these candidates were once in the Senate. The lower half of the table shows that sitting senators have a poor success rate (just .14) in winning the nomination, whereas former senators have an almost 50 percent chance (.43). Only two sitting senators have ever won the presidency: Warren Harding in 1920 and John Kennedy in 1960. Winning the nomination would be difficult for Edwards, Graham, Kerry, or Lieberman; winning the presidency would be downright historic.

A key liability of the Senate is that it ties candidates to a long series of roll call votes on difficult and complicated issues. Kerry's record in particular did him more harm than good. He voted for Bush's No Child Left Behind initiative, then criticized it for the way it was implemented. After voting to authorize military action in Iraq in 2002, he famously explained why he later voted against a war funding bill by saying, "I actually did vote for the $87 billion before I voted against it," a line the Bush campaign would repeat frequently. Congressional observers understood what Kerry meant: he supported funding the military effort but not by the particular means proposed by Republicans. But to the average voter it was disconcerting. Kerry did best when he eschewed his senatorial manner of speaking, with its long sentences and big words, for a more direct style.

Each of the four senators had something unique to offer Democratic primary voters. Edwards had the advantage of being a southerner and a charismatic orator. But as a first-term senator from North Carolina he had little experience in public life and almost no foreign policy credentials. Graham, also a southerner, was experienced both as a senator and as governor of Florida. Health problems delayed his entry into the race, however, and his personal style was not especially engaging. Kerry, of Massachusetts, brought stature and experience plus an impressive combat record in Vietnam. Finally, Lieberman had been on the ticket in 2000. But Al Gore, who had selected Lieberman as his running mate, did not endorse him, and many considered Lieberman too boring or too moderate to win the Democratic nomination.

Richard Gephardt's chances were not much better. Gephardt had served in the House for twenty-eight years, much of it as his party's leader. He had long been connected with bread-and-butter economic issues such as protection of entitlements and support for labor unions. His experience running for president in 1988 was probably an advantage, but being a member of the House, with deep roots in the Democratic Party of the past, was almost certainly a hindrance. Gephardt had won Iowa in 1988; a repeat would be essential.

Wesley Clark was the least traditional of the top-tier contenders. He had never held elective office, jumped into the campaign remarkably late, and had only a weak commitment to the Democratic Party before deciding to seek its presidential nomination. Clark had voted Republican until recently and had not cultivated support in the Democratic Party. His lack of experience in electoral politics quickly showed when he made some amateur mistakes. Confusing statements about his position on the congressional vote authorizing the use of force in Iraq muddled his message. But after 9/11 there was a great deal of enthusiasm for a former general who could confront the Bush administration on foreign policy. Like astronaut John Glenn in 1984, Clark performed better when he was a noncandidate than after he entered the field.

Finally, there was Howard Dean. Dean's main advantage was being the only governor in the field. Every candidate faces the problem of "product differentiation"—that is, distinguishing himself from others in the field yet remaining credible enough to compete. Because there were three southern candidates, none of them could claim being from that region as an advantage. Clark might have benefited from his military record, especially in the context of the "war on terror," but Kerry was a decorated Vietnam veteran. Dean lacked military experience and national name recognition, but he was the governor of a state—the same credential that Bill Clinton offered in 1992. Indeed, governors had won all but one of the last seven presidential elections.

Not having a roll call record to defend, Dean was outspoken in his criticism of President Bush. As a governor, he could take credit for accomplishments in office, such as balancing the budget, expanding health care, and adopting same-sex civil unions in Vermont. No other candidate could claim so many concrete accomplishments. Although many considered Dean the most liberal of the top-tier candidates, his conservative record on fiscal issues and gun control broadened his appeal.[12]

One reason that an insurgent like Dean could emerge was that party elites did not organize behind a single, established candidate. DNC chair

McAuliffe refused to support a candidate. The Clintons might have been considered kingmakers, but they purposely stayed quiet. As expected, several unions and many members of Congress got behind Gephardt early. Clark was supported by some members of Congress, too, as well as by celebrities such as Michael Moore. Firefighters and, informally, veterans lined up behind Kerry. But Dean was endorsed by Gore, two big unions, and Hollywood luminaries such as Rob Reiner and Martin Sheen. In a competitive field, party leaders did not coalesce behind any single contender.

It's All in the Timing

The beginning of the "invisible primary" stage often looks radically different from the end. Early polls typically measure nothing more than name recognition. An insurgent can ride high for a while, as can an establishment candidate. The point is to peak at the right time. Like athletes training for a competition, candidates hope to hit their stride just as the first nominating events in Iowa and New Hampshire approach. To do so any earlier would make them targets for opponents and raise expectations too high; any later might be too late to recover. The shortest explanation for why Kerry won the nomination is that he peaked at exactly the right moment. Kerry's stock was rising and Dean's was falling when the Iowa caucuses hit. These were not independent events: Dean built momentum for the party that Kerry seized from him at just the right time.

Howard Dean was on fire in the latter half of 2003. He signed up hundreds of thousands of "Deaniacs" on the Internet, drew tremendous crowds, and raised enormous sums of money. Although the four candidates from the Senate, particularly Edwards and Kerry, dominated the money chase in early 2003, Dean set a blistering pace thereafter. In the third quarter of 2003 he raised almost $15 million; no one else raised even $5 million. Dean spent rapidly, too, going on an expensive, multicity "Sleepless Summer Tour" across the country. In October his campaign supporters decided that he would opt out of federal matching funds in return for not being bound by spending limits. By the time Gore endorsed him in mid-December, Dean seemed unbeatable. If momentum exists in contemporary presidential nominating campaigns, Dean had it. As the left side of Figure 2-2 shows, Dean's prospects for winning the nomination rose dramatically throughout the fall, dwarfing the other Democrats' by the end of year.[13]

Dean's early success consisted of filling the void left by the other candidates. Most of the top-tier Democrats had voted for or endorsed the Iraq war resolution. With an eye on November, they were already looking toward the center rather than appealing to the Democratic base. They offered little criticism of No Child Left Behind, the PATRIOT Act, or other Bush initiatives. As members of Congress, they spoke in Washington lingo rather than words that would resonate with Democratic primary activists. Dean did none of these things.

Figure 2-2 Democratic Candidate Standings, October 1, 2003–March 3, 2004

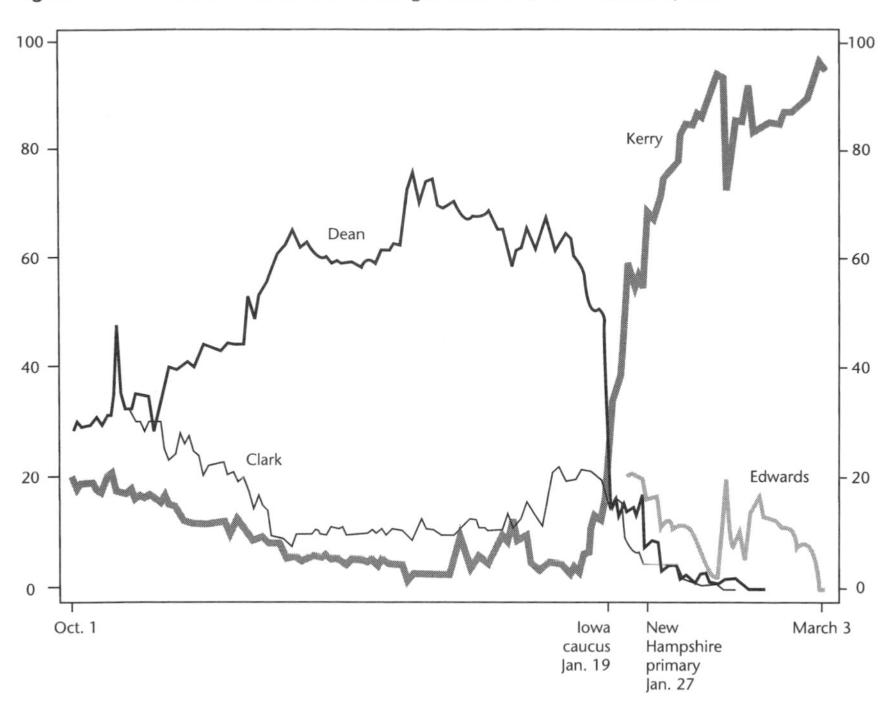

Source: Data are from the Iowa Electronic Market Democratic National Convention Market.

Note: The Iowa Electronic Market allowed investors to buy futures in candidates seeking the Democratic nomination. A candidate contract paid $1.00 if the candidate won the nomination. The figure shows the value of each candidate relative to the $1.00 payoff. The values are equivalent to the perceived likelihood that each candidate would win the nomination. For example, Dean's value of .619 on December 3, 2003, indicates that investors gave him roughly a 62% chance of winning the party nomination at that point; www.biz.uiowa.edu/iem/markets/DConv04.html.

Dean also used new technology in a way that no previous campaign had. Although John McCain and Bill Bradley had made some use of the Internet to raise money in 2000, Dean took the fund-raising technology to a new level. He organized "meetups," house parties, road trips, blog discussions, and letter-writing campaigns among his supporters, largely via the Internet. Independent political groups, such as MoveOn.org, had been successful Internet organizations, but Dean's was the first campaign to take advantage of the Internet's organizational possibilities. Most politicos had never heard of the small Meetup.com when Dean for America began using it to set up simultaneous monthly meetings for supporters around the nation.

After entering the race early and with low expectations, Dean rose impressively throughout 2003. In the American Research Group tracking poll, his standing among Democrats increased from 19 percent in July to 45 percent in early December. During the same period Kerry's fell from 25 percent to 13 percent, essentially tied with Clark. By the second week of January, Dean continued to hold firm at 35 percent, but Kerry fell to 10 percent, and Clark rose to 20 percent.

What about the other candidates? As Figure 2-2 shows, Clark burst onto the scene in October 2003 with great fanfare, giving Dean a short-lived run for the money. Clark even rose briefly to the top of some national polls. But his lack of organization and occasional stumbles on the campaign trail quickly deflated the excitement. Among other things, Clark seemed to make contradictory statements about whether he would have voted for the Iraq war if he had been in Congress; he also failed to denounce supporter Michael Moore for labeling Bush a "deserter." Lieberman never became competitive. Like Bruce Babbitt in 1988, neither his moderate message nor his laconic style ever connected with Democratic primary voters. Eventually Lieberman decided to camp out in New Hampshire, forgoing Iowa entirely. But still he could not compete with the other two New Englanders in the race—or anyone else in the top tier, for that matter. Similarly, Bob Graham failed to gain much traction. It was difficult for voters to identify Graham with many policy positions or accomplishments, and personality quirks such as the minute-by-minute diary of his life that he kept did not help. Graham dropped out in early October, admitting that he "could not be elected."

Meanwhile, Gephardt built a union-based organization in Iowa. Although he bonded with the Teamsters and other traditional unions, some other labor organizations supported his competitors. Gephardt hoped that a strong performance in Iowa would energize his campaign. Edwards gained support in Iowa, but not in New Hampshire or anywhere else. His early prowess at fund raising, mostly from his fellow trial lawyers, was dissipating. But his friendly style and speech-making ability quietly allowed him to win over voters at face-to-face events. Finally, Kerry slid from the front to near the rear of the pack. His campaign was in financial trouble and in general disarray. Staff members were leaving, and Kerry's message was muddled. No one, it seemed, could catch Dean.

The invisible primary of 2003 ended badly for Dean. In a ten-day period in December, Gore made his surprise endorsement, Kerry took out a personal loan on his home for $6.4 million to pay campaign expenses, and Saddam Hussein was captured by coalition forces in Iraq. Gore's support undermined Dean's status as the outsider candidate. It also gave his opponents a clear target.[14] Joe Trippi (Dean's campaign manager) believes that this was the first time that both the press and fellow competitors simultaneously criticized a presidential candidate.[15] In a December interview Dean quipped, "If you wrote the headline 'Blank Attacks Dean,' you could fill that in with any number of names." [16] And though union leaders endorsed Dean, the three million rank-and-file members were actually divided among the candidates.[17] Dean was the loudest critic of the U.S. action in Iraq, and his statement that America was no safer with Hussein in custody provoked an avalanche of criticism. Kerry's taking out a personal loan demonstrated his commitment to the campaign and allowed him to bring in veteran staff to compete with Dean's less-experienced team. Kerry's new campaign slogan, the "Real Deal," seemed the right contrast with the brasher and less-experienced Dean.

Kerry's Turnaround: Iowa and New Hampshire

Kerry's turnaround changed everything. He made real progress in Iowa, partly because of the support he received from veterans and firefighters. Both groups are important vote mobilizers in the Iowa caucuses and are conveniently spread across the state. Instead of building a grassroots organization in Iowa, Dean trucked in several thousand out-of-state volunteers, who were not especially credible when talking with locals on their doorsteps.[18] Clark's presence helped focus Democrats on the need for a candidate with military credentials, but Kerry became the beneficiary when Jim Rassman, a Republican veteran who served with him in Vietnam, appeared at an Iowa event. Their bear-hug reunion resonated with Iowans.

Dean's support nationwide held into the new year, and he actually gained a bit in New Hampshire. No single opponent was able to break from the pack to turn it into a two-candidate race. The opponent who took Dean on most directly in January was Dick Gephardt. Gephardt was not polling well nationally and had difficulty raising funds. Feeling desperate in must-win Iowa, he committed what has been called the "murder-suicide" of the campaign, taking Dean down hard and going down with him. As Dean later put it, "We chose to engage in back and forth with Dick Gephardt and we both ended up at the bottom." [19] Most front-runners win at least a primary or two before faltering, but Dean's rise and fall occurred before a single vote was cast.

As shown in Table 2-3, caucus night in Iowa produced a strong victory for Kerry, who won 38 percent of the vote. With the support of the *Des*

Table 2-3 2004 Democratic Caucus Results

State	Date	Turnout	Clark (%)	Dean (%)	Edwards (%)	Kerry (%)
Iowa	Jan. 19	124,331	0	18	32	38
New Mexico	Feb. 3	102,096	21	16	11	43
North Dakota	Feb. 3	10,558	24	12	10	51
Michigan	Feb. 7	163,769	7	17	13	52
Washington	Feb. 7	105,000	3	30	7	48
Maine	Feb. 8	18,259	4	27	7	47
Dist. of Columbia	Feb. 14	9,126	1	18	10	47
Nevada	Feb. 14	9,000	0	17	10	63
Hawaii	Feb. 24	4,073	1	7	13	47
Idaho	Feb. 24	4,920	0	11	23	55
Minnesota	March 2	54,931	0	2	27	51
Kansas	March 13	2,000	1	7	9	72
Alaska	March 20	500	0	11	3	48
Wyoming	March 20	665		3	4	77
Colorado	April 13	12,000	0	3	1	64
North Carolina	April 17	17,809		6	52	27

Source: Caucus turnout numbers are estimates reported as of June 8, 2004, by Rhodes Cook, www.rhodescook.com/analysis.html. The District of Columbia also held a nonbinding primary on Jan. 13.

Note: Empty cells indicate data not available.

Moines Register and a good stage presence, Edwards ran a surprising second, just a few points behind Kerry. Dean earned only 18 percent of the vote, and Gephardt received 11 percent, not even winning most of the union households. Gephardt withdrew the following day. In all, the Iowa results placed Kerry and Edwards on a higher plateau than the other top-tier candidates. Kerry bested Dean among union members (29 percent to 19 percent), senior citizens (43 percent to 15 percent), first-time caucus goers (36 percent to 22 percent), and late deciders (37 percent to 18 percent). He won with voters looking for electability and experience, whereas Dean did well among those concerned about the war in Iraq and looking for strong stands.

Dean took the stage the night of his loss in Iowa intending to fire up the 3,500 supporters in the room. In front of a national television audience, he rattled off a list of states where the campaign would go next. After shouting that his campaign would "take back the White House," he let out a red-faced "Yeeeeaaaah!" The "I Have a Scream" speech, as it came to be known, was delivered at an unfortunate time. It made the candidate look desperate rather than confident, angry rather than resolute. The scream got tremendous play on late-night talk shows and the Internet. The media used it to label Dean an unelectable failure. For voters just starting to pay attention to the nominating contests, it provided little reason to join his cause. More important, replays of the scream dominated the news about Dean for several days, inhibiting his ability to get back on message.

The New Hampshire primary came just eight days after Iowa, but the dynamics in New Hampshire were different: Clark and Lieberman were actively campaigning there, and Dean had a thirty-point lead as late as December. Yet Kerry's bounce out of Iowa gave him the edge on primary day. As Table 2-4 shows, Kerry took 39 percent of the vote, to Dean's 26 percent. Clark and Edwards finished next, with around 12 percent each, not bad for southerners running against three New Englanders. Lieberman could not manage double digits. For the first time since 1976, a candidate who was not already president won both Iowa and New Hampshire. Nevertheless, Dean pledged to march onward and win the nomination by accumulating delegates in key states.

The next major nominating events took place on February 3, dubbed "Junior Tuesday" because it had fewer events than "Super Tuesday" on March 2. In an unorthodox move, Dean skipped all seven of those events to focus on the February 7 contests in delegate-rich Michigan and Washington. Kerry won five of the seven Junior Tuesday primaries and caucuses, while Edwards easily took South Carolina and finished a close second to Clark in Oklahoma. Lieberman's poor showing pushed him out of the race, and at this point the news media began to paint Kerry as the likely Democratic nominee.

Although Dean did not win the Michigan or Washington caucuses, he dimmed Edwards's star by finishing second to Kerry in both. Dean then set the February 17 Wisconsin primary as his last stand. Meanwhile, Kerry won southern contests in Virginia and Tennessee, prompting Clark to withdraw and narrowing the race to just three candidates: Dean, Edwards, and Kerry.

Table 2-4 2004 Democratic Primary Results

State	Date	Turnout	Clark (%)	Dean (%)	Edwards (%)	Kerry (%)
New Hampshire	Jan. 27	219,761	12	26	12	39
Arizona	Feb. 3	238,942	27	14	7	43
Delaware	Feb. 3	33,291	10	10	11	50
Missouri	Feb. 3	418,339	4	9	25	51
Oklahoma	Feb. 3	302,385	30	4	30	27
South Carolina	Feb. 3	293,843	7	5	45	30
Tennessee	Feb. 10	369,385	23	4	27	41
Virginia	Feb. 10	396,181	9	7	27	52
Wisconsin	Feb. 17	826,250	2	18	34	40
Utah	Feb. 24	34,854	1	4	30	55
California	March 2	3,107,629	2	4	20	64
Connecticut	March 2	130,023	1	4	24	58
Georgia	March 2	626,738	1	1	41	47
Maryland	March 2	481,476	1	3	26	60
Massachusetts	March 2	614,296	1	3	18	72
New York	March 2	715,633	1	3	20	61
Ohio	March 2	1,221,014	1	3	34	52
Rhode Island	March 2	35,759	1	4	19	71
Vermont	March 2	82,881	3	54	6	32
Florida	March 9	753,762	1	3	10	77
Louisiana	March 9	161,653	4	5	16	70
Mississippi	March 9	76,298	3	3	7	78
Texas	March 9	839,231	2	5	14	67
Illinois	March 16	1,217,515	2	4	11	72
Pennsylvania	April 27	787,034		10	10	74
Indiana	May 4	317,211	6	7	11	73
Nebraska	May 11	71,572		8	14	73
West Virginia	May 11	252,839	4	4	13	69
Arkansas	May 18	266,848				67
Kentucky	May 18	229,916	3	4	15	60
Oregon	May 18	368,544				79
Idaho	May 25	379		11	23	55
Alabama	June 1	218,574				75
South Dakota	June 1	84,405		6		82
Montana	June 8	93,543	4		9	68
New Jersey	June 8	208,176				92

Source: Rhodes Cook, www.rhodescook.com/analysis.html.

Note: Empty cells indicate data not available.

Foiling Dean's plan, the Wisconsin primary pruned the field to two. Despite spending ten days in the state, Dean finished a disappointing third to Kerry and Edwards. He ended his campaign the following day, leaving Edwards as the only serious alternative to Kerry. Then Edwards's chances ended as a result of the ten Super Tuesday contests of March 2. Kerry won nine of the ten, including the Georgia primary, where the southerner Edwards needed a win. (Now a noncandidate, Dean picked up his only victory in his home state of Vermont.) Edwards withdrew from the race the next day, making Kerry the de facto nominee.

Spirited competition and an insurgent candidate were not enough to boost voter turnout in the 2004 primaries. Although the Democratic turnout rate in New Hampshire was the highest since 1960, overall turnout was the third-lowest since that year.[20] Iowa saw impressive caucus attendance, but participation in later events was much lower. An early victory for a nominee leaves voters in the states that have not already voted disengaged.

Both Kerry and Bush clinched their parties' nominations by reaching the number of delegates they needed to be nominated on March 9. This date is notable for two reasons. First, it is apparently the earliest that both major parties have settled their nominating contests.[21] As a result, the general election campaign between Bush and Kerry effectively began eight months before election day. Resolving the intraparty battles so early in the year added yet another stage to the presidential selection process. Because the selection of running mates and the national party conventions do not occur until the summer, the nominees have more than four months to fill between clinching and accepting their parties' nominations.

Second, it is remarkable that Bush and Kerry both clinched their nominations on the same date. As an incumbent popular within his party, Bush faced no opposition in the primaries. Moreover, the Republicans mostly use a winner-take-all system for allocating delegates to the candidate who wins a primary, whereas the Democrats tend to allocate delegates proportionally. So even though Kerry and Bush were both winning primaries, Kerry often received only half of the Democratic delegates in states where he won the popular vote, while Bush received all of the Republican delegates. In addition, the large Democratic field should have extended the nomination battle. Yet a little serendipity coincided with the front-loaded schedule in 2004 to produce the Democratic nominee just as early as the Republican.

The Rise and Fall of Howard Dean

Many attributed Dean's collapse to his ranting performance the night of the Iowa caucuses. But "the scream" occurred after he had already been losing ground for a couple of weeks. Some have called Dean the "dot-com candidate," since his candidacy paralleled the rise and fall of the technology companies in the late 1990s. The hard reality of the Iowa results caused a massive sell-off of his stock and a return to more tried-and-true ("bricks-and-mortar") candidates. But however compelling the analogy, there must have been reasons for Dean's reversal of fortune. Specifically, a combination of four factors was responsible.

First, as has already been noted, expectations for Dean became unreachable. Because a candidate's success in the nominating contests is largely defined as beating expectations, a standard tactic of front-runners' campaign managers is to lower expectations for how many votes their candidates will receive. Dean and campaign manager Joe Trippi did this, saying on many occasions in 2003 that Dean could not possibly lock up the nomination when a single primary vote had yet to be cast. But the Dean people also broadened their ambitions beyond their capabilities. Dean spent too much of the money he raised in 2003, and a good deal of it went to states other than Iowa and New Hampshire. The campaign's ambitious behavior overshadowed its verbal attempts to downplay expectations. Gore's endorsement, which one reporter called "Mr. Inside's" embrace of "Mr. Outside," put a bull's-eye on Dean's back.[22] As Dean put it on more than one occasion, he spent that latter part of 2003 "picking a fair amount of buckshot out of my rear end."

Second, Dean suffered the contradiction of the insurgent who becomes the establishment. He initially succeeded by offering a different message than the other Democrats, promising to empower regular people instead of the elite. As a governor he spoke from outside the Beltway rather than from the corridors of influence. Yet the very qualities that brought excitement and momentum to his candidacy also led to his downfall. His attacks on the Democratic Party (and, earlier, on the Iowa caucus system) did not sit well with many Democratic voters. The casual, unrehearsed style that worked so well early in the process did not hold up well over the long haul. He made mistakes, such as his offhand comment, "I still want to be the candidate for guys with Confederate flags in their pickup trucks." [23] He seemed disingenuous when he talked about his religious values or brought his wife, Judy, to the campaign trail at the last minute. His amateur supporters in Iowa were particularly maladroit at gauging Dean's support in the caucuses. Their optimism and lack of experience created a false confidence. In the end the Dean campaign won only two counties in Iowa, despite having predicted that he would win over 70 percent of them.[24] Dean morphed from a successful, momentum candidate, to a failed, organization candidate in just a few weeks.

Third, Dean and Trippi's commitment to the Internet worked beautifully in 2003, but it might have been a hindrance when the real nominating events approached. Caucuses, in particular, are won by mobilizing supporters to attend a time-consuming set of face-to-face meetings. The twenty-somethings who readily gave the campaign small monetary donations and maintained pro-Dean Web sites did not embrace the old-fashioned world of political shoe leather. Point-and-click activists are not the same as grassroots mobilizers.

Fourth, Dean's early surge made the other Democrats better campaigners. Partly out of desperation, Gephardt became feistier in attacking Dean, a strategy that hurt them both. Kerry learned to better coordinate his message and organization. Most important, Dean convinced the rest of the candidates that taking on President Bush was the best way to make one's mark. Together, the Democratic contenders aired several months of anti-Bush criticism, which lowered the president's approval ratings about ten points. Once Democratic voters were persuaded that Bush could be beaten, they began moving away from the candidate who had first expressed their frustration and to the candidate they thought could win. By making the party seem electable, Dean had directed Democratic voters to electability as a criterion. And electability was one domain where Kerry, with his Vietnam record in particular, dominated. Bumper stickers bore the painful but realistic mantra, "Dated Dean, Married Kerry." Dean drew Democratic voters into active involvement in the process, but they provided Kerry with the victory.

The Dean Legacy

Howard Dean's campaign spurred enduring changes both in the Democratic Party and in the way all campaigns will be run in the future. Unlike other populist insurgencies, such as Gary Hart's in 1984, or ideological movements, like Pat Buchanan's in 1992, Dean's left a footprint that party leaders cannot ignore.

Perhaps Dean's most obvious innovations are the Internet tactics that his movement introduced. Although the Web had been widely available for a decade, no candidate until Dean made serious use of it to organize, raise money, and share information with supporters. Now, the 2004 party conventions officially hosted Internet bloggers for the first time. After wrapping up the nomination in March, Kerry used his own Web site and advertisements placed on other sites to raise money. The techniques Dean developed reconfigured not only his candidacy but others, demonstrating that horizontal campaign organizations based in the World Wide Web can perform functions that traditional hierarchical organizations cannot.[25]

Dean for America created the most successful grassroots fund-raising machine in recent political history. Dean raised $40 million in a short time; more astonishingly, his average donor gave less than $100. No candidate since McGovern in 1972 had such a wide donor base. In fact, since 1972, fund-raising trends had been moving in the opposite direction, toward a smaller number of larger donors. The BCRA's doubling of hard money limits from $1,000 to $2,000 and the front-loaded calendar of primaries and caucuses in 2004 seemed certain to push candidates further in that direction. The Bush campaign, for example, received many $2,000 donations and recruited volunteer supporters who could raise $100,000 or more from their friends and business associates. When Democrat Jerry Brown declared during the 1992 campaign that he would only take donations of less than $100, his credibility evaporated. When Dean proposed raising $200 million in $100 increments, from two million people on the Internet, he seemed arrogant yet visionary at the same time.

The Republicans

In most election years, nominating races occur only within one party. Usually the other party is supporting a president running for reelection or a vice president seeking the nomination. In the former case especially, it is rare for a serious contest to take place.

Republicans were enthusiastic about renominating Bush in 2004, but that is not to say the party was united on everything. There were internal disagreements about Iraq, the economy, and whether Dick Cheney ought to be replaced as Bush's running mate. But the level of commitment to building a unified campaign machine far surpassed what Bush's father had managed in 1992, when similar disagreements existed.

George W. Bush spent the invisible-primary stage of the campaign raising money. He gathered well over $100 million by the end of 2003. (More astounding, considering that Bush was unopposed, is that the campaign *spent* roughly $40 million in 2003.) As noted above and in stark contrast with Dean and most of the other Democrats, Bush relied heavily on a small number of donors. Volunteer fund-raisers became "Pioneers" if they could raise $100,000 and "Rangers" if they assembled $200,000. One report indicated that a quarter of the $34 million Bush raised in the first half of 2003 was funneled through Pioneers and Rangers.[26] By the time of the Republican convention in September 2004, Bush had raised $260 million, more than double the record amount he accumulated in 2000. Raising money in 2000 had been a means to scare off opposition, as Bush drove Elizabeth Dole and others from the race. Raising—and spending—such sums so early in the 2004 cycle was something else. Perhaps it was intended to discourage Democrats from seeking the nomination or was a way to require fund-raisers and other supporters to demonstrate their early commitment.

Ralph Nader

Nader's declaration of candidacy for the presidency on February 21, 2000, was scarcely a media event. Many newspapers decided not to cover the press conference at all. The *New York Times* gave Nader's entrance into the race just 331 words, buried on page A18. When Nader announced in 2004—almost four years to the day after his 2000 declaration—journalists turned their eyes toward him. His announcement got 1,441 words on the front page of the *Times* and was covered amply in every other major news outlet.

The Nader campaigns of 2000 and 2004 were quite different. Nader had run as the Green Party nominee in 2000, hoping to build a new, progressive party to challenge the Democrats and Republicans. He aimed to get the 5 percent of the national popular vote that would earn the Greens federal campaign funds in 2004, a goal he failed to achieve.[27] Democrats were upset when Nader's share of the vote appeared to throw the election to Bush in Florida.

This sour backdrop strongly colored Nader's 2004 run. Progressives in the entertainment business, such as filmmaker Michael Moore, abandoned his cause. Nader decided he was no longer interested in growing the Green Party and chose to run as an independent instead. He later pursued the nominations of the Green and Reform Parties but won only Reform's support, despite choosing a Green running mate. In contrast to his complaints about both Bush and Gore in 2000, Nader claimed to be assisting Kerry by opening up a "second front" against Bush in 2004.

While Democrats tried to keep Nader off the ballot in as many states as possible, Republicans helped him in various ways. FEC filings showed that roughly one in ten of Nader's $1,000–plus donors were Republicans. In all, Nader received almost $300,000 from GOP donors in the first five months of 2004.[28] Republican support was also instrumental in gaining him ballot access. Much of the first six months of Nader's campaign was devoted to getting on the ballot in enough states to compete seriously. In 2000 he had missed only seven state ballots, but that was with the assistance of the Green Party and without Democratic interference. This time Nader had to face scrutiny from Democratic activists every time his campaign delivered petitions to a secretary of state. But he also had conservatives helping him in Arizona, Michigan, Washington, and elsewhere.[29]

A New Stage

With all the nominations settled in early March but the nominating conventions still months away, a new stage of the presidential campaign opened. This "interregnum" phase, as Mayer and Busch call it, is neither nominating contest nor general election campaign. The challenge for each candidate is to select a running mate and develop an organization for the general election.

In 2004 Bush took the bull by the horns. He began attacking Kerry in February, even before the Democrat had sewn up the nomination. This was apparently the earliest that an incumbent president had ever mentioned his opponent by name. Bush's father, for example, had waited until August 1992 to mention Bill Clinton. In 1984 President Reagan did not utter Mondale's name in public until October.[30]

The interregnum poses different challenges for the two major-party nominees. One candidate comes out of a primary battle with an image to reconstruct, a running mate to select, and money to raise. The president, on the other hand, arrives not having spent much money or needing to select a vice-presidential candidate. Moreover, he has spent the last year planning a general rather than a primary election campaign.

The news vacuum created by the new space between the primaries and the convention provides an opportunity for events to play a large role in the campaign. The candidates must try to stay on message and in the headlines without boring voters or revealing too much about their strategies for the general election. Campaign news can be sparse. In the 2004 interregnum Bush was stung by developments in the Iraq conflict. Casualties of the war continued to mount, and Michael Moore's harsh documentary *Fahrenheit 9/11* was released. In addition, the 9/11 Commission appointed by Bush continued its inquiry. The periodic release of economic numbers provided a confusing portrait of where the economy was going. In this atmosphere Kerry gained ground in April and May, making the race a statistical dead heat by the start of summer.

Raising money occupied the Kerry campaign for most of the interregnum. Kerry's coffers were nearly empty when he wrapped up the nomination in early March. During the next four months before the convention, Kerry raised a staggering $233 million, nearly the same amount as Bush. Indeed, 2004 was the first time in the thirty-year history of the Federal Election Commission that both major-party nominees chose to raise money privately, and both easily surpassed the more than $100 million raised by Bush in 2000. Following the conventions, Bush and Kerry each received $75 million from the federal government to fund their general election campaigns.

The Conventions

For much of American history the national nominating convention was the forum at which state party leaders would broker a deal over who would represent the party in the presidential election. Conventions sometimes were marked by long stalemates, multiple ballots, and disputes on the floor. This tradition changed after the McGovern-Fraser Commission spurred the states toward more democratic methods for choosing delegates. The rise of television also motivated parties to use the conventions to woo undecided voters. The 2004 conventions were tightly choreographed media events that received just three hours of network television coverage each, spread over four nights.

As the Democrats' nominating convention approached, speculation grew about a running mate for Kerry. His short list included New Mexico governor Bill Richardson, Iowa governor Tom Vilsack, friend and also-ran Dick Gephardt, and John Edwards. Each provided something that Kerry lacked. Richardson would help with the Latino vote and in the Southwest. As governors, he and Vilsack would provide a counterweight to Kerry's career inside the Beltway, and each was from a swing state. Gephardt would help in battleground Missouri and with organized labor. Yet it was Edwards who won the nod from Kerry, mainly because he could help the campaign among lower-income and rural voters. The Kerry-Edwards ticket was the first since 1960 to feature two sitting senators.

The Democrats gathered in Boston in late July to launch the general election campaign, the first time the city had ever hosted a major-party convention. Although union protests and the city's Kennedyesque, liberal image threatened to interfere with the party's unified, centrist message, the convention unfolded without much trouble. In addition to the central speeches by Edwards and Kerry, the convention gave prominence to Democratic mainstays such as Bill Clinton and Ted Kennedy and introduced Theresa Heinz Kerry and Illinois Senate candidate Barack Obama. Speakers emphasized Kerry's Vietnam record, neglecting his twenty years in the Senate. Flanked by fellow veterans, Kerry arrived to salute the crowd and announce, "I am John

Kerry, and I am reporting for duty." At Kerry's direction, the convention avoided Bush-bashing in an attempt to be seen as the party of optimism.

Because the Republican convention would not take place until five weeks later, the Democrats worried about a fund-raising disadvantage. Concern stemmed from FEC rules that apply differently to the primary and general election campaigns. Once a nominee is officially chosen, funds raised for the primary campaign can no longer be spent. Because Bush would not be nominated until the GOP met in September, he could continue to raise and spend primary money for a month longer than Kerry.

It is a truism of presidential campaigns that a nominating convention provides the candidate with a "bounce" in the polls. This seems to happen because the convention introduces the candidate to voters who previously did not know him, presenting the nominee in the best light and without much audible criticism from the other party. The excitement of learning who will run for vice president contributes to the lift as well. Bounces have averaged six or seven points in recent campaigns.[31] Kerry, who was running about even with Bush before the convention, was hoping for a "double bounce"—one from the announcement on July 6 of Edwards as his running mate and the other from the convention itself.

Instead, the Democrats got almost no immediate bounce from either the Edwards announcement or the convention. Four different national polls showed Bush and Kerry remaining almost in a dead heat from the beginning to the end of July. This was the first time a bounce had failed to appear since 1972, when liberal George McGovern was nominated around midnight by a severely divided party. Why the well-scripted 2004 Democratic convention had no punch is unclear. Perhaps the Democrats did not hit Bush hard enough, or there may have been fewer undecided voters to persuade than in previous elections.[32] Or the bounce might have surfaced later, when Kerry's standing improved in early August despite little advertising.

The Republicans held their convention in New York, just a stone's throw from Ground Zero, the site of the September 11, 2001, attacks. The location gave the GOP ample opportunities to connect Bush to the patriotism aroused by the "war on terror." Despite large anti-Bush protests in the streets of New York, the Republicans largely executed their convention as planned. They highlighted popular centrists in the party, including maverick senator John McCain, former New York City mayor Rudy Giuliani, California governor Arnold Schwarzenegger, and Sen. Zell Miller, a conservative Democrat from Georgia. All of the speakers praised Bush's handling of terrorist threats and his removal of Saddam Hussein from power in Iraq. Yet they also turned their sights on Kerry to a greater extent than the Democrats had focused on Bush. Zell Miller, the first person ever to be a keynote speaker at both a Democratic (1992) and a Republican (2004) convention, angrily attacked Kerry for not supporting military spending. Vice President Dick Cheney amplified the indictment in his address. Bush's speech combined listing his first term successes, such as the No Child Left Behind Act, and promising a simplified tax code and partial privatization of Social Security in his second term. He also vowed to extend freedom to the Middle East and the rest of the world by defeating terrorism.

In contrast to the Democrats, the Republicans seemed to generate a substantial bounce in the polls with their convention. Their focus on foreign policy and Kerry's record took the race from a dead heat to a five to ten point Republican advantage, according to several polls. Kerry was not helped by new allegations from a 527 group calling itself "Swift Boat Veterans for Truth," which immediately ran television ads challenging his record in Vietnam.

Conclusion

The 2004 nominations fit most of the patterns established in recent elections but also introduced some new dynamics. Delegates and early events continued to be critical. The Democratic field was quickly winnowed, with most of the contenders bowing out of the race as soon as their chances looked bleak. The winnowing that took place was mostly, but not exclusively, the result of the front-loaded primary calendar. Different in 2004 was that so much of the winnowing happened before a single vote was cast and without much prodding from party leaders. This helped the Democrats in several ways. First, it provided the party with an early nominee and time to regroup before the general election. Second, the debates among the candidates and other invisible-primary events gave the party several months to hone its critique of the Bush administration. Despite a hard-fought contest, the Democrats emerged from the nominating process stronger than when they entered it.

Finally, much of the Democrats' success had to do with Howard Dean's transformation of the electoral environment. He managed to raise large sums of money in ways that few had expected to be successful. Unburdened by the baggage of a Washington career, he effectively trumpeted a list of grievances about Bush's policies and performance in office that emboldened other Democrats. In challenging his own party, Dean made Kerry a better campaigner and attracted new supporters. Finally, he handed the party new technological tools for organizing, fund raising, and spreading its message. Party leaders, who had come to play a larger role in nominations in recent years, were upstaged at least for a while by Dean, who forced the party to reevaluate its message and strategy. Kerry won the nomination because, in time of war, the Democrats wanted a nominee with military credentials, but the party he inherited had been invigorated by Dean.

Bush spent much of the nomination period preparing for the general election, raising money to build a campaign organization across the country. In several respects he aimed to avoid his father's mistakes in 1992: beginning the campaign too late, downplaying domestic policy, and allowing the Democrats to focus the election on the economy. Bush engaged Kerry even before the Democrat secured the nomination. For a while Kerry had to confront the administration while finishing off Edwards.

More than anything else, the 2004 nominations will be remembered for the dramatic transfer of momentum from Dean to the Democratic Party and then to Kerry. After several months of building support, raising money, and changing the terms of the debate during the invisible primary, the Dean machine folded as the Iowa caucuses approached. By making the party believe it was viable against Bush, Dean unintentionally turned Democratic voters toward the contender who appeared most electable.

Notes

I thank Sunshine Hillygus for helpful comments and Mike Nelson for editorial guidance.

1. William G. Mayer and Andrew E. Busch, *The Front-Loading Problem in Presidential Nominations* (Washington, D.C.: Brookings Institution Press, 2004).
2. Specifically, since 1968 it has happened only twice. In 1972 Edmund Muskie won both Iowa and New Hampshire but lost the nomination to George McGovern. In 1992 Tom Harkin won Iowa and Paul Tsongas won New Hampshire, but Bill Clinton won the nomination.
3. Arthur T. Hadley, *The Invisible Primary* (Englewood Cliffs, N.J.: Prentice Hall, 1976).
4. William G. Mayer, "The Basic Dynamics of the Contemporary Nomination Process: An Expanded View," in *The Making of the Presidential Candidates 2004,* ed. William G. Mayer (Lanham, Md.: Rowman and Littlefield, 2004).
5. John H. Aldrich, *Before the Convention: Strategies and Choices in Presidential Nomination Campaigns* (Chicago, Ill.: University of Chicago Press, 1980); and Larry M. Bartels, *Presidential Primaries and the Dynamics of Public Choice* (Princeton, N.J.: Princeton University Press, 1988).
6. Marty Cohen, David Karol, Hans Noel, and John Zaller, "Beating Reform: The Resurgence of Parties in Presidential Nominations, 1980 to 2000" (paper presented at the annual meeting of the American Political Science Association, San Francisco, 2001).
7. Mayer and Busch, *The Front-Loading Problem in Presidential Nominations.*
8. Andrew E. Busch and William G. Mayer, "The Front-Loading Problem," in *The Making of the Presidential Candidates 2004,* ed. William G. Mayer (Lanham, Md.: Rowman and Littlefield, 2004).
9. David Postman, "Legislators Cancel '04 Primary," *Seattle Times,* December 6, 2003.
10. In addition to the occupations shown, other backgrounds include activists and celebrities (10.3 percent of contenders), federal appointees (6.4 percent), and a few others.
11. Barry C. Burden, "United States Senators as Presidential Candidates," *Political Science Quarterly* 117 (Spring 2002): 81–102.
12. Michael Powell, "As Governor, Dean Was Fiscal Conservative," *Washington Post,* August 3, 2003.
13. Figure 2-2 shows the candidates' standings according to the Iowa Electronic Market (www.biz.uiowa.edu/iem/). Among other things, these political markets allowed investors to bet on which candidate would win the Democratic nomination. The operation has been forecasting election outcomes since 1988 and has

been a better gauge of expected success than are traditional polls. See S. G. Kou and Michael E. Sobel, "Forecasting the Vote: A Theoretical Comparison of Election Markets and Public Opinion Polls," *Political Analysis* 12 (Summer 2004): 277–295; and Daron R. Shaw and Brian E. Roberts, "Campaign Events, the Media and the Prospects of Victory: The 1992 and 1996 U.S. Presidential Elections," *British Journal of Political Science* 30 (April 2000): 259–289.

14. Diane Cardwell and David M. Halbfinger, "After Gore Endorsement, Attacks on Dean Are Sharper," *New York Times,* December 11, 2003.
15. Joe Trippi, personal interview, September 16, 2004, Harvard University.
16. Jodi Wilgoren, "Dean, under Attack, Revives Feisty Style," *New York Times,* December 25, 2003, A4.
17. Roger Simon, "Turning Point," *U.S. News & World Report,* July 19–26, 2004.
18. Ibid.
19. Jodi Wilgoren and Jim Rutenberg, "Missteps Pulled a Surging Dean Back to Earth," *New York Times,* February 1, 2004, 1
20. Katherine Q. Seelye, "Democratic Primaries' Turnout Is Said Not to Have Been Strong," *New York Times,* March 10, 2004.
21. Mayer and Busch, *The Front-Loading Problem in Presidential Nominations*; and Harold W. Stanley, "The Nominations: The Return of the Party Leaders," in *The Elections of 2000,* ed. Michael Nelson (Washington, D.C.: CQ Press, 2001).
22. Todd S. Purdum, "Mr. Inside Embraces Mr. Outside, and What a Surprise," *New York Times,* December 9, 2003.
23. Jill Lawrence, "Staffers Fill in Details of the Decline of Dean," *USA Today,* February 18, 2004, 1A.
24. Simon, "Turning Point."
25. Samantha M. Shapiro, "The Dean Connection," *New York Times Magazine,* December 7, 2003, Section 6, 56.
26. David Firestone, "Bush Loyalists Jockeying against Each Other to Raise Money," *New York Times,* July 21, 2003.
27. Barry C. Burden, "Ralph Nader's Campaign Strategy in the 2000 U.S. Presidential Election," *American Politics Research,* forthcoming.
28. Carla Marinucci, "GOP Donors Funding Nader," *San Francisco Chronicle,* July 9, 2004.
29. Michael Janofsky and Sarah Kershaw, "Odd Alliances Form in Efforts to Place Nader on Ballot," *New York Times,* July 1, 2004.
30. Dana Milbank, "The Challenger Gets Mentioned Early," *Washington Post,* March 9, 2004.
31. John R. Zaller, "The Statistical Power of Election Studies to Detect Media Exposure Effects in Political Campaigns," *Electoral Studies* 21 (June 2002): 297–329.
32. Adam Nagourney, "Polls Show Tight Race with a Few Gains for Kerry," *New York Times,* August 3, 2004.

3

The Presidential Election: The Ills of American Politics After 9/11

Gerald M. Pomper

Four years earlier, the question was, Did George W. Bush win the presidential election? In 2004, the question became, Why did Bush win the election?

The incumbent chief executive now had clear title as president of the United States. In the largest free election ever conducted in the world, Bush gained a transparent majority of the popular vote—reversing his trailing position in 2000, when Vice President Al Gore outpolled him by half a million votes. In the decisive electoral vote, Bush won a certain majority of 286 to 252 over his Democratic opponent, Sen. John F. Kerry—displacing the doubtful count of the previous contest.[1]

The popular and electoral tallies, however, were notably different in dimension. Although Bush won a clear popular vote majority, his actual selection as president by the Electoral College came from his victory in one state, Ohio, where he led Kerry by less than 120,000 votes. Without that narrow margin, Bush would have lost the White House (dropping twenty electoral votes), even while leading the national popular tally. Through the grace of Ohio, Bush dodged an ironic reversal of the 2000 election, when he took power even though Gore won the total popular vote.

The Electoral Map

The dominant characteristic of the 2004 election was the stability of the vote over four years. The geographic voting pattern virtually replicated that of the earlier election. Only three states shifted their overall preference: Iowa and New Mexico moved into Bush's column, and New Hampshire moved into Kerry's. But even these visible changes in the electoral map (Figure 3-1) were less impressive than they seemed. It took only a shift of half a percent in the vote to turn narrow Democratic victories in Iowa and New Mexico in 2000 into narrow Bush victories in 2004. The change in New Hampshire showed no true shift in sentiment but resulted from the virtual disappearance of Ralph Nader, whose vote had cost Gore the state in 2000.

Although the 2004 vote closely paralleled that of 2000, the small differences carried vital political significance. Bush's areas of support in the two elections were almost identical, yielding an astonishing correlation of .97, the high-

Figure 3-1 The Electoral Map of 2004

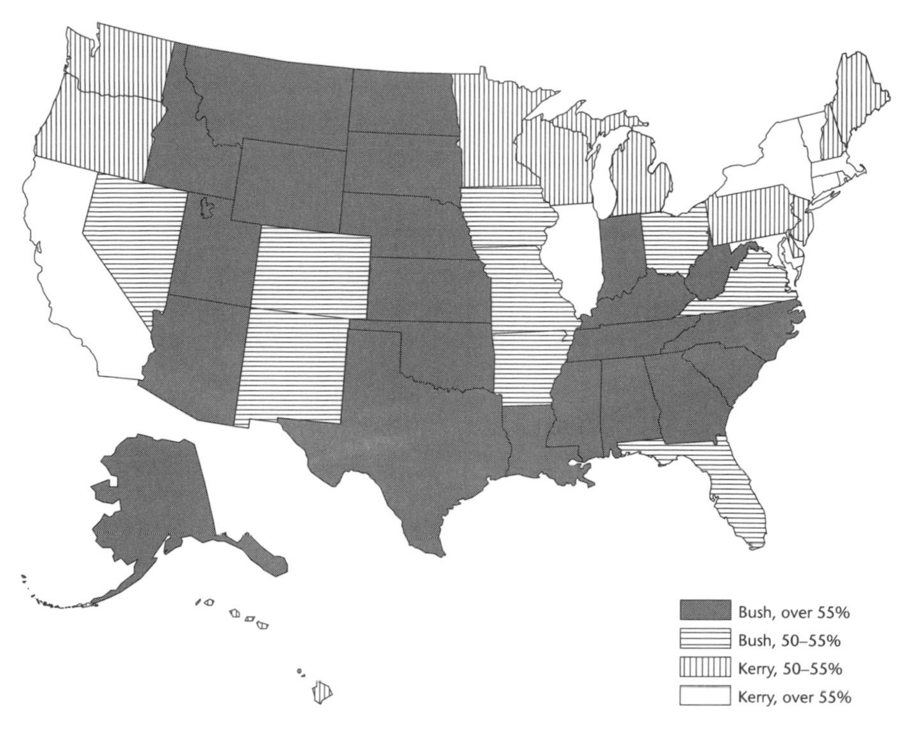

Sources: Curtis Gans, "Turnout Exceeds Optimistic Predictions," Committee for the Study of the American Electorate, press release, January 14, 2005, http://election04.ssrc.org/research/csae_2004_final_report.pdf; Michael P. McDonald, George Mason University, elections.gmu.edu/President_2004.htm.

est statistical association between successive elections in American history.[2] But his votes (detailed in Table 3-1) were higher in most states, and even if they were only marginally higher, that margin made all the difference. Nationally, the president gained only a bare edge, an additional 1.5 percent of the major-party vote. On a state-by-state basis, Bush's gain was even smaller, on average only 1.0 percentage points. But Bush lost significant ground (3 percent or more) in just three sparsely, populated states—Alaska, Montana, and Vermont—while gaining significantly in ten states, including the reputedly liberal states of Connecticut, New Jersey, and New York, the metropolitan area of the World Trade Center, destroyed on September 11, 2001.

When the results are presented on television with a colored map, the nation appears sharply divided geographically, with states colored Republican red and Democratic blue.[3] That map appears to be a sea of red, with scattered islands of blue. Bush won every state south of the Ohio River and every state lying entirely between the west bank of the Mississippi River and the rim of the Pacific coast, along with the Midwest states of Ohio and Indiana, a total of thirty-one. The visual impact is reinforced by the large acreage of the Republican states. Kerry's support was confined to nineteen states (and

Table 3-1 The Presidential Vote of 2004

State	Electoral vote		Popular vote		Two-party vote (%)		Two-party vote (%), 2000	
	Bush	Kerry	Bush	Kerry	Bush	Kerry	Bush	Gore
Alabama	9		1,176,394	693,933	62.9	37.1	57.6	42.4
Alaska	3		190,889	111,025	63.2	36.8	67.9	32.1
Arizona	10		1,104,294	893,524	55.3	44.7	53.3	46.7
Arkansas	6		572,898	469,953	54.9	45.1	52.8	47.2
California		55	5,509,826	6,745,485	45.0	55.0	43.8	56.2
Colorado	9		1,101,255	1,001,732	52.4	47.6	54.5	45.5
Connecticut		7	693,826	857,488	44.7	55.3	40.7	59.3
Delaware		3	171,660	200,152	46.2	53.8	43.3	56.7
Dist. of Columbia		3	21,256	202,970	9.5	90.5	9.5	90.5
Florida	27		3,964,522	3,583,544	52.5	47.5	50.0	50.0
Georgia	15		1,914,254	1,366,149	58.4	41.6	56.0	44.0
Hawaii		4	194,191	231,708	45.6	54.4	40.2	59.8
Idaho	4		409,235	181,098	69.3	30.7	70.9	29.1
Illinois		21	2,346,608	2,891,989	44.8	55.2	43.8	56.2
Indiana	11		1,479,438	969,011	60.4	39.6	58.0	42.0
Iowa	7		751,957	741,898	50.3	49.7	49.8	50.2
Kansas	6		736,456	434,993	62.9	37.1	60.9	39.1
Kentucky	8		1,069,439	712,733	60.0	40.0	57.7	42.3
Louisiana	9		1,102,169	820,299	57.3	42.7	53.9	46.1
Maine		4	330,201	396,842	45.4	54.6	47.2	52.8
Maryland		10	1,024,703	1,334,493	43.4	56.6	41.6	58.4
Massachusetts		12	1,071,109	1,803,800	37.3	62.7	35.2	64.8
Michigan		17	2,313,746	2,479,183	48.3	51.7	47.4	52.6
Minnesota		10*	1,346,695	1,445,014	48.2	51.8	48.7	51.3
Mississippi	6		672,660	457,768	59.5	40.5	58.6	41.4
Missouri	11		1,455,713	1,259,171	53.6	46.4	51.7	48.3
Montana	3		266,063	173,710	60.5	39.5	63.6	36.4
Nebraska	5		512,814	254,328	66.8	33.2	65.2	34.8
Nevada	5		418,690	397,190	51.3	48.7	51.9	48.1
New Hampshire		4	331,237	340,511	49.3	50.7	50.7	49.3
New Jersey		15	1,670,003	1,911,430	46.6	53.4	41.8	58.2
New Mexico	5		376,930	370,942	50.4	49.6	50.0	50.0
New York		31	2,962,567	4,314,280	40.7	59.3	36.9	63.1
North Carolina	15		1,961,166	1,525,849	56.2	43.8	56.5	43.5
North Dakota	3		196,651	111,052	63.9	36.1	64.5	35.5
Ohio	20		2,859,764	2,741,165	51.1	48.9	51.8	48.2
Oklahoma	7		959,792	503,966	65.6	34.4	61.1	38.9
Oregon		7	866,831	943,163	47.9	52.1	49.8	50.2
Pennsylvania		21	2,793,847	2,938,095	48.7	51.3	47.9	52.1
Rhode Island		4	169,046	259,760	39.4	60.6	34.4	65.6
South Carolina	8		937,974	661,699	58.6	41.4	58.2	41.8
South Dakota	3		232,584	149,244	60.9	39.1	61.6	38.4
Tennessee	11		1,384,375	1,036,477	57.2	42.8	52.0	48.0
Texas	34		4,526,917	2,832,704	61.5	38.5	61.0	39.0
Utah	5		663,742	241,199	73.3	26.7	71.7	28.3
Vermont		3	121,180	184,067	39.7	60.3	44.6	55.4
Virginia	13		1,716,959	1,454,742	54.1	45.9	54.1	45.9
Washington		11	1,304,894	1,510,201	46.4	53.6	47.1	52.9
West Virginia	5		423,550	326,541	56.5	43.5	53.2	46.8
Wisconsin		10	1,478,120	1,489,504	49.8	50.2	49.9	50.1
Wyoming	3		167,629	70,776	70.3	29.7	71.0	29.0
Totals	286	252	62,028,719	59,028,550	51.2	48.8	49.7	50.3

Sources: Curtis Gans, "Turnout Exceeds Optimistic Predictions," Committee for the Study of the American Electorate, press release, January 14, 2005, http://election04.ssrc.org/research/csae_2004_final_report.pdf; Michael P. McDonald, George Mason University, elections.gmu.edu/President_2004.htm.

Notes: The total national vote was 122.3 million, 60.7% of those eligible. The total minor-party vote was 1.2 million, 1% of the total vote for 16 candidates, including independent Ralph Nader, 440,513.

*One Democratic elector in Minnesota cast a presidential vote for Edwards, not Kerry.

the District of Columbia)—the Pacific Coast, most of the Midwest, and the northeast corner of the nation, where he won all of the New England and Middle Atlantic states, relatively small in geographic size.

In an earlier time—as with John Kennedy's victory in 1960—the states Kerry carried would have brought him to the White House.[4] But the American population has been moving—to the South, the Southwest, the Rocky Mountains, and the Pacific. Only the last of these regions has been friendly to the Democrats. With the population changes have come shifts in electoral votes. In 2004, the population shift meant that the states that Bush carried in 2000 now had seven more electoral votes. Even before the campaign began, the decennial Census had converted his earlier 271 electoral votes to 278; this was the arithmetic equivalent of taking Oregon out of the Union.

The two-color map presents a dramatic picture, but it is also deceptive. Most of the nation is actually neither red nor blue (nor black and white in our monochromatic map), but a mixed blend of purple (or gray), as can be seen in maps of counties, rather than states. When the map is drawn in proportion to the actual populations of counties, "only a rather small area is taken up by true red counties, the rest being mostly shades of purple with patches of blue in the urban areas." [5]

Bush's narrow victory was reflected in most regions. The vote tallies were within 5 percent of a tie (45 to 55 percent) in twenty states, while Bush and Kerry together gained "blowouts" (over 60 percent) in only seventeen states and the District of Columbia. This more complex picture, including the variation in the results, is shown in Figure 3-1.

In fact, the attitudes of voters in these states are actually more alike than different, as Morris Fiorina and his associates showed in a preelection study. On most policy issues, red state and blue state residents share similar views. There are almost as many Democrats in both groups (36 percent in the blue states, 32 percent in the red), and almost as few liberals (22 percent in the blue and 18 percent in the red). In both kinds of states, residents attend church regularly (50 percent blue and 65 percent red), yet they are also tolerant of others' moral views (62 percent in both areas) and oppose job discrimination against gays (73 percent blue and 62 percent red). At least until the 2004 election, the regional data provide "little that calls to mind the portrait of a culture war between the states." [6]

Sources of the Vote

The most striking aspect of the vote for president in 2004 is its size; the election brought a vast increase in turnout over 2000 of close to 17 million participants. More than one in six voters in 2004 had not cast a ballot four years earlier. More than one in ten, primarily young voters, had never voted before.

The youth vote—those aged eighteen to twenty-nine—increased considerably, both in actual numbers—an additional 4.6 million, for a total of nearly

21 million—and in the proportion participating—an increase from 42 percent to 51 percent.[7] Kerry had hoped this would happen, taking his campaign to college campuses with rock idols such as Bon Jovi and Bruce Springsteen. In its own terms, the effort worked: more young people voted, they ignored Ralph Nader, and they chose Kerry, by a 54–45 margin, a considerable improvement over Gore's showing among young voters in 2000.

Democrats tried to win this vote, and they succeeded. But the new young voters did not elect Kerry because Republicans also succeeded in mobilizing other votes for Bush. As young people came to the polls, they were met by older citizens who were also energized by the campaign, so that the proportion of younger voters in the total electorate was unchanged from 2000, remaining at 17 percent.

Responding to the competing mobilization efforts, turnout rose in virtually every demographic group and region. New votes from Christian evangelicals may have totaled four million—the publicized goal of Bush strategist Karl Rove.[8] This new evangelical vote almost equaled that of the new young voters but was far more cohesive, with 77 percent supporting Bush. The overall result worked to the advantage of the Republicans: previously a lower proportion of the turnout, they reached parity with Democrats at the voting booths.

The great increase in turnout had many causes. Voters were far more interested in the election than they had been four years earlier, probably reflecting the intensity and closeness of the contest, the barrage of television and other mass media campaigning, and a patriotic concern for the nation in the war environment created by the terrorist attacks of September 11, 2001, and the subsequent invasion of Iraq. In widespread mobilization campaigns, as many as two million people were involved in get-out-the-vote efforts.

Democrats, in particular, had placed their bets on mobilizing a large vote, since conventional wisdom taught that a large vote would be to their benefit. Their effort succeeded, at least in its own terms. Urban turnout, especially in minority areas, increased considerably. More voters reported contacts from the Kerry than from the Bush campaign. But again, that effort was matched or overmatched by Republican efforts.

Ohio provides the critical example. Democrats had close to 50,000 canvassers in the state. On election day, the encouraging result for Kerry was a substantial margin in the Democrats' strong areas. Kerry won Cuyahoga County (Cleveland) by over 200,000 votes, a 30 percent increase over Gore's margin in 2000.[9] The pattern also appeared in other industrial and urban areas; even in traditionally Republican Cincinnati, the Democrats cut their 2000 losses in half. The turnout of new Democratic voters provided enough additional ballots to virtually reverse Gore's loss of the state (by 165,000 votes) in 2000 (see Table 3-2).

But a Kerry victory also would have required that the vote be unchanged in the rest of the state, and Republicans and their allies were also active.[10] Concentrating on Ohio's smaller cities and on churchgoing white

Table 3-2 The Ohio County Vote, 2004 and 2000

	Kerry 2004	Bush 2004	Kerry 2004 margin	Gore 2000	Bush 2000	Gore 2000 margin	Kerry gain/loss
Counties adding to the Democratic vote							
Cuyahoga County: Cleveland	433,262	215,624	217,638	359,913	192,099	167,814	49,824
Northeast urban/ industrial area (10)	629,696	518,265	111,431	512,564	437,425	75,139	36,292
Other larger cities/ major universities (5)	750,690	679,608	71,082	599,695	594,874	4,821	66,261
Totals	1,813,648	1,413,497	400,151	1,472,172	1,224,398	247,774	152,377
Counties adding to the Republican vote							
Cincinnati area (3)	104,902	234,952	−130,050	86,459	182,034	−95,575	−34,475
South of Columbus (11)	89,476	131,463	−41,987	78,162	107,737	−29,575	−12,412
West of Columbus (7)	104,364	163,857	−59,493	91,393	132,213	−40,820	−18,673
Totals	298,742	530,272	−231,530	256,014	421,984	−165,970	−65,560

Source: Compiled by the author from preliminary data from the office of the Ohio secretary of state, www.sos.state.oh.us.
Note: Bush margins: 2004 = 118,599; 2000 = 165,019.

Protestants and Catholics, the GOP brought its own new voters to the polls and recruited established voters to their cause. In the small town and suburban counties in southwestern Ohio alone, Bush's margins increased by 65,000 over 2000, more than half of his ultimate edge statewide and more than enough to hold Ohio to its traditional Republicanism. As academic observers had long noted, many previous nonvoters were social conservatives and thus unlikely to cast Democratic ballots; the Ohio results of 2004 vindicated their analysis.[11]

Nationally the vote revealed sharp divisions among American voters, although the divisions did not fall along geographic lines. Republican support was particularly high among whites, regular churchgoers, evangelical Christians, residents of smaller communities, married people, those not in union households, those with a family income above $50,000, and southerners. Voters in these groups gave Bush at least 10 percent more of their vote than did matched groups in the various demographic categories (as listed in Table 3-3).[12]

The more extreme differences among voters fell along lines of race, class, and church attendance. The racial disparity in candidate support was enormous between whites and blacks, forty-seven percentage points, and was considerable—at least fourteen points—between whites and Hispanics. Class also mattered: Poorer Americans voted Democratic; those around the median income split their votes evenly; and the wealthy gave Bush strong support. Those attending church frequently also declared their Republican faith, voting twenty-four percentage points more for Bush than did those who avoid houses of religious worship.

Table 3-3 Social Groups and the Presidential Vote, 2004 and 2000

2004 voters (%)	2000 voters (%)	Characteristic	2004 For Bush (%)	2004 For Kerry (%)	2000 For Bush (%)	2000 For Gore (%)
		Party and ideology				
1	2	Liberal Republicans	78	22	67	31
13	14	Moderate Republicans	89	11	88	11
23	19	Conservative Republicans	97	3	95	4
5	5	Liberal independents	17	79	17	68
15	15	Moderate independents	47	51	41	48
6	6	Conservative independents	76	21	79	17
14	13	Liberal Democrats	4	95	5	91
19	20	Moderate Democrats	13	87	12	86
3	5	Conservative Democrats	23	76	26	73
		Ethnic group				
77	82	White	58	41	54	42
11	10	Black	11	88	8	90
8	4	Hispanic	44	53	31	67
2	2	Asian	44	56	41	54
		Sex/ethnicity				
36	39	White men	62	37	60	36
41	43	White women	55	44	49	48
5	4	Black men	13	86	12	85
6	6	Black women	10	90	6	94
		Sex/marital status				
30	32	Married men	60	39	58	38
32	33	Married women	55	44	49	48
16	16	Unmarried men	45	53	46	48
22	19	Unmarried women	37	62	32	63
		Age				
17	17	18–29 years old	45	54	46	48
29	33	30–44 years old	54	46	49	48
30	28	45–59 years old	51	48	49	48
24	22	60 years and older	54	46	47	51
		Education				
4	5	Not a high school graduate	49	50	39	59
22	21	High school graduate	52	47	49	48
32	32	Some college education	54	46	51	45
26	24	College graduate	52	46	51	45
16	18	Post-graduate education	44	55	44	52
		Religion				
		Protestant				
40	47	White Protestant	58	40	63	34
22		White evangelical	77	22		
42		Attend church weekly	70	29		
27	26	Catholic	52	47	47	49
12		Attend church weekly	55	44		
3	4	Jewish	25	74	19	79
		Family income				
8	7	Under $15,000	36	63	37	57
15	16	$15,000–$29,999	42	57	41	54

(Continues)

Table 3-3 Social Groups and the Presidential Vote, 2004 and 2000 *(Continued)*

2004 voters (%)	2000 voters (%)	Characteristic	2004 For Bush (%)	2004 For Kerry (%)	2000 For Bush (%)	2000 For Gore (%)
		Family income (cont.)				
22	24	$30,000–$49,999	49	50	48	49
58	53	Over $50,000	56	43	52	45
32	28	Over $75,000	57	42	53	44
18	15	Over $100,000	58	41	54	43
24	26	*Union household*	40	59	37	59
18		*Veterans*	57	41		
		Size of place				
13	9	Population over 500,000	37	62	26	71
19	20	Population 50,000–500,000	49	50	40	57
45	43	Suburbs	51	48	49	47
8	5	Population 10,000–50,000	50	49	59	38
16	23	Rural areas	58	40	59	37

Source: National exit polls conducted by the National Election Pool.

The divisions among Americans, however, can be exaggerated—we are not "two nations." [13] The vote was similar (that is, the differences were less than ten percentage points) between many paired groups, including men and women, those who did and did not attend college, the young and the old, Protestants and Catholics, veterans and nonveterans, working women and homemakers, the middle class and the wealthy, urbanites and suburbanites, parents and the childless, and residents of regions outside the South.

The demographic differences that did exist suggested to some disheartened Democrats a simple explanation of the vote: the election was decided by personifications of the fictional Snopes family created by William Faulkner. These voters are poor, uneducated, southern white men, using their votes unintelligently to advance bigotry, racism, and physical aggression. The explanation may provide solace to cynics, but it is wrong, for three reasons.

First, the actual vote does not fit the story. Poor voters actually supported Kerry, as did those who had not completed high school. If they had been the only voters, the Democrats would have won the election handily.

Second, voting among these groups reflected past patterns rather than a unique reaction to the electoral environment of 2004: the "Snopes vote" was already firmly Republican. To the extent that it changed, the trends were not consistent. In fact, Kerry won slightly more support than Gore did from white men, the poor, and residents of smaller communities. He did only slightly worse than Gore among Catholics, white Protestants, and gun owners.

Third, rather than a sudden onslaught of the boorish and the foolish, the election evidenced a thin, but broad, shift toward Bush over the four years of his administration. His greatest gains (4 percent above his 2000 vote) occurred among many groups not fitting the Snopes stereotype: women, residents of large and medium-sized cities, seniors, persons without children, infrequent churchgoers, residents of the Northeast, married people, and possibly Hispanics.[14] The vaunted gender gap—the differing preferences of men and women—decreased considerably from 2000 to 2004. The more significant marriage gap—the difference between those married and those single—increased. Just as the president gained a few votes in most states and regions, he increased his support—marginally but critically—among most demographic groups.

In the politics of 2004, demography was not destiny. Far more important were Americans' political attitudes: their partisan loyalties, ideological commitments, and policy preferences. Partisan divisions among citizens were already severe a year before election day,[15] confirming recent trends toward a more committed electorate.[16] Always the best indicator of electoral behavior, party loyalty was especially firm in 2004. Kerry won 89 percent of Democrats; Bush won even more, 93 percent, of Republicans; and the two candidates split the votes of independents almost exactly in half.

These party loyalties incorporated ideological attachments. In recent decades, Republican Party leaders have become coherently conservative and Democratic leaders coherently liberal. These philosophical commitments could be seen in attitudes of party convention delegates and in congressional roll calls.[17] Taking their cues from these leaders, voters aligned their party loyalties. There were very few liberal Republicans or conservative Democrats in the 2004 electorate, and the proportion of conservatives among Republican voters expanded significantly.

When the two conflicted, voters' party loyalties were far stronger than their ideology. Bush swept even the few liberal Republicans; Kerry, improving over Gore, held more than three-fourths of conservative Democrats. The election outcome turned not on partisan disloyalty but on partisan mobilization. Bush won simply because there he secured a greater increase in turnout among Republicans and conservatives.

In party terms, as in the geography of the vote, the election was largely a repetition of the 2000 results. Yet, as can be seen in Figure 3-2, there also were dynamic elements. New voters entered the lists, barely favoring Kerry; Nader's disruptive vote of 2000 disappeared, again slightly favoring Kerry; and small—and offsetting—proportions of Gore and Bush voters switched sides. Bush won in 2004 because there were more consistent, "standpat" Republicans than Democrats. This group appears as the largest segment in Figure 3-2, again demonstrating the mobilization of party loyalists.[18]

Voters in 2004 were strongly loyal to their parties, but their partisan behavior meant more than simple party loyalty. Citizens now choose their parties not on incoherent emotional grounds but because their party expresses their policy attitudes. As a young scholar writes, "mass partisanship . . . is now based significantly more on a rational assessment of differences between the parties (and, as such, on policy considerations) than on inherited, affective considerations." [19]

Figure 3-2 Dynamics of the 2000–2004 Presidential Vote

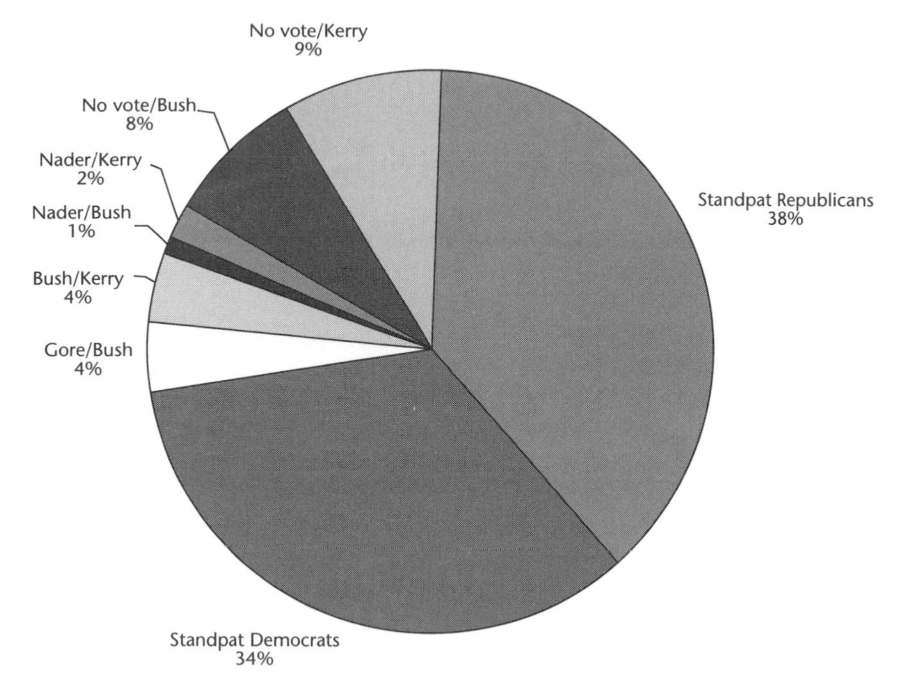

Source: Author calculations based on national exit polls conducted by the National Election Pool.

The Campaign

The Setting

The election of 2004 was constrained by the long-standing social memberships, party loyalties, and ideological commitments of the voters. But it was also affected, as is every contest, by the particular events, issues, and candidates of the time. These short-term factors made for an exciting and closely fought campaign.

Usually an incumbent president has a distinct advantage when running for reelection. He can control the agenda of national politics; establish foreign policy, the budget, and the multiple policies of the executive departments; nominate all federal judges and administrators; garner immediate publicity for any actions; and provide benefits to favored areas and groups—as Bush did—from hurricane relief in Florida, to higher steel tariffs in Pennsylvania, to restrictions on abortion.

After gaining control of the White House in 2001, George Bush vigorously deployed all the resources of incumbency. Construing his selection as a mandate, he secured major legislation to lower taxes, particularly for those in the higher income brackets, to redirect national education policy, and to create a limited prescription drug program for seniors. He formulated assertive foreign and defense policies—most obviously in invading Iraq but also in declaring a readiness to launch preemptive military attacks on potential adversaries and in repudiating international agreements on global warming and missile defenses. The judges he nominated leaned distinctly to the right, as did his policy statements on social issues such as abortion, stem cell research, and the legalization of marriage between homosexuals.

In a reelection campaign, the focus is typically on the record of the incumbent, as the electorate passes a retrospective judgment on the president's four years in office. Bush's record made him vulnerable. He took office without the legitimacy of a popular vote majority and with a disputed electoral vote majority, dependent on the frail authority of a 5–4 decision by the Supreme Court.[20] Early in his term he had only a bare and declining favorable majority in job approval ratings. Just as he took office, the economy entered a downturn, and eventually the nation endured the first decline in jobs over a presidential term since the Great Depression of the 1930s. The war in Iraq turned from a quick military triumph to a chaotic insurgency, including suicide bombings, the deaths of over a thousand U.S. military personnel, revelations of the torture of Iraqis in American prisons, and refutation of administration claims that Iraq possessed weapons of mass destruction. The tide of events threatened Bush's hold on power.

Except for one event: On September 11, 2001, terrorists crashed hijacked airliners into the World Trade Center and the Pentagon, killing almost 3,000 Americans. The president launched the "war on terror." Soon, Afghanistan was conquered and Iraq invaded. Congress passed the "PATRIOT Act" and established the new Department of Homeland Security, bolstering executive authority. The nation, now facing threats both intimate and uncertain, rallied behind the war president; Bush's approval ratings briefly soared to 90 percent, the highest ever recorded.

September 11 created a new reality of American politics; it became the newly central element of the electoral environment of 2004. A change of president would represent not only a transition in government but a basic choice between continuity and uncertainty. Americans would need to resolve Hamlet's famous dilemma, whether they would

> . . . rather bear those ills we have
> Than fly to others that we know not of?
> Thus conscience does make cowards of us all. . . .[21]

In the post 9/11 environment, the election became as much an existential as a political decision, one that matched disappointment with Bush against uncertainty about Kerry. By the last week of the campaign, two journalists reported, "A general consensus exists among strategists from both parties that a majority of voters appear willing to oust Bush. At the same time, though, many voters tell pollsters that although they do not approve of the president's performance in office, they are not sold on replacing him with Kerry during such tumultuous times." [22]

Bush versus Kerry

The campaign was long and intense but did not itself determine the outcome. Political scientists predicted the results long before election day, and their forecasts of a Bush victory proved correct, if exaggerated.[23] As Figure 3-3 illustrates, no evident trend emerged in the polls during the campaign. The two candidates ran close to each other throughout the election year, and their ratings over the course of the campaign were essentially as flat as the temperature chart of a stabilized patient.

The candidates' campaign strategies offset each other. Kerry gained a small lead at the end of July, just after he selected John Edwards as his running mate and gained formal ratification of his nomination at the Democratic National Convention. His lead was short-lived, soon reversed by a carefully managed Republican convention. Bush was artfully staged—in New York City—as the nation's savior after the terrorist attacks on the World Trade Center. Kerry came back to life in the presidential debates; the public judged

Figure 3-3 Trend in 2004 Election Polls

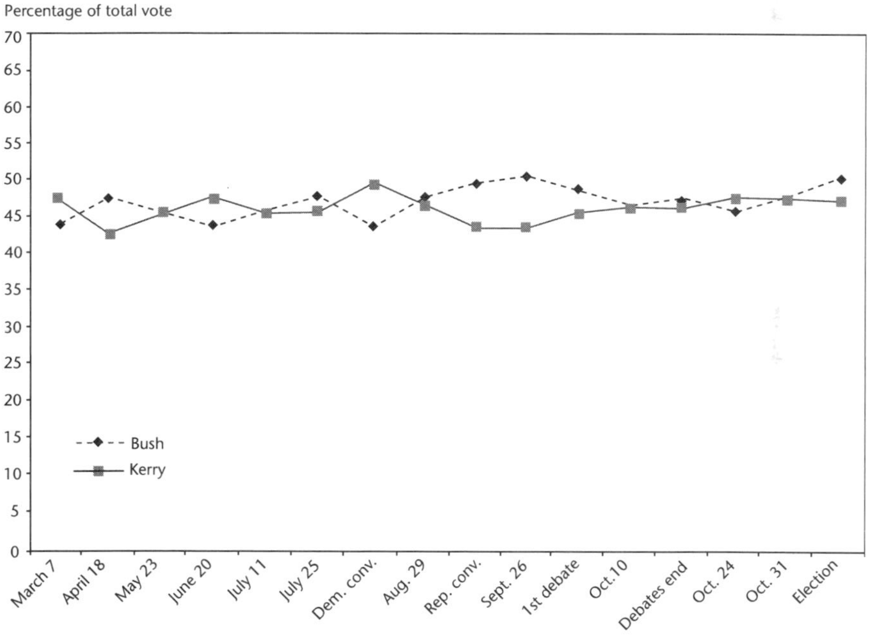

Source: Net leaned vote of registered voters, Washingtonpost.com.

him the "winner" in all three engagements, particularly the first. In the final weeks, the race was essentially tied in the polls, until Bush finally pulled in his small majority on election day.

The candidates deluged voters with their appeals, through rallies, policy statements, appearances on national television programs and local radio stations, and repetitive advertisements in battleground states. The issues of the campaign (see Table 3-4) were sharply different from those in 2000. Iraq and terrorism dominated the news reports, in contrast to the domestic issues that predominated four years earlier. Although Bush and Kerry did carry on a debate about Iraq, their other emphases were quite different. Terrorism was frequently the unanswered focus for Bush. Kerry emphasized the shape of the economy, while Bush dwelt only generally with domestic issues. But, surprisingly, neither candidate gave priority in their daily speeches to the moral issues that apparently concerned many in the electorate, such as gay marriage.

Although the candidates ranged widely on the issues, they confined their travels, as well as their advertising, to the relatively few states seen as competitive. As shown in Table 3-5, the candidates dogged each other's tracks in the battleground states, sometimes even appearing literally within earshot of

Table 3-4 Campaign Issues, 2004 and 2000

	2004		2000	
Topic	Bush	Kerry	Bush	Gore
Foreign and defense policy issues				
Iraq	14	15		
Terrorism	7	1		
Diplomacy	1		3	2
Military defense	2	1	2	
Leadership, character	6	5	8	4
Domestic issues				
Education/family policy/women	3	1	8	10
Health coverage	4	4	1	2
Social Security	1	4	5	3
Medicare, prescription drugs			4	5
Crime, gun control, drugs		2	1	
Economic management, jobs	1	11	1	8
Taxes, budget, ideology	7	1	11	9
Environment/energy/science		2	4	5
Social issues				
Gay marriage				
Morality, pornography, media			2	3
Campaign finance			1	1
Civil rights				2
Abortion				
Totals	46	47	51	54

Source: Lead issue reported daily in the *New York Times;* days spent at home or on the television debates excluded.

Table 3-5 Candidate Visits in the 2004 Campaign

State	Electoral votes	Number of visits			
		Bush	Kerry	Cheney	Edwards
Alabama	9	1			
Alaska	3				
Arizona	10	2	2		1
Arkansas	6			1	
California	55				1
Colorado	9	4	4	2	1
Connecticut	7				
Delaware	3				
Dist. of Columbia	3				
Florida	27	11	14	5	13
Georgia	15				
Hawaii	4			1	
Idaho	4				
Illinois	21			1	1
Indiana	11				
Iowa	7	8	7	9	8
Kansas	6				
Kentucky	8				1
Louisiana	9		1	1	
Maine	4	2			3
Maryland	10				1
Massachusetts	12				
Michigan	17	5	3	5	5
Minnesota	10	4	3	6	5
Mississippi	6				
Missouri	11	3	2	2	1
Montana	3				
Nebraska	5				
Nevada	5	2	4	4	1
New Hampshire	4	3	3	1	3
New Jersey	15	1		1	2
New Mexico	5	3	5	4	1
New York	31	3	1		1
North Carolina	15	1	1		3
North Dakota	3				
Ohio	20	10	16	11	16
Oklahoma	7			1	
Oregon	7	1		2	3
Pennsylvania	21	10	9	6	7
Rhode Island	4				1
South Carolina	8				1
South Dakota	3				
Tennessee	11				
Texas	34	1			
Utah	5				
Vermont	3				
Virginia	13				
Washington	11				
West Virginia	5	2		3	5
Wisconsin	10	8	13	6	7
Wyoming	3			1	
Totals	538	85	88	73	92

Sources: Daily reports in the *New York Times* and at abcnews.com; days in Washington, D.C., or home visits excluded.

each other, in the same city on the same day. But thirty states, from the most populous, California, to the most spacious, Alaska, received no more than a single visit by a single presidential or vice-presidential candidate.

In the end, the outcome would depend on what was uppermost in the voters' minds: If voters focused on "those ills we have," then their disappointment with Bush—reflected in mediocre job approval ratings and a predominant opinion that the nation was "on the wrong track"—would likely lead to his defeat. But if voters thought mainly of their uncertainty about Kerry as the alternative, they would be less likely to "fly to others that we know not of."

The Republican campaign successfully shifted much of the focus from Bush to Kerry. Vice President Dick Cheney led the assault on the senator as weak and vacillating on issues of national security, both at home and abroad, going so far as to suggest that terrorists would be encouraged to attack the nation again if Kerry were elected. The tactic succeeded sufficiently to give Bush large advantages over Kerry among the third of the electorate that most wanted the president to be a "strong leader" with "clear stands on issues" (as detailed in Table 3-6 below).

The Republicans continued, in more restrained language, a line of attack opened in August by Swift Boat Veterans for Truth, an independent group possibly allied to the Bush-Cheney reelection effort. In inexpensive advertisements freely replayed in the mass media without verification, the group

Table 3-6 Issue and Candidate Traits in the 2004 Election

	% voting for		% contribution to vote	
	Bush	Kerry	Bush	Kerry
Issue and % citing as most important				
Taxes, 5%	56	44	3	2
Education, 4%	25	75	1	3
Iraq, 15%	25	74	4	12
Terrorism, 19%	86	14	18	3
Economy/jobs, 20%	18	80	4	17
Moral values, 22%	79	18	19	4
Health care, 8%	22	78	2	7
Totals			50	49
Candidate quality and % citing as most important				
Cares about people like me, 9%	24	75	2	7
Strong religious faith, 8%	91	8	8	1
Honest and trustworthy, 11%	70	29	8	3
A strong leader, 17%	86	13	16	2
Intelligent, 7%	8	91	1	7
Bring about needed change, 25%	5	95	1	25
Clear stands on issues, 17%	78	21	14	4
Totals			50	49

Source: Author calculations based on national exit polls conducted by the National Election Pool.

accused Kerry of lying about his war record in Vietnam and of fraudulently receiving medals for his war wounds. Kerry added to the problem by waiting three weeks to answer the charges (perhaps wanting to preserve his campaign's funds for the later months), far too long in a world of instantaneous cable and internet communications.[24] The accusations were later shown to be undocumented lies. But by reinforcing the Republicans' broader critique of Kerry's personal traits, they did him great damage.

Kerry also had some inherent deficiencies as a candidate. He never established a warm, personal connection to the voters, losing to Bush even among his fellow Catholics. His nomination owed much to his heroic record in Vietnam, because Democrats required a candidate with a credible appeal on issues of military strength. But Vietnam was thirty years in the past, and Kerry's record there could not alone establish his present-day qualifications. Kerry also bore the handicap of his service in Congress, providing critics with a twenty-year record that would inevitably show changed positions, apparent inconsistencies, and political compromises. His complicated explanations were joyfully trumpeted by Republicans as admissions that he was no more than a "flip-flopper," unreliable as a potential commander in chief.

In contrast, the Bush effort was managed skillfully. It extended organizational discipline from its national headquarters in Virginia to every locality, raised money in extravagant amounts, and produced evocative television advertising. The president stayed relentlessly on message in his speeches, conveyed personal warmth through appearances with his family, suggested strength as he rolled up his sleeves at rallies, and invoked piety in his secular homilies. Despite a strategy that emphasized attacks on his opponent (75 percent of his messages, compared with 40 percent of Kerry's), he convinced the public that he conducted the fairer campaign.[25]

Yet even in the face of the efficient Republican campaign, Kerry ran well. In the television debates, he impressed the public as confident, competent, and better informed than the incumbent president. Forced by the nature of the times to focus on Bush's war agenda, he still fought him almost to a draw. Learning from Howard Dean, Kerry used the new technology of the Internet to amass an e-mail list of three million supporters and to bring the Democrats close to financial parity with the GOP. In a rare feat for a Democrat, he won the endorsement of most of the nation's daily newspapers, including forty-three that switched from supporting Bush in 2000.[26] On the bottom line, the senator brought out over eight million more Democrats than Gore did, increased his party's share of the total electorate to the highest level since 1964, and won more popular votes nationally than any previous candidate—winner or loser—in American electoral history. Kerry did well; Bush did better.

Any losing candidate is apt to be blamed for his party's defeat.[27] Yet with a very few more votes in a few critical states, Kerry would probably now be seen as a political genius. Although his campaign had many organizational deficiencies, it would be overly simple to blame him personally for the loss. As senator from Massachusetts, he bore the unpopular label of a Northeast liberal. He was attacked without pause—relentlessly by the Republican Party, slanderously by independent groups. Despite these handicaps, he still came close to unseating a determined and politically adept incumbent president in time of war. Even a partisan opponent, former Republican Speaker Newt Gingrich, credits Kerry: "I think he did the best he could. I think he actually overperformed his natural vote by four or five percentage points." [28] Elections are draconian in their judgments—you win or you lose—and Kerry lost. But a broader verdict would be more forgiving to him: not bad, but not good enough.

Influences on the Vote

Elections are decided by the agenda that is dominant more than by the candidates' positions on issues. The candidate who can get the voters to focus on his or her priorities is more likely to win the contest.[29] The election of 2004 was fought primarily on Bush's agenda: foreign policy and terrorism. The Republican campaign focused on those questions, both as substantive policy questions and as choices about which candidate would be the better commander in chief. Kerry could not avoid the centrality of these issues, given the trauma of 9/11 and the subsequent war in Iraq. In the circumstances, what is remarkable is not that he lost but that he came so close.

As can be seen in Table 3-6,[30] the voters preferred Kerry on most issues of domestic policy—education, health, and the economy—and he almost matched Bush's support on tax policy. A majority of voters believed that Bush paid more attention to the interests of large corporations than those of ordinary Americans, that the national economy was not in good shape, and that the cost and availability of health care were a major worry. These domestic concerns are the "normal" issues of most elections and typically are Democratic strengths. Kerry also gained from the unpopularity of the Iraq war, which most Americans thought was going badly, reprising past national opposition to wars in Korea and Vietnam. Among those whose first concern on election day was Iraq, the senator was strongly favored.

But 2004 was not a normal year. It was marked by an entirely different issue—the 9/11 terrorist attacks and the resulting national fear. Among the overwhelming majority of voters who worried about a new terrorist attack (74 percent of the electorate), Bush won a clear majority, 52 percent to 47 percent. Among those who regarded terrorism as the nation's most important issue, Bush gained an overwhelming advantage—fifteen percentage points—enough to overcome all of Kerry's strengths. The effect of terrorism was also reflected in the candidate qualities the electorate emphasized. Voters who most wanted a president to be "honest and trustworthy," a "strong leader," or one who takes "clear stands on issues" all regarded terrorism as the most important issue of the election.

Both campaigns recognized, and attempted to exploit, the fears created by the terrorist attacks, even imitating each other in their appeals. A Republican television spot featured a teenager whose mother was killed at the World

Trade Center. The attractive girl endearingly says of the president, "All he wants to do is make sure I'm safe." Democrats matched with a mother whose husband was killed at the same time, pleading Kerry's cause, "I want to look in my daughter's eyes and know that she is safe." [31]

One other issue affected the election, "moral values"; much postelection commentary emphasized, applauded, or deplored its impact. Concern for moral values was often seen as equivalent to social conservatism, as exemplified by opposition to gay marriage. It is true that "moral values" was the issue most frequently cited by respondents to the national exit poll. Yet its effect is neither new[32] nor predominant in 2004.[33]

In general, the partisan effect of moral values is unclear; their invocation does not necessarily entail a simple affirmation of conservative morality.[34] All politics is based on morality, perhaps particularly in the United States, which declared its independence on the moral principle that "all men are created equal . . . endowed by their Creator with certain inalienable rights." The great social movements of American history—abolition, civil rights, feminism, and even temperance—have been animated by moral values. The nation's religious traditions may include prescriptions regarding marital practices, but they also include the Social Gospel of Protestantism, the egalitarian precepts of Catholicism, and the Jewish call of Isaiah "to share your bread with the hungry." [35]

For Americans in 2004, morality meant much more than opposition to gay marriage or abortion. In a postelection survey, only one of six identified abortion as the nation's most urgent moral problem, and only one of eight gay marriage. In contrast, a third stressed "greed and materialism," and another third emphasized "poverty and economic justice." In explaining their choice on election day, "42 percent of voters cited the war in Iraq as the 'moral issue' that most influenced their choice of candidates," twice as many as cited either abortion or same-sex marriage.[36] In fact, 63 percent of voters expressing an opinion in the national exit poll supported either marriage or civil unions for same-sex couples.

In Ohio, the swing state in the election, "moral values" also had a broader meaning. It was the main concern both of those who supported a state constitutional restriction on gay marriage and of those who opposed it (see Table 3-7). The two candidates drew mostly from one side or the other, but one-fifth of Bush's Ohio vote came from opponents of the state constitutional amendment, and two-fifths of Kerry's vote came from supporters of the gay marriage ban. The advantage went to Bush; in this close state in a close election, the issue can be read as the source of his victory. But he would have fallen short, both in the state and nationally, without the gains he derived from other issues, particularly terrorism.

Gay marriage affected the election through its mobilization of Republican voters, not as a new attitude. The issue did not create Republicans but rather reinforced their more traditional attitudes. But it was still politically important, its momentum accelerated by the legalization of same-sex mar-

Table 3-7 Comparison of Ohio Votes to Restrict Gay Marriage to Votes for President

Most important issue	Total selecting (%)	Yes on ban (%)	No on ban (%)	Yes Voters: For Bush (%)	Yes Voters: For Kerry (%)	No voters: For Bush (%)	No voters: For Kerry (%)
Taxes	6	7	5	7	7	13	3
Education	5	5	7	3	7	3	8
Iraq	13	9	20	6	16	14	23
Terrorism	17	20	10	29	4	32	3
Economy/jobs	24	20	32	7	46	11	39
Moral values	23	29	12	42	3	18	10
Health care	5	4	7	2	8	3	9
Totals	93	94	93	96	91	94	95

Presidental vote	Bush (%)	Kerry (%)
Total	51	49
Yes voters	80	19
No voters	41	58

Source: Author calculations based on Ohio exit poll conducted for the National Election Pool.

riages in Massachusetts and the publicity given to flamboyant gay and lesbian wedding ceremonies in San Francisco. With eleven states holding (and passing) referenda to outlaw same-sex marriage, the issue drew more traditional Republicans to the polls.

Moral disputes will persist, but their effects on future elections are likely to be broader than the narrow issues of 2004. Bush made a deliberate, and successful, effort to cast his campaign in moralistic terms. Voters responded: Those who emphasized the personal qualities of "strong religious faith" or "honest and trustworthy" also deemed moral values their most important substantive concern. The president built his victory on this combination of related attitudes, not on one issue alone.

Indeed, Bush did convey a substantive moral message, even if his vision was unrealistic. In the ideal domestic world he pictured, marriages would be stable unions of a man and a woman, sexual abstinence before marriage would prevent teenage pregnancy, and all children would pass tests of their educational competence. Abroad, the example of American democracy would transform the world:

> We'll continue to spread freedom. I believe in the transformational power of liberty. . . . I believe that a free Afghanistan and a free Iraq will serve as a powerful example for millions who plead in silence for liberty in the broader Middle East. . . . We've been challenged and we've risen to those challenges. We've climbed the mighty mountain. I see the valley below, and it's a valley of peace.

The president's vision may well be distorted, and critics would say that he was engaging in a messianic "crusade" (the word he first maladroitly used for his war against Islamic extremists). Yet his message was also principled in content and religious in phrasing. It would understandably draw support from those voters most concerned with moral values.

Senator Kerry was more restrained in his rhetoric, reflecting both his personal style and a Catholic and Jewish emphasis on good works rather than a Protestant belief in pure faith. He appealed to the voters' interests more than their emotions, to realism in foreign policy more than idealism. The difference between him and Bush could be seen in Kerry's basic position on Iraq:

> We have a different set of convictions about how to make our country stronger here at home and respected again in the world. . . . You want to know who could be a commander in chief who could get your kids home. . . . I have a plan for Iraq. I believe we can be successful. I'm not talking about leaving. I'm talking about winning. And we need a fresh start, a new credibility, a president who can bring allies to our side.[37]

Kerry echoed his Massachusetts mentor, Michael Dukakis, as he tried to move voters away from ideological enthusiasm to an instrumentalist emphasis on competency. A Kerry presidency would be better, rather than different, he argued. His attractiveness to many voters mirrored this appeal. A considerable proportion (at least 40 percent) of his vote came from those who were voting against the record of the Bush administration, rather than for Kerry personally. In contrast, the overwhelming proportion of Bush voters (85 percent) were for the president, not against the senator.

The Democrats—and not only Kerry personally—did not develop a broader moral appeal, even on the question of Iraq, which abounded in moral issues. At the elementary level, they had trouble selecting a campaign slogan. Of course, slogans are only catchwords, but they still may convey some sense of direction. Bush campaigned for "compassionate conservatism" and "the ownership society." Some might consider these appeals only cynical ploys to snare a gullible electorate, but Kerry lacked an effective or even a consistent response at this shallow level.

The senator's final slogan—"A Fresh Start"—did have some campaign advantages: It focused on Bush's record rather than his own, and it reflected the inherent optimism of Americans. Yet there was no implied issue content in the appeal; it promised voters nothing beyond trying someone or something new. In its lack of content, it resembled FDR's promise, "A New Deal for the American People." But Kerry was not a new Roosevelt.

The Future of American Elections

The 2004 election carries implications for the long-term future of American politics. On the partisan level, Republicans hope that it was a critical, or realigning, election, establishing a new basis for party loyalties that will persist for a generation.[38] Their supporting evidence includes the high intensity of the election, sharply increased Republican turnout, the shifted political focus to issues of morality, and the expansion of Republican control of both houses of Congress. One-party government will probably lead to policies that reward Republican groups, cementing their loyalties, as well as the addition of conservatives to the Supreme Court, leading to further endorsement of the party's philosophy.

The political map of the United States has certainly shifted. The parties now comprise stable geographic coalitions, which are virtually mirror images of their support as long ago as the critical election of 1896: Of the forty-five states in the Union at that time, all but six have reversed their partisanship. Rock-ribbed, Republican New England has become the Democrats' strongest bastion; the Democratic Solid South of yore has now become just as solidly Republican.[39]

Change is clearly evident, but Republican dominance is not assured. Over the course of the seven most recent presidential elections, the parties' geographic coalitions have shown great stability,[40] but it is a stability of close competition, bending toward the Republicans, who won popular victories in four of seven contests. George Bush benefited from this stable alignment, yet he won by less than 2.5 percentage points, the smallest popular vote margin of victory for a reelected president since the beginning of competitive party elections in 1828 and the second smallest in the Electoral College.[41] Bush clearly has the power to govern, and the intention to govern conservatively, but his thin margin provides no electoral mandate and no assurance of a long-term Republican majority.[42] His consistent conservatism "has left him with a firm hold on about half the country, but with the other half increasingly beyond his reach." [43]

Moreover, the parties' geographic coalitions are less fixed than they appear. In reality, each of the major parties is competitive in virtually every state, and each controls half of the state legislative chambers. In recent statewide elections for U.S. senator or governor, Democrats have won at least once in all of the Plains states, all but two of the Mountain states, and a majority of the states in the South. Republicans have matched their opponents by winning such elections in all but two states of the Northeast.

Demographic trends do not clearly favor one party or the other. Slowly, Republicans have gained support among groups that previously leaned Democratic, including men, Hispanics and other Catholics, Jews, and seniors (as the New Deal generation is replaced). In the opposite direction, Democrats maintain majorities among several groups that are growing larger in the population, including working women, the unmarried, minority groups (including Hispanics), and the youngest voters. Democrats can also take heart from the growth of the postindustrial professional class of "knowledge workers"—highly educated, secularist in outlook, environmentally "green," and moderate in their politics.[44]

New issues will surely arise in the coming years, and they may work to the benefit of the Democrats. Even terrorism, the Republicans' winning issue in 2004, is likely to have lessened impact in the future. In 2004, the first election after the 9/11 attacks, terrorism was a new issue, and the incumbent president benefited from the fears aroused by the real threat to the nation. Although the war on terror, unfortunately, will probably never end in a clear victory, it may well become a "normal" issue, a familiar part of the political landscape. With both parties obviously on the same side against terrorism, they will come to be judged not by their philosophy but by their competence in meeting such threats.

Cultural issues also hold some promise for Democrats, despite their losses in 2004.The general trend in American life has been irrevocably toward more secularist lifestyles and more tolerant attitudes. In recent decades, traditionalist views have eroded on such issues as the role of women, abortion, racial equality, marriage, sexual behavior, religious authority, and homosexuality. Conservatives may lament that the nation is not as ethically upright as in the past, but the political significance of these changing views is clear: no party can build a lasting majority by standing for values that are losing public support. In light of these varied trends, the overall pattern we may predict for future elections is continued close party competition.

But elections are more important to the voters than to the parties. Whether the Republicans or Democrats win is of less consequence than the opportunity that elections provide for Americans to govern themselves, to choose leaders and policies responsive to their interests and their values. The election of 2004 revealed dangers to this basic process of self-government.

One part of the problem is the Electoral College, now notorious as an undemocratic method to select the chief executive of the world's most prominent democracy. The argument for its abolition is philosophically strong, yet politically futile.[45] So long as smaller states think they benefit from its workings, they will be able to use their votes in the Senate to block a constitutional amendment to replace it. And, despite the Electoral College's shortcomings, there are some reasons to keep it. A pure popular vote would probably mean that campaigns would be conducted principally through television advertising, depriving voters of the direct contact they now have with presidential candidates.[46] A close contest, moreover, might trigger nationwide replications of the Florida controversy of 2000, with disputes extending over many months.

Even without abolition, however, Congress could improve the Electoral College through legislation. As it now stands, the system gives disproportionate weight to the small states because each receives two electoral votes corresponding to its seats in the Senate. Enlarging the House—achievable through ordinary legislation and justifiable on its own terms as a means to provide better representation for local areas—would make the relationship between population and electoral votes more appropriate. Any such legislation should take care that the total number of electoral votes is an odd number, to prevent the disruptive possibility—quite real in 2000 and 2004—of a tied electoral vote.

The possibility of "faithless electors," electors who do not vote for the candidate who wins their state, also should be curbed. One Kerry elector from Minnesota reneged on his pledge in 2004, and a Bush elector from West Virginia threatened to do the same. There is no justification for allowing an unknown individual to override the wishes of the citizens of their state. Making such faithless voting a federal crime would probably be an effective deterrent.

The voting process itself also needs improvement. As the results in 2000 demonstrated, the administration of American elections has many faults, ranging from clumsy technology, insufficient polling locations, and deficient registration methods to deliberate efforts to exclude voters and manipulate the reporting of the returns.

In the light of the Florida debacle of 2000, a bipartisan commission stimulated Congress to pass the Help Americans Vote Act and to provide nearly $4 billion to states to upgrade election machinery.[47] In response, many states, including Florida, revised their ballot statutes, technology, and administration. These efforts did improve the electoral process in 2004, and the numerous snags that developed on election day did not affect the ultimate outcome.

Despite the technical improvements, however, voting is still beset with problems. Many states, including Ohio, still rely on outdated technology such as punch-card machines; others have adopted computer voting systems that are insufficiently secure against hackers and lack a paper record that would be available for any necessary recounts. Voters are discouraged by long waiting lines—particularly evident in 2004 in Ohio's Democratic cities—that result from having too few election clerks, or are handicapped by complicated registration requirements and partisan interpretations of election laws. Four million Americans are completely barred from voting because they have been convicted of a felony, many even after they have served their sentences and their paroles.[48] Our presidents are still not the clear choice of the American people that our democratic commitment promises.

But democratic elections require yet more than reasonable rules and efficient processes. Elections are meant to be dialogues in which prospective leaders talk with the voters in an honest conversation. A democratic dialogue requires a candid presentation of facts, an appeal to the voters' reason, and a respectful debate among the contenders.

The dialogue of 2004 was flawed. Much of the information provided to the electorate, particularly on the Iraq war, was wrong, and sometimes deliberately wrong—as, for example when the administration continued to imply that there was collaboration between Saddam Hussein and the terrorists of Al Qaeda, even though the 9/11 Commission specifically denied the assertion.[49] The threat of terrorism was manipulated to promote a fearful, rather than a rational, electoral environment, as in the yo-yo raising and lowering of terrorism alerts. Senator Kerry's loyalty was called into question by the smears of the Swift Boat Veterans and by the sneers of the vice president. Anti-Bush groups planted false reports that the president was a military deserter from his service in the National Guard. Politics can be a bruising contest, but the campaign of 2004 was less worthy than a rough-and-tumble yet decent wrestling match. It was nasty, brutish, and far too long.

Campaigning can be made both more civil and more helpful to voters, even as we recognize the value of vigorous partisan debate and the primacy of free speech. Campaign spending reforms have already turned the parties away from their previous dependence on large contributors and toward reliance on smaller donors and face-to-face mobilization of voters. Limiting independent committees' spending would accelerate these desirable trends and perhaps even discourage smear tactics. More television debates, in a greater variety of formats, would give voters more opportunities to judge the candidates in balanced, face-to-face forums. Free television time for the candidates would allow them to address the electorate more seriously than is possible in spot advertisements.[50] But ultimately, improved campaigning requires that candidates value their nation more than their triumph.

The republic still stands; the United States will endure. But its citizens may well worry that they will suffer more elections like that of 2004. Such campaigns would bring[51] peace only to the victors but leave a political wilderness in the land once praised as America the Beautiful.

Notes

I gratefully acknowledge the editorial help of Miles Pomper, Dr. Marlene Pomper, Robert Cohen, and Dr. Milton Finegold and assistance on exit poll data from Dr. Kathleen Frankovic, director, and Jennifer De Pinto of CBS News.

1. For analysis of the disputed election of 2000, see Gerald M. Pomper, *The Election of 2000* (Washington, D.C.: Chatham House/CQ Press, 2001), 126–132; and "The Final Florida Recount," at my Web site: www.rci.rutgers.edu/~gpomper.
2. Removing the extreme value of the District of Columbia hardly affects the statistical relationship, barely lowering the correlation to .96.
3. The choice of colors has no significance beyond the whims of graphic artists. Still, it is somewhat ironic that Republicans have been assigned the red color of the historic left, and Democrats the traditional color of aristocratic "blue bloods."
4. Richard Scammon argued, accurately at the time but no longer, that presidential elections are won in "Quadricali," the combination of the Northeast, Midwest, and California. See *The Real Majority* (New York: Coward McCann and Geoghegan, 1971).
5. Michael Gastner, Cosma Shalizi, and Mark Newman, "Maps and Cartograms of the 2004 U.S. Presidential Election Results," www-personal.umich.edu/~mejn/election. For the same point on the 2000 election map, see Philip Klinkner, "Red and Blue Scare," *The Forum* 2, no. 1 (2004).
6. Morris P. Fiorina, with Samuel J. Abrams and Jeremy C. Pope, *Culture War?* (New York: Pearson Education, 2004), 16–26.
7. Jose Antonio Vargas, "Vote or Die? Well, They Did Vote," *Washington Post,* November 9, 2004, C01.
8. Alan Cooperman and Thomas B. Edsall, "Evangelicals Say They Led Charge for the GOP," *Washington Post,* November 8, 2004, A01. The actual increase is difficult to determine, because the exit poll question changed from 2000 to 2004, as

described in a sidebar by Edsall accompanying the article. In 2000, respondents were asked, "Do you consider yourself part of the conservative Christian political movement, also known as the religious right?" In 2004, the question was changed to, "Would you describe yourself as a born-again or evangelical Christian?" The proportion identifying themselves as members of these groups changed from 14 percent to 22 percent, surely an effect more of question wording than of conversion. Another indicator is found in the increase in the proportion of voters who attend church more than once a week, from 14 percent in 2000 to 16 percent in 2004.

9. Previous votes are available in virtually any conceivable breakdown from an excellent Web site, www.uselectionatlas.org. The 2004 vote by county can be found on many newspaper sites. I have relied on www.washingtonpost.com. Demographic data on the counties can be found at quickfacts.census.gov.
10. For a good journalistic account, see Karen Tumulty, "Fighting for Every Last Vote," *Time,* 164, October 18, 2004, www.time.com.
11. Raymond R. Wolfinger and Steven J. Rosenstone, *Who Votes?* (New Haven: Yale University Press, 1980); Ruy A. Teixeira, *The Disappearing American Voter* (Washington, D.C.: Brookings Institution Press, 1992).
12. This analysis is based on the exit polls conducted for the National Election Pool, a consortium of news organizations. Although premature reports of the exit polls on election day were inaccurate, predicting a solid Kerry victory, the final reports replicated the national tabulated vote. For poll details, see many news Web pages, such as cnn.com/ELECTION/2004. Richard Morin provides a good account of the polls' problems in "Surveying the Damage," *Washington Post,* November 21, 2004, B1.
13. Alan Wolfe reaches a similar conclusion in regard to social attitudes more generally. See *One Nation After All* (New York: Viking Penguin, 1998).
14. The vote of Hispanics may be seriously misestimated because of sampling discrepancies in the exit polls. A truer assessment will require further academic research. See Darryl Fears, "Pollsters Debate Hispanics' Presidential Voting," *Washington Post,* November 26, 2004, A04.
15. David S. Broder, "Partisan Gap Is at a High, Poll Finds," *Washington Post,* November 9, 2003, A06.
16. See Larry Bartels, "Partisanship and Voting Behavior, 1952–1996," *American Journal of Political Science* 44 (January 2000): 35–50
17. CBS News/*New York Times* Polls: "Democratic Delegate Survey," June 16–July 17, 2004, and "Republican Delegate Survey," August 3–22, 2004, www.cbsnews.com; John Cochran, "Legislative Session Drawn in Solid Party Lines," *CQ Weekly* 62 (January 3, 2004): 10–21.
18. In the exit poll, 42 percent reported that they had voted for Bush in 2000, and 38 percent that they had voted for Gore. These reports are certainly inaccurate, given the actual, even division of the two-party vote that year. Reports of past votes are inherently questionable, given the fading of memories and the inclination to remember voting for the winning candidate. To correct these errors, I characterize these groups as "standpatters," adapting the term from V. O. Key, *The Responsible Electorate* (Cambridge: Harvard University Press, 1966).
19. Marc D. Weiner, "Fifty Years On: The American Electorate's Evolving Participation in a More Responsible Two-Party System" (PhD diss., Rutgers University, 2005), chap. 4, 26.
20. *Bush. v. Gore,* 121 S, Ct. 525 (2000). For early discussion of the case, see the collection by Cass R. Sunstein and Richard A. Epstein, *The Vote* (Chicago: University of Chicago Press, 2001).
21. William Shakespeare, *Hamlet,* 3:1, 83–85.
22. Jim VandeHei and Mike Allen, "Kerry Speaks of Faith's Role; Bush Touts 'Record of Results,' " *Washington Post,* October 25, 2004, A07.

23. See the diverse, but consensual, predictions in "Forecasting the 2004 Presidential Election," *PS* 37, October 2004, 733–768. The success of the predictions was in marked contrast to the academicians' universal failure in 2000 but in keeping with the cautious skepticism of Andrew Gelman and David King, "Party Competition and Media Messages in U.S. Presidential Elections," in *The Parties Respond,* 2nd ed., ed. L. Sandy Maisel (Boulder, Colo.: Westview, 1994), chap. 11.
24. His hesitancy seemingly mirrored that of the last Democratic nominee from Massachusetts, Michael Dukakis, who also failed to respond to personal attacks in August from a nonparty group, in his case focusing on the prison furlough of William Horton, a convicted murderer. For discussion of the distortions in this attack, see Kathleen Hall Jamieson, *Dirty Politics* (New York: Oxford University Press, 1992), chap. 1.
25. As monitored by the authoritative University of Wisconsin Advertising Project, close to two-thirds of the Bush spots were "attack" ads, and the remaining negative messages were "contrasts" between Bush and Kerry. Of Kerry's messages, less than 5 percent were "attacks," and the remaining negative messages were "contrasts." See *New York Times,* November 1, 2004, A19. The same differences are evident in speeches at the parties' national conventions. Kerry was attacked by name thirty-nine times at the Republican convention, Bush only five times at the Democratic conclave: Todd S. Purdum, "G.O.P., Last to Bat, Swings Freely for the Fences," *New York Times,* September 2, 2004, A1. In the national exit poll, 21 percent thought that only Kerry attacked his opponent "unfairly," while 15 percent had the same criticism of Bush. Of the remainder, 46 percent criticized both candidates; another 13 percent—who are either perpetual optimists or very tolerant of politicians—thought neither did.
26. Greg Mitchell, "Daily Endorsement Tally," October 31, 2004, www.editorandpublisher.com.
27. For some early Wednesday morning quarterbacking of the campaign, see Howard Kurtz, "Kerry's Troubled Campaign," November 15, 2004, www.washingtonpost.com.
28. Todd S. Purdum, "An Electoral Affirmation of Shared Values," *New York Times,* November 4, 2004, A1.
29. Hans-Dieter Klingemann, Richard I. Hofferbert, and Ian Budge, *Parties, Policies and Democracy* (Boulder, Colo.: Westview, 1994), chap. 2.
30. The calculation for the last columns is a simple multiplication of the percentage of all responses citing the specific issue or trait by the percentage in that group voting for a particular candidate. Since all respondents did not answer these questions, the resulting figures are then normalized to a base of 100. For example, 5 percent cited taxes as the most important issue, 56 percent of this group voted for Bush, and all responses summed to 93 percent. The contribution to the Bush vote then = 05 * 56 / 93 = 3 percent.
31. Katherine Q. Seelye, "Polls Show Gains for Kerry among Women in Electorate," *New York Times,* October 20, 2004, A24.
32. In 1992, "moral values" was included as one of the policy choices in an exit survey by the *Los Angeles Times*. It was selected by 23 percent of respondents, essentially the same proportion of voters as in 2004 (while only 2 percent chose abortion as their major issue). Of particular note is that the partisan breakdown on this issue closely paralleled that in 2004: 73 percent of those emphasizing "moral values" voted for the elder George Bush. See study no. USLAT1992-303, available through the Roper Center for Public Opinion Research archives at www.ropercenter.uconn.edu. I am indebted to Professor David Weakliem, of the University of Connecticut, for this material.
33. According to one report, the emphasis on moral values "is much lower than it was in the two previous presidential elections," when 35 percent in 2000 and 40

percent in 1996 gave priority to ethical issues, even aside from abortion. "Thus, in those two elections, almost half of the electorate said they voted on moral matters; this time, only a fifth did." "The Triumph of the Religious Right," *The Economist,* November 11, 2004, www.economist.com.

34. Question wording can be determinative. Offered a more specific choice by Rasmussen Reports, only 10 percent of voters emphasized "cultural values such as same-sex marriage and abortion." They voted for Bush by a 73–26 margin. Using these data, cultural issues gained Bush only five percentage points in the vote, rather than the fifteen points calculated in Table 3-4. See www.rasmussenreports.com.
35. Isaiah 58:7, in *The Prophets* (Philadelphia: Jewish Publication Society, 1978), 488.
36. The data are from a national poll of over 10,000 voters conducted by Zogby International, reported by Alan Cooperman, "Liberal Christians Challenge 'Values Vote,' " *Washington Post,* November 10, 2004, A07.
37. The quotations come from Bush's and Kerry's concluding statements in the first presidential debate, as reported in *New York Times,* October 1, 2004, A23.
38. This hope is grounded on a classic scholarly article by V. O. Key Jr., "A Theory of Critical Elections," *Journal of Politics* 17 (February 1955): 3–18. The theory has been severely undermined by David Mayhew, *Electoral Realignments* (New Haven: Yale University Press, 2002).
39. Gary Miller and Norman Schofield, "Activists and Partisan Realignment in the United States," *American Political Science Review* 97 (May 2003): 245–260.
40. The correlation of the two-party vote with the preceding contest shows increasing stability in the vote; specifically, 1980, .84; 1984, .87; 1988, .94; 1992, .89; 1996, .91; 2000, .94; 2004, .97.
41. Ronald Brownstein, "GOP's Future Sits Precariously on Small Cushion of Victory," *Los Angeles Times,* November 15, 2004, www.latimes.com.
42. For an incisive analysis of electoral mandates, see Stanley Kelley Jr., *Interpreting Elections* (Princeton: Princeton University Press, 1983).
43. Ronald Brownstein, "After 4 Years, Bush Is No Closer to Building a GOP Majority," *Los Angeles Times,* November 1, 2004, www.latimes.com.
44. This is the partisan hope expressed by John B. Judis and Ruy Teixeira, *The Emerging Democratic Majority* (New York: Scribner's, 2002).
45. See George C. Edwards, *Why the Electoral College Is Bad for America* (New Haven: Yale University Press, 2004); Paul D. Schumaker and Burdett A. Loomis, *Choosing a President* (Washington, D.C.: Chatham House/CQ Press, 2002).
46. See John Tierney, "Imagine if Texas and the Bronx Mattered," *New York Times,* October 31, 2004, Sec. 4, 4.
47. National Commission on Federal Election Reform, *To Assure Pride and Confidence in the Electoral Process* (Charlottesville, Va.: Miller Center of Public Affairs, 2001). The report of the commission, headed by former presidents Gerald Ford and Jimmy Carter, is available at www.reformelections.org.
48. See Elizabeth A. Hull, *Aliens in Their Native Land* (Philadelphia: Temple University Press, 2005).
49. The commission found "no evidence" that Iraqi and Al Qaeda "contacts ever developed into a collaborative operational relationship. Nor have we seen evidence indicating that Iraq cooperated with Al Qaeda in developing or carrying out any attacks against the United States." See National Commission on Terrorist Attacks upon the United States, *The 9/11 Report* (New York: St. Martin's, 2004), 97.
50. For further discussion, see Richard R. Lau and Gerald M. Pomper, *Negative Campaigning* (Lanham, Md.: Rowman and Littlefield, 2004), chap. 7. The best standards for rational campaigning are still found in Stanley Kelley Jr., *Political Campaigning* (Washington, D.C.: Brookings Institution Press, 1960), chap. 2.
51. The allusion here is to the description by Tacitus, the historian of the Roman Empire, of the invasion of Scotland by Agricola.

4

Voting Behavior: The 2004 Election and the Roots of Republican Success

Nicole Mellow

After hundreds of speeches and three debates and interviews and the whole process, where you keep basically saying the same thing over and over again, when you win there is a feeling that people have spoken and embraced your point of view.

—President George W. Bush, Thursday, November 4, 2004[1]

After the close and contested presidential election in 2000 and a campaign in 2004 that seemed to promise more of the same, President Bush's reelection was relatively clear-cut. The president won 286 Electoral College votes, 16 more than he needed and 35 more than his rival, Democratic candidate John Kerry. Just as important, the 2004 election sent no mixed signals. Unlike 2000, when the winning candidate lost the popular vote, three million more Americans chose George Bush than John Kerry in 2004, awarding the president 50.7 percent of their votes. Bush claimed in a press conference two days after the election that he had "earned some [political] capital" from the people.[2] Adding bite to his bark, Republicans made significant gains in both houses of Congress, ensuring that the president and his party retained unified control of the government.

The 2004 election was a high-stakes contest with clear differences between the parties, making the voters' endorsement of Republican leadership especially significant. Any election in which an incumbent is running is largely a referendum on the job he or she has done in office.[3] But this one was especially so, partly because questions lingered about the fairness of the 2000 election, but mostly because the tasks that confronted President Bush in his first term were substantial and his stewardship, although controversial, was unwavering. At the end of the president's first term, with the country still at war and the state of the economy uncertain, voters gave a plain, if cautious, signal for him to continue along the same path.

From a more historical perspective, however, the voters' approval of President Bush and his Republican colleagues in Congress has a different significance. For the first time in fifty-two years, a majority of Americans chose Republicans to control both the legislative and executive branches of the government. This represents a major step forward for a party that has long been on the rise but had been consistently denied the ultimate fruits of electoral victory: total control of the national government. It is especially significant because, despite the new terrain of politics since September 11, the president's victory built on the electoral base that his Republican predecessors established.

The New Deal Democratic regime that reigned from the 1930s to the 1960s thrived by providing economic and national security. The Republican order constructed after its demise has succeeded not just by emphasizing national security but also, in contrast to the Democrats, by promoting traditional social values. In the face of rapid social and economic change, the Republican regime has offered a new form of domestic security, one grounded more in social conservatism than in economic management. The party has found its greatest support in the South and West.

During his first term, President Bush consolidated the Republican base by emphasizing traditional values and the war on terrorism and minimizing the potential influence of economic issues with efforts to reform Medicare and education. Because the key issues in the campaign involved both foreign policy and economic concerns, the election was close. Yet "moral values" emerged as a significant factor in voters' choices, and this helped the president to victory. In this chapter I explore the 2004 election results in light of important electoral trends of the last forty years. The president's reelection has given Republicans, after years of sharing power with Democrats, their first legitimate claim to majority-party status since the 1920s.

Building the Republican Majority

From the 1930s to the 1960s, the dominant ideas and interests in American politics were those of the New Deal Democratic Party. National institutions reflected the Democrats' commitments. Keynesian fiscal policy, the bureaucratic welfare state, a social contract between labor and capital, and containment of Soviet communism were regularly reauthorized by a majority of Americans. Simply put, Democrats prevailed by using government activism to promote security at home and abroad, and Republicans were hard-pressed to compete. As political analyst E. J. Dionne has written, "To many in the late 1940s, it appeared that conservatives were doomed . . . to crankiness, incoherence, and irrelevance." [4] The one Republican president of the era, Dwight Eisenhower, was a moderate whose governance was more in step with the New Deal than with the conservatives in his own party.

By the 1970s, Democratic dominance was gone. The social disruptions of the 1960s from the civil rights and feminist movements, dissension over the war in Vietnam, and economic deterioration upended the political order. To many, Democratic solutions appeared obsolete or wrongheaded. Richard Nixon was the first Republican to capitalize on the weakness, and by 1980, with Ronald Reagan's election, the country seemed poised to embrace a new governing philosophy. A revitalized national defense was one of its pillars.

Domestically, Republicans stressed the benefits that would accrue from unfettering capital. Yet when the effects of this approach appeared volatile, conservative social values became the Republicans' new ballast. Churning economic and social change, they argued, was best answered with the stability and security of traditional values.[5] In the new Republican agenda, deregulation of industry, monetary policy over Keynesian fiscal policy solutions, and tax cuts were coupled with an emphasis on race-neutral individual rights, a resurrection of traditional "family" values, and support for law and order. Along with a reinvigorated national defense apparatus, these became the themes around which the interests and institutions of the newly emerging Republican majority were constructed.

The New Deal Democratic and earlier party orders had been ratified by the voters' clear endorsement, but the public appeared ambivalent about the new Republican state. Despite Republican dominance of the presidency in the 1970s and 1980s, the party could not wrest control of Congress from the Democrats. When it finally did so in 1994, by reiterating in the Contract with America themes that earlier Republican presidents had articulated, the electorate had chosen a Democrat, Bill Clinton, to be president. Until Bush's election in 2000, divided government was the norm.

Accustomed to seeing decisive shifts in party governance in American history, scholars have described the post-1968 era in equivocal terms. Realignment theorists described a new "interregnum" state characterized by split-ticket voting and indecisive results.[6] Others described a bitter deadlock between the parties and their activist bases, but one in which average voters increasingly chose not to go to the polls, withholding their endorsement from both parties.[7] Some speculated that voters strategically split their tickets to produce a moderate, divided government and to take advantage of each party's perceived strengths: Republican foreign policy in the White House and Democratic domestic policy in Congress.[8] Still another, broader perspective held that Reagan did indeed build a new Republican regime but one that was limited in its ability to move aside the older Democratic order because of the massive growth and ossification of the state and its related, entrenched interests during the twentieth century.[9] All agreed, however, that the dominant discourse in American politics had shifted rightward, so much so that Clinton had to tack right in order to survive.

For Republicans, the evolution of their new order may have been gradual, even halting, but it has been relentless. As William Kristol claimed in the aftermath of the 1994 Republican takeover of Congress, "The nation's long, slow electoral and ideological realignment with the Republican party is reaching a watershed." [10] From this perspective, much significance was attached to the upset victory in 2000 of George W. Bush, a candidate with little elected experience, over Al Gore, who had a long, rich political resumé and represented the incumbent party at a time of prosperity. Because President Bush in his first term established himself clearly as a conservative president, the 2004 election seemed to represent electoral ratification of the Republican realignment.

The closeness of the 2000 and 2004 elections and the deep partisan divide in the country suggest that the Republicans' hold on the national government is still tenuous. Yet the electoral bases on which the party has been building were fortified in 2004, and new gains were made among groups, such as Hispanics, that had previously been identified as Democratic. In the rest of this chapter I trace—first by geography and then by issues and groups—the electoral trends that have contributed to Republican dominance and that figured in President Bush's reelection.

The Geographic Building Blocks

As the words of President Bush at the beginning of this chapter suggest, a modern presidential campaign involves a good deal of repetition, and as a candidate, the president was nothing if not steadfast. Although he won the election, his message was not embraced equally around the country. As in the 2000 election, states in the South and interior West responded far more favorably to President Bush's appeals than did states in the Northeast, Great Lakes, and Pacific Coast regions. As in 2000, too, these latter states, by and large, voted for the Democratic nominee.

Regional divisions between the parties have a long history. Distinctive regional voting patterns have characterized American presidential elections since the earliest days of mass party politics, reflecting the significance of geographic disparities in the means of economic production and in social conditions.[11] In fact, the election of 1896 closely mirrors those of 2000 and 2004: In 1896 states in the industrial and financial centers of the North and the Pacific Coast voted Republican, while states in the agrarian South and West voted Democratic. In the 1930s politics became nationalized as a result of the nationwide depression and the emergence of a dominant political cleavage along class lines. Further nationalization occurred during the New Deal and World War II, as the economies of the South and West modernized and began to converge with that of the North. Augmenting this process of nationalization were the civil rights movement and the passage of the 1965 Voting Rights Act, which overturned centuries-old restrictions imposed on African Americans in the South and thus equalized voting conditions around the nation.

Although these trends of the twentieth century worked to suppress regional politics, it is abundantly clear from the last several elections that distinctive regional patterns have not disappeared. Rather, they have reemerged as a potent political reality. As Figure 4-1 illustrates, the basic *L*-shaped pattern, of red states in the country's interior flanked by blue states on the coasts, characterizes the last five elections.

This is not to say that the new red state–blue state pattern has been inviolable. In 1988, Republican George H. W. Bush won most of the blue states, and in 1992 and 1996, Democrat Bill Clinton won a number of red states. Yet when the number of Republican victories in the five elections from 1988 to 2004 is added up for each state, the states in the South and interior West

Figure 4-1 The Geography of Presidential Election Results, 1988–2004

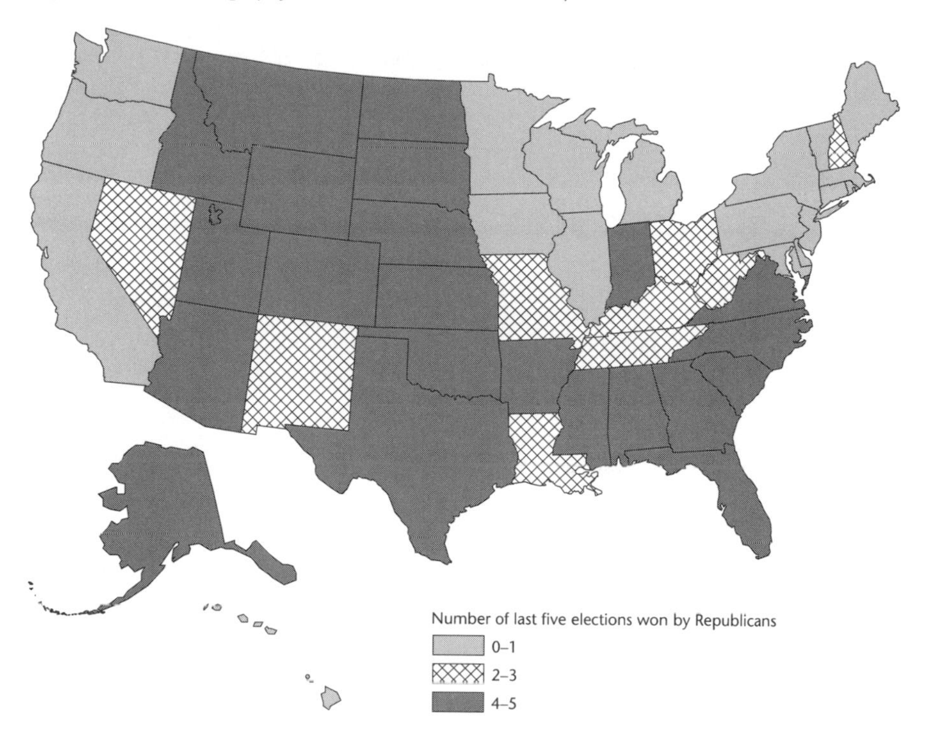

Source: Presidential Elections, 1789–2000 (Washington, D.C.: CQ Press, 2002); 2004 data, CNN.com, www.cnn.com/ELECTION/2004/pages/results/president/.

emerge as the most consistently Republican. These states chose the Republican presidential nominee at least four times in the last five elections. Conversely, states on the East and West Coasts and in the upper Midwest chose the Republican nominee one time at most. If the 2000 and 2004 elections were flukes or represented an entirely new development, far fewer states would fit these patterns. That they do fit suggests that a more durable pattern of regional division has emerged.

In the 2004 election, Bush won the states in the South and West that already were consistently trending Republican, while Kerry won those that had been trending Democratic in the North and the Pacific Coast area. Each candidate also picked up the states that had split between the parties in recent elections (the crosshatched states) but that are located in their party's regional strongholds. Thus Bush won New Mexico, and Kerry won New Hampshire.

In a closely divided nation, the significance of swing states has increased substantially. In the final days of the 2004 campaign, three swing states—Florida, Ohio, and Pennsylvania—seemed to hold the keys to victory for either candidate. But on election day these states broke the way one might have expected based on recent trends. Pennsylvania, which had voted Republican only once in the previous four elections, stayed Democratic in 2004. Florida, which had voted Democratic only once, stayed Republican. From this perspective, only Ohio was a true swing state: it had split the last four elections evenly, twice voting for the Democrat and twice for the Republican. Not surprisingly, then, it was Ohio on which the 2004 election hinged, and when it went Republican, so too did the nation.

Part of the starkness of the red-blue map derives from institutional contrivances; simple majorities dictate how nearly all states cast their electoral votes. The fact that majorities in one set of states have voted in a consistently different fashion from majorities in the other set of states is compelling by itself. Yet further evidence of these long-standing geographical trends can be seen in Figure 4-2, which shows the percentage of major-party voters in each region who supported the Republican presidential candidate from 1960 to 2004.[12]

As is clear from the figure, voters around the country behaved rather similarly at the beginning of the period and then gradually diverged. The trend lines tend to move in the same direction, reflecting the idiosyncrasies of each election, yet clearly voters in the South and West have more regularly supported Republican candidates than voters in the North and Pacific Coast.

Figure 4-2 Percentage of Major-Party Voters Selecting Republican Presidential Candidate, 1960–2004, by Region

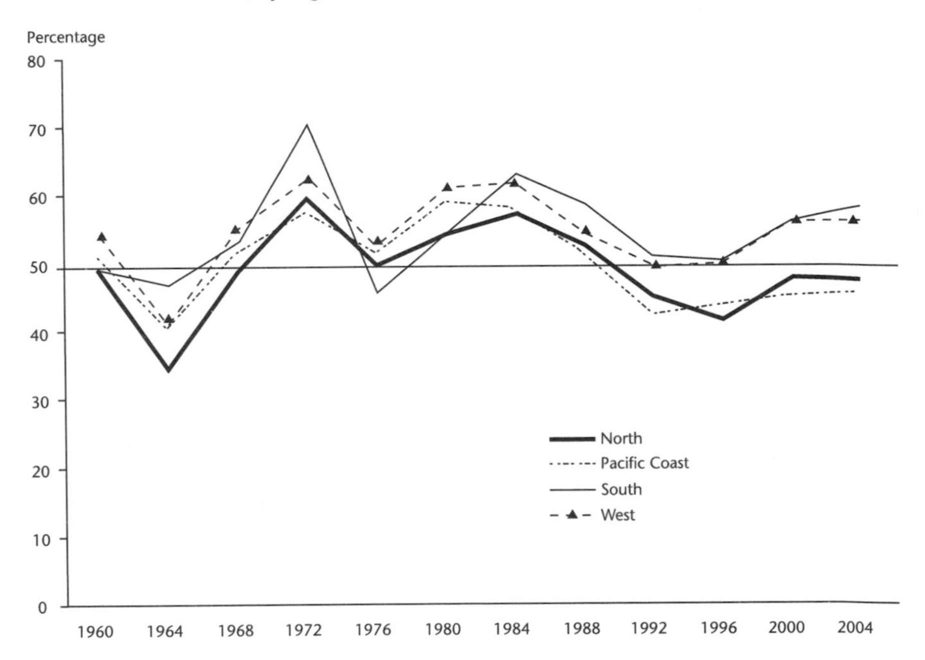

Source: Presidential Elections, 1789–2000 (Washington, D.C.: CQ Press, 2002); 2004 data, CNN.com, www.cnn.com/ELECTION/2004/pages/results/president/; regional calculations are the author's.

The only exception was in 1976, when Jimmy Carter, a Georgian, ran on the Democratic ticket and brought southern voters back to the party fold. By the 1990s, the red-blue partisan division among the regions that became famous in the 2000s was already becoming apparent. Democrat Bill Clinton won easily in the North and Pacific Coast, despite being a southerner, and he struggled in the South and West.

Most significant, the new regional patterns of presidential support accentuate the uniqueness of the New Deal era. The elections from the 1930s to the mid-twentieth century represent the only sustained period since the Civil War in which northerners and southerners voted for the same party. They did so, in large part, because the divisive issue of race was suppressed. Instead, issues on which the regions agreed—an internationalist foreign policy and economic activism—formed the dominant lines of party conflict, keeping North and South together and Republicans and Democrats apart. The recent return to regional voting indicates that the issues that animated the New Deal era have been displaced.[13]

Eroding New Deal Democratic Strength: The Decline of Class Politics

When asked whether President Bush cared more about average Americans or large corporations, 54 percent of voters in the 2004 exit poll said "large corporations"; of these, 16 percent voted for the president nonetheless.[14] For a president to win an election when a majority believes that he sides more with big business than with ordinary Americans suggests that economic self-interest is not the primary voting rationale for a significant portion of the electorate. Indeed, only 37 percent of voters identified an economic issue (jobs, health care, education, or taxes) as the most important in the election.

One of the great successes of the New Deal Democratic Party was its ability to convince voters that it could "put America back to work" and that government was both responsible and able to ameliorate the vicissitudes of capitalism. This is still the Democratic Party's strong suit. Of those voters who chose an economic issue as the most important one in the election, the overwhelming majority voted for John Kerry.[15] Yet, as in 2000, dominance on economic issues was not enough to win the Democrat the election.

Part of the Democrats' difficulty in 2004 was that voters seemed unconvinced that either of the candidates was especially capable of, or committed to, successful economic management. When asked about the state of the economy, 52 percent said that it was in poor shape. But neither candidate received majority support when voters were asked which one they trusted to handle the economy: only 45 percent said they trusted Kerry and only 49 percent said they trusted Bush. Clearly, Democratic candidates are no longer automatically considered economic saviors in the same way that Franklin D. Roosevelt and his successors were. But it is also the case that the groups to which such an economic appeal would have been most important—the New

Deal Democratic coalition of small farmers, working-class whites, and ethnic and racial minorities—have become much less unified since the late 1960s. One of the hallmarks of Ronald Reagan's success was his ability to woo working-class whites away from the Democratic Party, and the two parties have battled over this group since.

Democrats are increasingly unable to mobilize voters along economic class lines because these lines have been obscured. This is reflected in how voters identify themselves in class terms. As Figure 4-3 indicates, fewer and fewer Americans see themselves as part of the working class. Asked in 1960 to choose whether they were working or middle class, 66 percent of Americans said "working class." [16] By 2000 the percentage had fallen to just 46 percent. This may have to do with the steady decline of unions, long a bulwark of working-class consciousness. Membership in unions declined from 25 percent of the labor force in the late 1960s to just 11 percent in 2000.[17] Union strength also varies regionally; it is greater in the North and Pacific Coast states than in the South or West, where right-to-work laws prevail. Not surprisingly, the regions where unions are stronger are the ones where Democrats still tend to do well. But what is especially surprising about the decline in working-class identification is that actual income inequality increased over this period. For example, the percentage of households considered low-income increased from 20.7 percent in 1969 to 22.2 percent in 1996.[18]

The erosion of political identification along class lines has hurt the Democrats. In response, many of the party's leaders have forsaken traditional allies in attempts to reposition themselves. President Clinton's abandonment

Figure 4-3 Working-Class Identification, 1960–2000

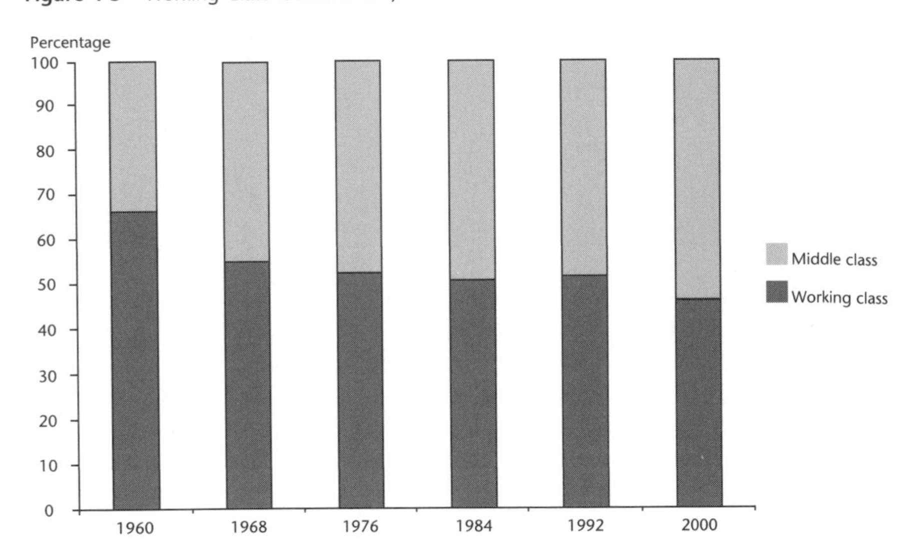

Source: American National Election Studies data, cumulative data file, 1948–2000, Inter-University Consortium for Political and Social Research, Ann Arbor, Mich., www.icpsr.umich.edu.

of labor in the pursuit of free trade legislation is one example; his willingness to overhaul welfare, a New Deal program supported by labor and minorities, is another. In 2004, John Kerry also tried this type of repositioning, most notably through his stated commitment to continuing and expanding middle-class tax cuts and by repeatedly emphasizing that his health care initiative was "not a government program." If setting the terms of debate is the province of the winner in politics, Franklin Roosevelt's Democrats have surely lost.

From the Cold War to the War on Terrorism: Further Democratic Decline

One of the reasons that Democrats have not been able to build a successful new coalition around middle-class economic interests is that, just as working-class identification has declined, so too has the importance that voters assign to economic problems when forming their loyalties. Foreign policy and, increasingly, social policy concerns have become much more salient for the voting public. Figure 4-4 shows the changing nature of Americans' concerns since the early 1970s. As the figure suggests, Democratic candidates have performed well in recent decades when economic concerns were the voters' main priority. In 1972, the nation was struggling with economic problems, social unrest, and conflict over Vietnam; all three commanded equal attention from the electorate. But after the 1973 oil crisis, concerns about

Figure 4-4 Voter Views of Most Important Issue Facing the Nation, 1972–2000

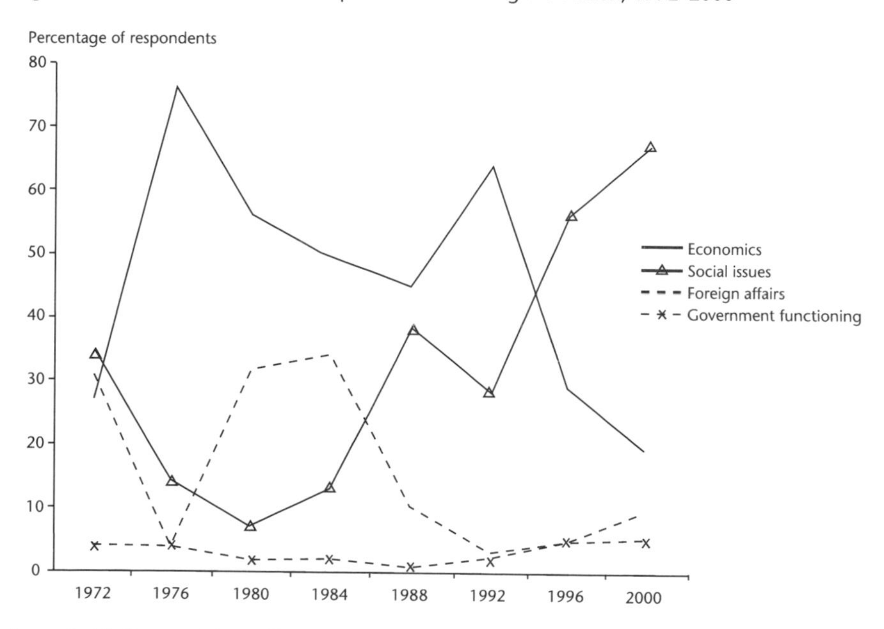

Source: Paul R. Abramson, John H. Aldrich, and David W. Rohde, *Change and Continuity in the 2000 Elections* (Washington, D.C.: CQ Press, 2002).

stagflation became paramount, and Democrat Jimmy Carter won the 1976 election. Since then, however, with the exception of 1992, economic issues have been declining in prominence.

During the 1980s, in the aftermath of the Iranian hostage crisis, public concern revived foreign policy issues, and this benefited the Republicans. Since Dwight Eisenhower in the 1950s, Republican success in presidential elections has been predicated on the party's perceived strength on national security issues.[19] Vietnam only enhanced voters' perceptions of Republican superiority to the Democrats on such issues.[20] As shown in Figure 4-4, since Vietnam, Republicans have done well when foreign policy issues have risen in importance. This was the case in 1972, as well as in 1980 and 1984 after Ronald Reagan labeled the Soviet Union the "evil empire." In this light, it is not surprising that the only Democrat to win the presidency since Reagan, Bill Clinton, did so in the brief interim between the end of the cold war and the start of the war on terrorism. Much as in 1976, the year Democrat Jimmy Carter was elected, Bill Clinton's victories in 1992 and 1996 occurred when foreign policy issues were not the most salient among voters.

Partly as a result of Reagan's massive defense buildup, the Soviet Union collapsed and cold war politics came to an end. But the attacks of September 11 brought national security issues immediately back to the fore. In the aftermath of the attacks, Gallup poll respondents identified the Republicans as the party they trusted more to fight terrorism by 61 percent to 23 percent, and as the party best suited to handle national defense generally by 65 percent to 24 percent.[21] Despite growing doubts about the war in Iraq, the 2004 exit poll makes it clear that Republicans continue to benefit from voters' concerns about national security. Iraq and the war on terrorism were cited as the most significant problems facing the nation by just over a third of all voters, and most of these supported President Bush. Specifically, 19 percent of voters in the 2004 poll identified the war on terrorism as most important, and 86 percent of them voted for President Bush. But of the 15 percent who said that Iraq was the most important issue, only 26 percent supported the president. This raises the possibility that the long-term consequences of the war could tarnish the Republicans' otherwise positive national security image.

Displacing the Economy with New Lines of Cleavage: Race, Religion, and the Republican Advantage

As a result of September 11, foreign policy issues benefited President Bush politically in much the same way that cold war concerns benefited President Reagan, although not to the same degree. The difficulty with foreign policy as a mobilizing device for elections, however, is that to the extent that the president is successful, the issue becomes less important to voters. Peaceful times mean that foreign policy concerns are less salient. In the domestic policy arena, Republicans have used more durable social, or cultural, issues to build their coalition. Indeed, perhaps the most compelling trend line in

Figure 4-4 is the escalating importance of social issues for Americans. The rise of these issues, especially since 1980, has by and large transformed the line of domestic political cleavage from one centered on the economy to one centered on social issues, including race, gender, and traditional religious values.

The results of the 2004 election make this transformation all the more pronounced. After a campaign that focused largely on the economy and the war, 22 percent of voters nonetheless identified "moral values" as the most important issue in the election. Although the term is vague (and not directly comparable to the "social issues" category in Figure 4-4), the vast majority of voters who selected it had the conservative Republican understanding in mind—a full 80 percent of them voted for the president. Interestingly, moral values were more important in some regions than others: 24 percent of southern and midwestern voters identified this as their top priority, while only 16 percent did so in the East.[22]

The advantages of emphasizing social issues first became apparent to Republicans in the 1964 election, when Barry Goldwater's racial conservatism in the midst of the civil rights movement helped him win several Deep South states that long had been solidly Democratic. The same Democratic Party embrace of civil rights that built support among African Americans also created an opportunity for Republicans to appeal to resistant white voters. Beginning with Goldwater's and, in 1972, Nixon's "southern strategy" and extending at least through the Willie Horton ad aired in 1988 to portray Democratic presidential candidate Michael Dukakis as soft on crime, Republicans used issues related to race to disrupt the class basis of blue collar white voting on which New Deal Democratic dominance had been built. These racial issues have ranged broadly, from the Republicans' promotion of race-neutral individual rights over race-based group rights to covertly racialized appeals for law and order, tough action against criminals, and the elimination of welfare programs.[23]

The enduring significance of racial, as opposed to class, electoral divisions is illustrated in Figure 4-5. This figure shows the difference between black and white voters' support for Republicans from 1960 to 2004, compared to the difference in Republican support between low- and middle-income white voters.[24] In 1960, white and black voters differed in their support for the Republican candidate by 26 percent: 52 percent of white voters supported Republican candidate Richard Nixon, and 26 percent of blacks did so. By the end of the 1960s, after the passage of civil rights legislation under Lyndon Johnson, this difference climbed to 56 percent. Since then African Americans have overwhelming supported Democratic presidential candidates, and a majority of whites have typically supported Republican candidates. The 2004 election was little different in this regard. President Bush captured only 11 percent of the black vote, compared to 58 percent of the white vote.

In contrast to the stark racial differences in presidential voting, the differences between low-income and middle-income white voters have been small since the 1960s. Only once was the difference greater than 10 percent—

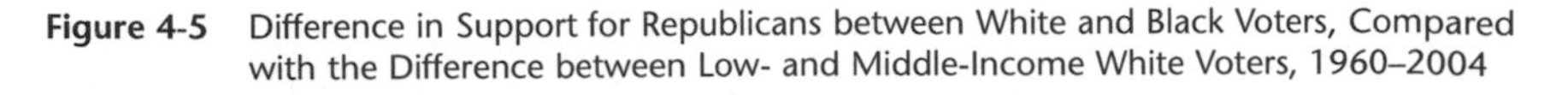

Figure 4-5 Difference in Support for Republicans between White and Black Voters, Compared with the Difference between Low- and Middle-Income White Voters, 1960–2004

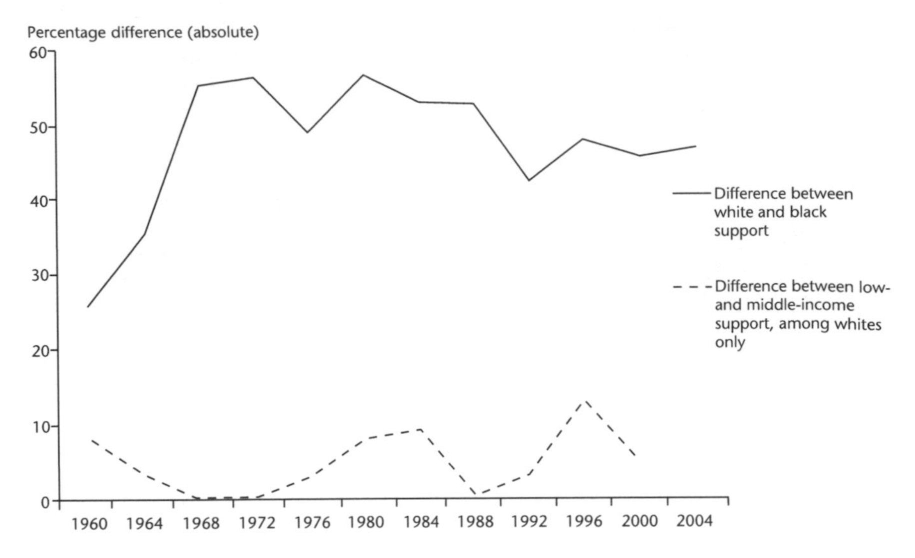

Source: American National Election Studies data, cumulative data file, 1948–2000, Inter-University Consortium for Political and Social Research, Ann Arbor, Mich., www.icpsr.umich.edu; 2004 data, CNN.com (NEP), www.cnn.com/ELECTION/2004/pages/results/president/.

in 1996, when low-income white voters increased their support for President Bill Clinton. Interestingly, however, the low-income and middle-income groups have crossed paths over the years. In the 1960s, low-income white voters were more supportive of Republican candidates than middle-income white voters. But by 1972, Republicans were finding greater support among middle-income whites, and it has stayed that way ever since. The slightly lower levels of support among low-income voters relative to middle-income voters after 1972 support the thesis, advanced by some, that income divisions still matter in party politics.[25] But racial differences remain much more politically significant than class differences among whites.

In recent years, the dynamics of racial politics have been altered by the growing ethnic and racial diversity of the country. Indeed, a recent argument about future Democratic prospects suggests that rising racial and ethnic groups, such as Hispanics, drawn to the party by its socially and economically progressive record, will play a pivotal role in the Democrats' return to majority status.[26] But the 2004 election results suggest that patterns of support among Hispanic voters are not yet established. Although President Bush made gains in 2004 among all ethnic groups, he increased his support most among Hispanics, from 35 percent in 2000 to 44 percent. The president's appeal for members of this group was apparently little different from his overall appeal. His stance on social issues, such as abortion and embryonic stem cell research, resonated well with the cultural conservatism of Hispanic voters, among whom the Catholic Church or evangelical Christian churches are highly influential. And since Hispanic Americans are disproportionately represented in the military, patriotism connected to the war on terrorism also won Bush some votes.[27]

To the extent that traditional values continue to appeal to Hispanic voters, Republicans will add to what already is perhaps their strongest base of support, that of religious conservatives. Invoking traditional values concerning gender and the family to court voters in the South and in parts of the West and Midwest has been a Republican strategy since the 1973 Supreme Court decision in *Roe v. Wade* began to energize religious conservatives politically. Catholic voters were an early target, particularly in many states in the Northeast and Midwest, where they are as much as 30 to 40 percent of the population. Since then, Republican attention has also focused on white evangelicals. By the mid-1990s, white evangelicals made up roughly a quarter of the adult population.[28] Heavily concentrated in the South and West, they make up 30 to 40 percent of the electorate in a number of states in these regions.

The Republicans' steady cultivation of religious conservatives has helped them woo these voters away from their traditional home in the Democratic Party, especially in the South and West.[29] Successful Republican presidential candidates since the 1980s have garnered roughly 80 percent of the white evangelical vote.[30] The 2004 election was no different in this regard. Despite a campaign that focused on the war and the economy, turnout among evangelicals increased, and as in 2000, they overwhelmingly supported President Bush.

Apart from religious affiliation, the growing importance of religion in general to the success of the new Republican order can be observed in Figure 4-6, which shows trends of support among those who attend religious services weekly, compared with those who never attend. Data in this figure reinforce those on issue priorities in Figure 4-4. Although there were some differences in 1972 between those who attended services weekly and those who never attended, the differences largely disappeared in 1976, 1980, and 1984—elections in which first the economy and then foreign policy were of greater concern. With the end of the cold war and the economic boom of the 1990s, the gap between the two groups widened considerably. In 1996, weekly worshippers voted for the Republican candidate by a margin 25 percent greater than those who never attended. The gap narrowed slightly in 2000 but returned to 25 percent in 2004, with weekly attendees increasing their support of President Bush and those never attending decreasing their support.[31]

Also noteworthy in Figure 4-6 is the *decline* in Republican support among those who never attend services. For John Judis and Ruy Teixeira, the authors of *The Emerging Democratic Majority*, it is trends like this, among the less religious, that make Democratic prospects bright. Not only do secularists tend to support Democrats much more strongly than Republicans, but they are growing in number: Those who attend services less than once a year, if at all, increased from 18 percent of voters in 1972 to 30 percent in 1998.[32]

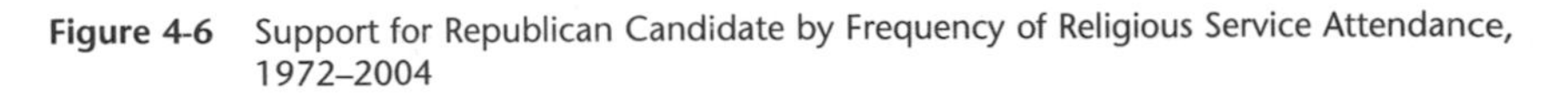

Figure 4-6 Support for Republican Candidate by Frequency of Religious Service Attendance, 1972–2004

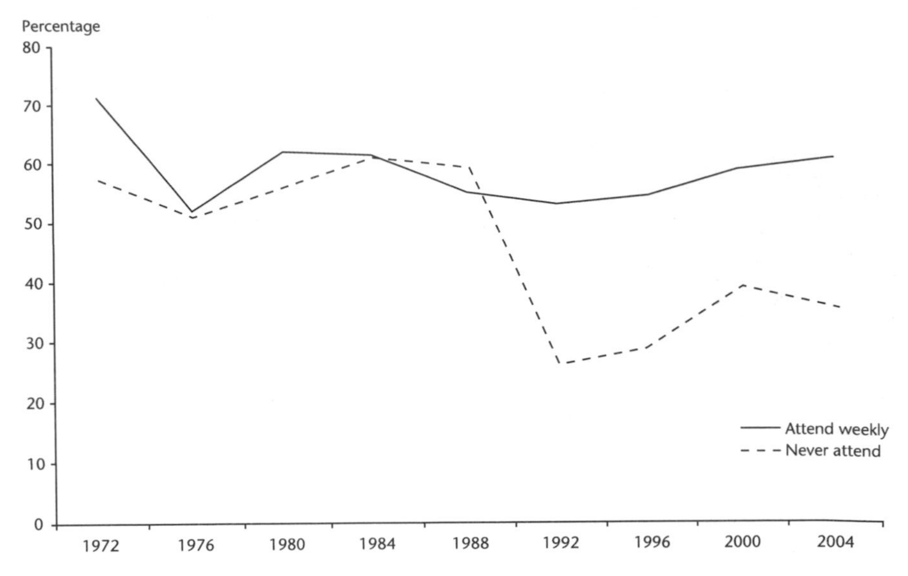

Source: American National Election Studies data, cumulative data file, 1948–2000, Inter-University Consortium for Political and Social Research, Ann Arbor, Mich., www.icpsr.umich.edu; 2004 data, CNN.com (NEP), www.cnn.com/ELECTION/2004/pages/results/president/.

In addition to the growth in the number of secularists that encourages Judis and Teixeira and other Democratic authors, they point to the rise in the number of highly educated professionals as additional evidence that the Democrats have a bright future. When political conflict was structured around economic class divisions, professionals were predominantly Republican. But Democrats have been making headway among these voters since the mid-1960s.[33] Some evidence for this appears in Figure 4-7, which tracks support for Republican candidates by voter level of education.

Until the 2000 election, voters with more education tended to be more supportive of Republicans than those with less education, in ways that are consistent with income divisions. For some time, however, support for Republicans has been declining among voters with a college degree. (Although not shown in the figure, the trend is even more pronounced among those with a professional or graduate degree.) In the 1990s, college-educated voters split roughly evenly between the two parties. By 2004, college graduates were more Democratic than high school graduates.

As the percentage of Americans with a college degree has increased, along with the percentage of professionals, and because members of these overlapping groups tend to be regular voters, the growth in their numbers may indeed be promising for Democrats. Any projections should be made with caution however. As a percentage of the population, these high-status groups

Figure 4-7 Support for Republicans by Level of Education, 1960–2004

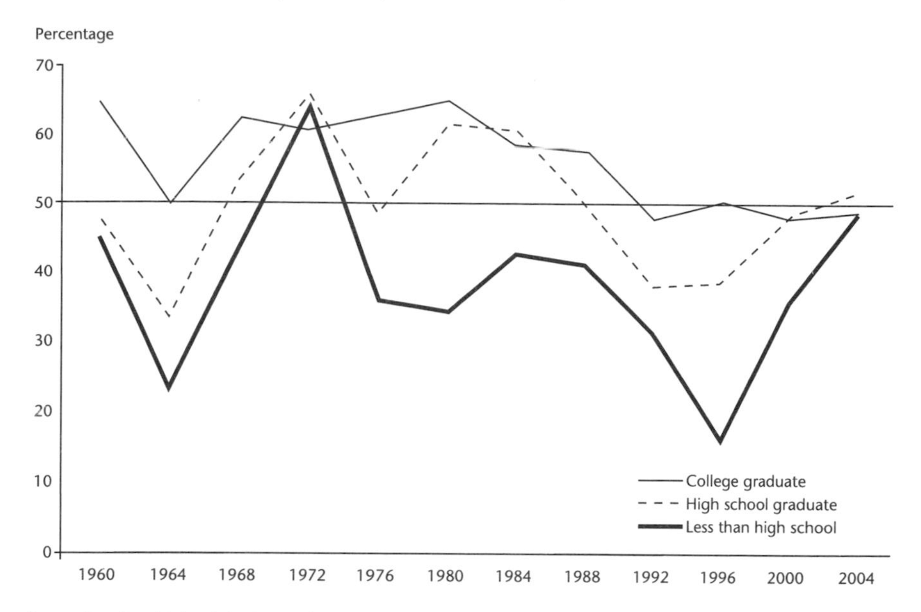

Source: American National Election Studies data, cumulative data file, 1948–2000, Inter-University Consortium for Political and Social Research, Ann Arbor, Mich., www.icpsr.umich.edu; 2004 data, CNN.com (NEP), www.cnn.com/ELECTION/2004/pages/results/president/.

are still small; roughly one in four Americans has a college degree and professionals make up only 15.4 percent of the workforce.[34] Just as important, these groups are not overwhelmingly Democratic, as Figure 4-7 makes clear. The attachment of many college-educated professionals to the Democratic Party is rooted in their coming of age after the 1960s, when issues of the environment, civil rights, and feminism figured prominently in the discourse on college campuses and in public life generally. Yet as Democratic pollster Stanley Greenberg makes clear, many college-educated voters, although sympathetic to the Democrats' social progressivism, dislike the party's traditional economic message.[35] These voters' continued attachment to the Democratic Party may vary directly with the degree of social conservatism of the Republican Party. And since social conservatives are much more vigorously supportive of the Republican Party than the college-educated are of the Democrats, the Democratic Party, at least for now, holds the short end of the stick.

Conclusion: Whither the Democratic Party?

From the 1930s until the 1960s, a majority of voters supported the New Deal Democratic regime because it provided security. In a political world defined largely in class terms, the security that mattered most was economic. In the face of what appeared to be the hopeless devastation of the Great

Depression, Franklin D. Roosevelt convinced voters that government activism would bring stability and an end to "nameless fear." Presidents Kennedy and Johnson built on this by promising to extend economic security to all Americans. The Democrats' economic message was buttressed by their commitment to providing national security as well, first in World War II and then during the early decades of the cold war. Despite occasional missteps, presidents from Roosevelt to Johnson used Keynesianism hand in hand with containment of communism to build and maintain the Democratic state.

Vietnam and stagflation undid Democratic promises of security. At the same time, the party's embrace of progressive social change further destabilized its traditional coalition. Beginning with President Nixon and accelerating under President Reagan, Republicans began to assume the mantle of the party of security. Reagan reasserted national security with an aggressive posture toward the Soviet Union. Equally important, he offered a new kind of security through the promotion of conservative social values, an appeal that was all the more meaningful because of rapid changes in the economic order. Mass consumption, capital mobility, and globalization brought social change, from closing factories and eroding unions, to two-income households, social diversity, and a wide-open popular culture. The more capricious the economic world appeared, the greater the appeal of traditional values as a means to offset those changes. Social conservatism became a type of security when the government seemed unable or unwilling to manage what had become an increasingly internationalized postindustrial economy.

President Bush was reelected in 2004 because he promised the sort of security that his Republican predecessors had established as the party's leading message. After attacks unprecedented in the American experience, the president's aggressive response to terrorism resonated well with traditional Republican national security appeals. And after eight years of greater social progressivism under President Clinton, President Bush's religious appeals, from faith-based initiatives to conservative court appointments to support for bans on gay marriage, resonated well with the party's socially conservative base. By reinvigorating traditional foreign and social policy appeals, President Bush reassembled the majority coalition that had put previous Republican presidents in power.

Although the complete control of the government that Republicans won in 2004 is a greater grant of power than the party has previously received, President Bush's margin of victory was slim, and the electorate remains narrowly divided between the two parties. To return to the quotation at the beginning of this chapter, the people may have endorsed the president's leadership, but they did so with skepticism and with 48 percent dissenting. Bush now faces the challenge of governing on behalf of a small majority that comprises several different factions, from social conservatives to foreign policy hawks to economic conservatives. Just as the Democrats in the 1960s struggled to hold together factions increasingly at odds with each other, President Bush will likely have to contend with factional strife within the Republican

Party. Catering too much to any one faction will jeopardize the support of the others. With such a small majority, few defectors can be afforded.

Democrats, for now, are the minority party. But that will change if Republicans overestimate the extent of the 2004 election's endorsement by moving too far in satisfying any particular constituency. And to the extent that Democrats can redefine security, that animating feature of modern American politics, they will be successful in recapturing the center.

Notes

1. Bush press conference transcript, November 4, 2004, www.washingtonpost.com/wp-dyn/articles/A25429-2004Nov4.html (accessed November 14, 2004).
2. Ibid.
3. See Martin P. Wattenberg, *The Rise of Candidate Centered Politics* (Cambridge: Harvard University Press, 1991).
4. E. J. Dionne, *Why Americans Hate Politics* (New York: Simon and Schuster, 1991), 152.
5. This is not new. Similar impulses have been observed in reactions against industrial modernization at the turn of the twentieth century. See Richard Hofstadter, *The Age of Reform: From Bryan to F.D.R.* (New York: Knopf, 1955).
6. Walter Dean Burnham, "Critical Realignment: Dead or Alive?" in *The End of Realignment?* ed. Byron Shafer (Madison: University of Wisconsin Press, 1991).
7. Benjamin Ginsberg and Martin Shefter, *Politics by Other Means,* 3rd ed. (New York: Norton, 2002); John Aldrich, *Why Parties: The Origins and Transformation of Political Parties in America* (Chicago: University of Chicago Press, 1995).
8. Gary C. Jacobson, "Congress: A Singular Continuity," in *The Elections of 1988,* ed. Michael Nelson (Washington, D.C.: CQ Press, 1989).
9. Stephen Skowronek, *The Politics Presidents Make: Leadership from John Adams to Bill Clinton* (Cambridge: Harvard University Press, 1993).
10. As quoted in John B. Judis and Ruy Teixeira, *The Emerging Democratic Majority* (New York: Scribner's, 2002), 30.
11. J. Clark Archer and Peter J. Taylor, *Section and Party: A Political Geography of American Presidential Elections, from Andrew Jackson to Ronald Reagan* (New York: Wiley, 1981).
12. Calculations are based on all major-party voters in each of the four regions. The South includes Alabama, Arkansas, Florida, Georgia, Kentucky, Louisiana, Mississippi, North Carolina, Oklahoma, South Carolina, Tennessee, Texas, Virginia, and West Virginia. The West includes Arizona, Colorado, Idaho, Iowa, Kansas, Minnesota, Missouri, Montana, Nebraska, Nevada, New Mexico, North Dakota, South Dakota, Utah, and Wyoming. The Pacific Coast includes California, Oregon, and Washington. The North includes Connecticut, Delaware, Illinois, Indiana, Maine, Maryland, Massachusetts, Michigan, New Hampshire, New Jersey, New York, Ohio, Pennsylvania, Rhode Island, Vermont, and Wisconsin. Alaska and Hawaii, which were added to the Union after World War II and which regularly vote Republican and Democratic respectively, are not included in the analysis.
13. This follows the logic of conflict displacement as described by E. E. Schattschneider, *The Semi-Sovereign People: A Realist's View of Democracy in America* (New York: Holt, Rinehart and Winston, 1961).
14. Data are from exit polls conducted by the National Election Poll (NEP). Except where indicated, data throughout this chapter are drawn from this source.

15. The breakdown is as follows: 20 percent said economy/jobs was the most important issue, and 80 percent of them voted for Kerry; of the 8 percent who said "health care," 77 percent chose Kerry; of the 5 percent who picked taxes, 43 percent chose Kerry; and of the 4 percent who picked education as the most important issue, 73 percent voted for Kerry.
16. American National Election Studies data, cumulative data file, 1948–2000, Inter-University Consortium for Political and Social Research, Ann Arbor, Mich., www.icpsr.umich.edu.
17. Harold Stanley and Richard Niemi, *Vital Statistics on American Politics* (Washington, D.C.: CQ Press, 2004).
18. U.S. Census Bureau, www.census.gov/hhes/income/mednhhld/ta5.html (accessed November 9, 2004). Another, more standard measure of income inequality, the Gini coefficient, increased 20.1 percent from 1968 to 2001. Calculated from data at www.census.gov/hhes/income/histinc/ie6.html (accessed November 19, 2004).
19. John Kenneth White, *The Values Divide* (New York: Chatham House, 2003), 204.
20. Norman Nie, Sydney Verba, and John Petrocik, *The Changing American Vote* (Cambridge: Harvard University Press, 1976).
21. White, *The Values Divide,* 204.
22. The number in the West was the same as the national average, 22 percent. This undoubtedly reflects differences between Pacific Coast and interior Western states.
23. On the "southern strategy," see Kevin Phillips, *The Emerging Republican Majority* (New York: Arlington House, 1969). For the use of race as a wedge issue against New Deal Democrats and to disrupt class politics, see, among others, Robert Huckfeldt and Carol Weitzel Kohfeld, *Race and the Decline of Class in American Politics* (Urbana: University of Illinois Press, 1989); Thomas Byrne Edsall and Mary D. Edsall, *Chain Reaction: The Impact of Race, Rights, and Taxes on American Politics* (New York: Norton, 1992); and Paul Frymer, *Uneasy Alliances: Race and Party Competition in America* (Princeton: Princeton University Press, 1999).
24. At the time of publication, the 2004 exit poll data that were available did not distinguish the categories of white low- and middle-income voters.
25. Jeffrey Stonecash, *Class and Party in American Politics* (Boulder, Colo.: Westview Press, 2000).
26. Judis and Teixeira, *The Emerging Democratic Majority.*
27. Kirk Johnson, "Hispanic Voters Declared Their Independence," *New York Times,* November 9, 2004.
28. John C. Green, "The Christian Right and the 1996 Elections: An Overview," in *God at the Grass Roots, 1996: The Christian Right in American Elections,* ed. Mark J. Rozell and Clyde Wilcox (Lanham, Md.: Rowman and Littlefield, 1997), 3.
29. For accounts that describe the evolution of the parties' positions on these issues, see Christina Wolbrecht, *The Politics of Women's Rights: Parties, Positions, and Change* (Princeton: Princeton University Press, 2000); and Greg Adams, "Abortion: Evidence of an Issue Evolution," *American Journal of Political Science* 41 (1997): 718–737.
30. Stanley B. Greenberg, *The Two Americas: Our Current Political Deadlock and How to Beat It* (New York: St. Martin's, 2004), 98. Also see Stanley and Niemi, *Vital Statistics on American Politics,* 124–125.
31. Because there is some reason to believe that, at least in exit polling, individuals exaggerate the frequency with which they attend services, the 2004 data in Figure 4-6 should be viewed cautiously (NES data are considered more accurate; see Judis and Teixeira, *The Emerging Democratic Majority,* 209, n. 6). Even so, however, this concern may not be entirely warranted. Individuals who feel sufficient

normative pressure to exaggerate their attendance, in all likelihood, are more responsive to religious cues, particularly in comparison to those who claim never to attend.

32. Based on a National Opinion Research Study survey, cited in Judis and Teixeira, *The Emerging Democratic Majority,* 150. Also see Greenberg, *The Two Americas,* 100.
33. Everett Carll Ladd, "Liberalism Upside Down: The Inversion of the New Deal Order," *Political Science Quarterly* 91 (1976–1977): 577–600.
34. Judis and Teixeira, *The Emerging Democratic Majority,* 39–49.
35. Greenberg, *The Two Americas,* 164–173.

5

The Media: The Challenge and Promise of Internet Politics

Matthew Robert Kerbel

It was Sunday, June 22, 2003. Howard Dean, the former governor of Vermont, had just endured one hour of abuse at the hands of Tim Russert on *Meet the Press,* giving a performance that could be described charitably as not ready for prime time. Halting and uncertain, Dean hemmed his way through questions about tax increases, the Iraq war, the death penalty, civil unions, and his draft history, failing to rebut Russert's questionable charge that Dean would preside over a 1,400 percent tax increase and unable to state the exact number of American troops in Iraq. Conventional wisdom inside the Beltway rapidly coalesced around the theme that the Dean candidacy, after experiencing monumental growth in media, money, and momentum during the previous few months, was severely weakened by the candidate's hour-long display of inexperience.

Eight days later Dean raised $819,531 on-line, to bring his take for the quarter to $7,500,000.[1]

What the national punditry had regarded as a raw performance Dean loyalists saw as a refreshingly spontaneous indictment of all that is wrong with television-centered politics. Perhaps their candidate was unpolished, but that was because he was unscripted. He would refuse to play Russert's game of "gotcha." And he could refuse—because he had his loyalists, and they had the Internet: the most democratic medium in American history. The Internet was the great equalizer, the tool that would permit otherwise disparate and far-flung "Deaniac" voices to be heard above the self-serving din of the chattering class. Far from destroying the Dean campaign, the candidate's appearance that Sunday morning brought forth from his supporters a deluge of epithets toward Russert and his peers, along with statements of defiance, commitments to soldier on—and lots of cash.

Something unprecedented was happening, although on that summer morning no one—not Russert or Dean or his supporters—could say exactly what it was. Under the standing rules of the television-centered political game, insider reaction to Dean's *Meet the Press* appearance should have spooked his contributors and doomed his candidacy. Were Dean's virtual community of supporters and the medium that bound them to one another powerful enough to rewrite those rules? Something had changed—but what was it? And how far-reaching were its effects?

Four years ago, in *The Elections of 2000,* I wrote that the Internet was "rough and raw" but preparing to take a seat alongside television, newspapers, and radio in the media campaign. "Four years from now," I suggested, "it may even give jaded political reporters something imaginative to think about." [2] And so it has. But the Internet remains a work in progress, more functional than it was four years ago but far from a decisive political force. The fate of the Dean candidacy is well known. The legacy of its digital exploits has yet to be written.

In September 2003, half the country went on-line—a record. Two-thirds of those who go on-line regularly seek out a news source at least some of the time, many of them using the Web sites of newspapers, broadcast and cable television news outlets, or Internet-only sources like AOL and Yahoo.[3] Sites like these, which represent the cyber component of conventional commercial news organizations, account for the largest share of news seeking on the Web. A smaller, less-commercial, less-predictable, and more free-form component, consisting of self-produced or narrowly focused Web sites, constitutes the frontier of Internet news, the Wild West of cyberspace. This is the portion of the Web where Dean loyalists dwelled.

The two groups of news sites combined are rattling the tectonic plates of journalism. The mainstream media of the twentieth century—large-circulation newspapers and news magazines, network and local television news broadcasts—still have the largest audiences, but they are losing market share while people move into an on-demand, on-line news environment. In the view of the Project for Excellence in Journalism, the result of these twin dynamics, circa 2004, "is that journalism is in the midst of an epochal transformation, as momentous probably as the invention of the telegraph or television." [4]

This One Was Different

The Internet picked a particularly propitious election in which to shed its larva. Weightier and more compelling than other recent elections, the 2004 presidential race emerged early as a call-to-arms for supporters and opponents of an administration that generated passionate feelings of loyalty and contempt. The Internet proved a natural fit to the moment: a hot medium in a political environment that was hotter than any in recent memory, a conduit for the political energy of the Bush and anti-Bush foot soldiers.

The emergence of those passions foreshadowed the arc of the presidential campaign. As a controversial war raged in Iraq, the public struggled with the political messages emanating from the two parties as much as the candidates struggled over what those messages should be. Democratic contenders first acquiesced to the war in Iraq, then—acknowledging the effectiveness of the Dean campaign—attacked President Bush, only to find themselves tongue-tied over their earlier acquiescence. President Bush first reigned as a war president, then saw his foundation for war systematically eroded by accumulating evidence of the nonthreatening state of Saddam Hussein's military. All the while, the Iraqi insurgency expanded. In time, Bush found himself changing his rationale for war, then insisting that things were going well in Iraq, to an American public to whom the war looked quite different on television.

Unlike the election of 2000, a campaign steeped in trivia, in spring 2003 the news media recognized that 2004 would offer a serious and important contest. To be sure, their coverage was as predictable as ever, depicting a horse race that seemed to stretch on infinitely, finding strategic nuance in every turn of events, teasing meaning from a hailstorm of polling data while largely misunderstanding the concept "margin of error." [5] But this time a lot appeared to be riding on the horses in the race, and as news from Iraq turned increasingly deadly it proved a sobering tableau for coverage that in past years looked like a cross between the Super Bowl and *Survivor.*

People were locked in. Against the backdrop of conventional coverage, a passionate argument raged about the veracity of the messages Americans were getting in the newspapers, from the networks, and on cable television. Conservatives took issue with the media's failure to show how democracy was taking root in Iraq. Liberals took issue with the failure to show the returning coffins of dead American soldiers. Conservatives denounced news stories suggesting that the president's Iraq policy was out of touch with reality. Liberals denounced news frames that spoke of a post-handover, "new Iraq" as perpetuating a fiction fabricated by the White House. Conservatives yelled that war coverage unfairly accentuated the negative. Liberals yelled that war coverage understated how disastrous the American intervention had become.

A lot of this yelling took place on-line. As the campaign rolled on, more and more Americans found their way to on-line political "weblogs" (or, in the unappealing vernacular of the initiated, "blogs")—virtual communities of like-minded individuals on the right and left that provided a safe haven for venting, planning, hoping, and—unlike television—acting on their wishes and frustrations. Andrewsullivan.com, Instapundit.com, MyDD.com, Talkingpointsmemo.com: in 2000 these blogs didn't exist. But as the leaves started to turn in fall 2004, traffic spiked to the point where the two most popular liberal blogs—Daily Kos and Eschaton—combined had more readers than the *Philadelphia Inquirer.*[6]

The traditional press took notice. Five weeks before election day, the *New York Times* featured the stories of several young, wired, and previously unemployed bloggers in its high-profile Sunday magazine, comparing their influence on the political process to that of the elite reporters of the previous generation:

> During the 1972 presidential campaign, Timothy Crouse covered the campaign-trail press corps in *Rolling Stone* magazine, reporting that he

> later expanded into his revealing and funny book, "The Boys on the Bus." Crouse described the way a few top journalists like R. W. Apple Jr., David S. Broder, Jack Germond and Jules Witcover, through their diligence, ambition and supreme self-confidence, set the agenda for the whole political race. This summer, sitting in the Tank [the space designated for bloggers covering the Republican National Convention] and reading campaign blogs, you could sometimes get a half-giddy, half-sickening feeling that something was shifting, that the news agenda was beginning to be set by this largely unpaid, T-shirt-clad army of bloggers.[7]

Like so many other observers, the *Times* knew the times were changing, but it didn't quite know how. Too much had transpired since March 15, 2003, the day Howard Dean's campaign manager, Joe Trippi, inaugurated the "Call for Action Blog" with the innocuous plea, "We are going to need as much support from the netroots and grassroots as we can possibly get. Please check back here regularly." [8]

What Dean Did

People checked back. For the remainder of March, Dean bloggers posted seventeen discussion "threads," averaging one new post per day. In June, when the Call for Action Blog was replaced by the more sophisticated "Blog for America," there were 206 discussion threads; in July, there were 306, and in August, 393. While the Dean campaign was collapsing the following January, the blog supported 507 separate discussions. During fund-raising drives, candidate debates, and the run-up to the primaries, new threads were posted several times per hour.

Deaniacs ate it up. Blog for America allowed users to post comments to the threads, permitting virtual conversations to emerge among hundreds of people across the country and around the world. In their discussions of all things Dean, blog enthusiasts engaged in a free-flowing discourse that was at once reflective of major themes in the mainstream media and, significantly, broader and more complete. Discourse on Blog for America ranged from the trivial to the serious and from the absurd to the insightful, touching on everything from the horse race, campaign strategy, and the candidates' personality traits to policy positions, media campaign coverage, and the on-line blog community itself.

Like the mainstream press, bloggers scrutinized opinion polls and paid meticulous attention to which candidates were rising (October saw a lot of angst about Wesley Clark's entering the race), falling (Bob Graham's departure from the race was met with a kind of tender regret), or wasting their time (read: Joe Lieberman). Mirroring the mainstream press, bloggers passed judgment on the strategic direction of the campaign and commented on every tactical device the campaign employed, from fund-raising drives and visibility events to printing posters and canvassing. Unlike television's version of the campaign, though, in which horse race and strategy stories were presented for viewers' amusement, bloggers who were invested in the outcome of the race were deadly serious about influencing the means to win it. Horse race threads served as morale boosters. Strategic discussion was a call to action—to give money, arrange events, and canvass. Unlike television, the point of the blog was to engage, not amuse.

Bloggers also discussed the issues, branching into substantive territory where mainstream media coverage is traditionally reluctant to dwell. Whenever Dean issued a policy statement, it was posted on his blog for discussion. Whenever he made a policy speech, the text was immediately available on the blog to serve as a point of conversation for interested participants. "Guest bloggers" who had worked on a cause or interest that reflected Governor Dean's agenda were invited to write about what they did, attracting feedback from interested parties.

At the same time, Blog for America resembled a mainstream medium in the way it consciously invoked itself while keeping one eye trained on its conventional counterparts. Endless discussion on the blog of the wonders of the blog paralleled the television reporter's tendency to cover—and thereby elevate—his or her role in the political process.[9] The mawkish nature of this self-celebration could appear cloying and off-putting to the outside observer. Echoing similar expressions too numerous to count, one blogger posted a response to a thread by Dean's head of Internet outreach, Zephyr Teachout: "Zeph, your posts always bring a lump to my throat and I get all misty-eyed thinking about how wonderful this campaign is." [10] Another wrote, in a direct appeal to the candidate,

> Thank you Dr. Dean for running a campaign I can believe in . . . . Just remember, we are watching, and we have faith in you. Remember those who have never seen you, and remind you [sic] the reasons why you are the one who will be president, and remember those who have seen you before, but haven't quite been won over. Talk to us Dr. Dean, we will talk back.[11]

If the blog shared television's self-referential characteristics, however, it did so for an entirely different and arguably nobler reason. The purpose of blogging about community is to define and defend community, and on that score blogger self-references served the purpose of maintaining the enthusiasm necessary for ordinary people to engage in a grueling presidential campaign. Conventional media self-references, on the other hand, come off more as puffery by journalists assuring themselves of their importance in the political hierarchy.

The same may be said about the way bloggers critiqued political coverage. An echo chamber effect can be created when reporters report about the reporting of other reporters, as in the ABC News on-line vehicle "The Note," the "Media Notes" column in the *Washington Post,* and similar vehicles. Blogging about media stories is less incestuous, partly because bloggers do not identify themselves as journalists but mostly because the point of the exercise is different. Bloggers relentlessly trumpeted and vigorously attacked reporting they deemed unjust or biased, reserving a special place in Hell for journalists they thought were trashing their candidate. They played defense on Dean's behalf whenever they perceived a hostile report, hoping to prevent the spread of negative news that might undermine the campaign and, by extension, the blog. "Many people have been sending e-mail to CNN, MSNBC, etc.," blogged one frustrated supporter. "[The news organizations] are not listening. It's probably time to start contacting their sponsors." [12] Wrote another, on the occasion of Iowa senator Tom Harkin's endorsement of Governor Dean, "The media flunkies are standing with their jaws on the ground. They can't believe that after all the hatchet jobs they've done on Dean that he is still getting endorsements." [13]

Much of the discourse among Dean bloggers was impassioned and heartfelt. In addition to scathing criticism of journalists perceived to be anti-Dean in their reporting, there was the requisite bashing of George W. Bush, Dick Gephardt, John Kerry, and Wesley Clark. Bloggers engaged in predictable amounts of whooping when polls looked good, of hunkering down when rivals attacked, and of bucking up when things looked bleak. When Dean failed in Iowa and New Hampshire and the finish appeared bitter, the blog served first as a forum for collective denial, then as a virtual couch for coping with defeat. It may have been a collection of disparate and isolated voices, but to the end, the blog was a community.

Journalists Take Note

Before long, the peculiar phenomenon of the Dean blog caught the attention of mainstream journalists, and the story of the virtual Dean community became part of the campaign narrative. "Simply, Howard Dean is running the most radical campaign in a generation," wrote a contributor to the *Baltimore Sun*. "The former Vermont governor's political team is reinventing how campaigns are run, rejecting a decade-long trend toward near-Orwellian campaign centralization (which has reached its apotheosis in the Bush administration) and trading that control for a more energized group of supporters." [14]

By late 2003, as Dean's campaign soared, observations like this were repeated in news and opinion pieces across the country. The Dean blog had become an item of curiosity to journalists and commentators, who approached it with a mixture of wonder, skepticism, and more than a little dread. Folklore about the blog's almost magical ability to rally supporters and raise money worked its way off the blog, where for months it had been an element of the campaign's self-narrative, and into the mainstream media.

In July 2003, for instance, Vice President Cheney scheduled a big donor luncheon in South Carolina to raise $250,000. The Dean campaign promptly initiated a "Dean Team vs. Bush-Cheney Challenge" to bloggers to match that figure with small contributions during the weekend leading up to the Cheney event. Over 9,600 contributors gave more than half a million dollars and, in not-too-subtle contrast with Cheney's luncheon, were treated to a picture of the governor at a computer, blogging while eating a turkey sandwich. The fund-raising event instantly became part of blog lore; several months later, as Dean surged, it became part of the narrative that mainstream journalists would spin about the campaign.[15]

On television and in newspapers the public learned the stories of people who were legendary in Blog for America circles for having been inspired by Internet portrayals of the candidate to move to Vermont to work for Dean. As the *Wall Street Journal* noted in October 2003,

> Mathew Gross, a 31-year-old environmental activist living in Moab, Utah, had been praising Mr. Dean on blogs for months. In March, he quit his job serving burritos and flew east to join the Dean campaign—without calling ahead. After stopping to buy a $10 tie, he took a cheap motel room in Burlington, near campaign headquarters. On his first day as a volunteer, he stuffed envelopes. That night he stayed up late writing a memo on the importance of blogs. The next morning, he marched toward Mr. Trippi's office to deliver it, pausing at the door just long enough for senior aides to start escorting him away. Mr. Gross threw the memo toward the boss. "I write on MyDD!" he shouted, guessing Mr. Trippi would understand [the reference to the liberal weblog]. Mr. Trippi's head shot up. "You're hired!" he yelled back.[16]

Through stories like this, Trippi became a pop culture figure as well, trading on the cult status he had earned within the campaign as the father of the blog. Reporters found Trippi—rumpled, scruffy, and tech-savvy—a compelling presence because of his colorful style and unconventional campaign methods. The *San Jose Mercury News* described Trippi as "a self-professed techno-junkie" who is also "a longtime political heavyweight." [17]

Trippi's theories of campaigning were almost as much a part of the story of the Dean campaign as Dean himself. Because Trippi's approach to Web campaigning had roots in software development, the Dean campaign found itself in the odd position of being covered by political reporters and technical reporters, as in this piece in the technical journal *Baseline:*

> The openness of the Dean campaign mirrors, in some ways, the "open-source" community that has built much of the software on which the Dean campaign runs. In this communal manner of creating industrial-strength software, a single developer or a core group produces a fundamental piece of programming and then donates the source code to all comers. The other developers then test, tweak, improve and add their contributions to the original program . . . . "I wanted to use the collaborative nature of open source, where more people filling holes makes it more stable and effective," says Trippi . . . . "I wondered how it would work in a political campaign."[18]

An opinion piece in *USA Today* picked up the theme of open-source campaigning, contending that although the Web belongs to everyone, Web-based campaigning will not work for everyone.[19] To be successful, candidates must be willing to relinquish significant control of their operation to a self-appointed group of bloggers in a manner that runs contrary to the structure of centralized, hierarchical campaigns and to the impulses of control-oriented politicians.

Less contested but widely discussed was the way Dean managed to connect several facets of the new technology with one another in a reinforcing web of high-tech tools for political action, outreach, and fund raising. Through the combination of an accidental partnership with the Web service Meetup.com, an attempted marriage with the on-line activist organization MoveOn.org, and a high-tech twist on fund-raising techniques on their own Web site, the Dean forces creatively expanded their base into cyberspace, often using cutting-edge technology in the service of surprisingly traditional campaign activities.

Meetup.com is the Internet service specializing in facilitating real-world meetings among like-minded people. Designed as a virtual commons where people with similar social interests would find each other and arrange to meet, it accidentally became an integral part of Dean's Internet effort when Dean meetups emerged spontaneously in early 2003. These gatherings later were facilitated by a Meetup.com icon on the Dean Web site, along with heavy promotion on the blog.

Membership numbers soared. In the early days, when only 3,000 Deaniacs subscribed to Meetup, one news report captured Joe Trippi compulsively refreshing his Web browser to watch the Dean Meetup number climb closer to the leading Meetup topic at that time—witches.[20] In a campaign that was obsessed with numbers—even a quick glance at blog postings would give anyone a good idea of how preoccupied Dean bloggers were with their Meetup figures, membership figures, fund-raising figures, polling figures, and endorsement figures—the trajectory of Meetup numbers was received enthusiastically, and they exceeded 160,000 by the end of 2003.

On the first Wednesday of every month of the campaign, thousands, or tens of thousands, or hundreds of thousands of people would gather in restaurants and libraries and bars to engage in old-fashioned, low-tech community politics. Loosely coordinated at Dean's national headquarters, Meetups were the nerve center for one of the signature activities of the campaign: writing pro-Dean, longhand letters to undecided voters in Iowa and New Hampshire. Through Meetup, the Dean campaign had stumbled on a twenty-first-century way to bring together disparate supporters in the service of old-style retail politics.

MoveOn.org, a liberal activist organization, was ancient by Internet standards, tracing its origins to the 1998 Clinton impeachment trial. In June 2003, MoveOn held a cyber primary: an on-line vote to determine which Democratic candidate it was going to support with its considerable membership and fund-raising muscle. The minimum for a MoveOn endorsement was 50 percent of the vote, a difficult mark to achieve in a nine-candidate field, and the Dean blog was alive with planning for the event. Dean's Internet brain trust pressed hard for a big turnout, believing that the combined Internet forces of Blog for America and MoveOn.org would be unstoppable. But the 50 percent threshold proved too difficult to meet; Dean won the primary with 44 percent of the vote, but a strong showing by Dennis Kucinich prevented him from getting the endorsement.[21]

Finally, there was Internet fund raising, the achievement for which Dean received the most mainstream media attention and which ultimately forced many traditional Democrats to grudgingly acknowledge Dean as the front-runner for their party's nomination. Like Dean's relationship to Meetup, his fund-raising juggernaut was the product of serendipity and luck more than planning, and it brought high-tech tools together with low-tech techniques. As the *Wall Street Journal* tells it,

> On June 28, [2003] top Dean staffers met in the storage closet that served as the Internet team's office. They decided to make an . . . online appeal by announcing that the campaign had raised $6 million but wanted $500,000 more for a show of strength. To encourage giving, they wanted a distinctive image to measure contributions for the Web site . . . . Larry Biddle, Mr. Dean's deputy finance director and a New York Yankees fan, suggested a slugger holding a baseball bat and pointing to the outfield fence à la Babe Ruth. Nicco Mele, the campaign's new Webmaster, launched the appeal at 3 a.m. on Sunday June 29. . . . A gusher ensued—$303,000 on that Sunday alone. At one point, the campaign's blog crashed as supporters egged each other on. "Wow! Keep on giving—we'll need it to defeat Bush's corporate money machine," posted one supporter.[22]

From that time on, bloggers responded to "the bat" with unprecedented numbers of small donations. The blog created an echo chamber in which contributions were amplified by the momentum-producing postings of Deaniacs who constantly reported their excitement at the prospect of setting fund-raising records through their collective action. At times, bloggers would insist that Dean's Burlington headquarters "put up a bat"—essentially demanding that the campaign ask them for money. To read what people posted to the blog's fund-raising threads is to get a sense of the excitement and deep gratification that the process created, a feeling that spread among bloggers like a wildfire. Watching the bat fill up with red ink as the blog edged closer to a fund-raising goal, in the same low-tech way that a church fund-raiser would post its progress by coloring a drawing of a thermometer with red ink, became a spectator sport built on the participant sport of giving money. And, as Dean achieved unprecedented fund-raising success, journalists became spectators, too.

Enter the Blogosphere

Meanwhile, elsewhere in cyberspace, a revolution of a different sort was taking place, and in the slow manner of the media's discovery of Blog for

America, journalists started to take note. As *USA Today* wrote in self-referential fashion, weblogs are "forcing the mainstream news media to follow the stories they're pushing." [23] In truth, it's hard to imagine how the "unpaid, T-shirt clad" amateurs described by the *New York Times* could "force" professional journalists to do anything. More accurately, by the start of 2004, as the Dean campaign was coming unhinged, a few noncampaign blogs attracted a wide enough following to draw the attention of political reporters. Once on their radar, it was inevitable that blogs would attract coverage.

In February 2004, the *Washington Post* explored the political and policy blogs listed on DCbloggers.com and concluded,

> There are plenty of gossipy teen blogs and "what-I-had-for-lunch" journals, but like the city itself, Washington's blog scene has a strong base of politicos . . . . Dedicated, like-minded bloggers have even founded circles of sites that link to one another and discuss similar topics. The Beltway Bloggers fall to the right. The Cato Blog Mafia consists of current and former employees of the Cato Institute. There are wonkish policy blogs, environmental blogs and libertarian blogs.[24]

A *Time* magazine feature appearing in June 2004 found the new blogs compelling enough to assert that they are an effective form of communication, to wonder aloud as to why that is so, and to offer a series of answers:

> They're free. They catch people at work, at their desks, when they're alert and thinking and making decisions. Blogs are fresh and often seem to be miles ahead of the mainstream news. Bloggers put up new stuff every day, and there are thousands of them. . . . Blogs have voice and personality. They're human. They come to us not from some mediagenic anchorbot on an air-conditioned sound stage, but from an individual. They represent—no, they are—the voice of the little guy.[25]

In other words, suggested *Time*'s reporters, blogs aren't us. But the distance between conventional and unconventional media was already starting to diminish when those words were penned. One month later, at the Democratic Convention, the presence of bloggers among credentialed reporters became the subject of public discourse. A piece in the *Wall Street Journal* described "Bloggers Boulevard" as the section of the convention hall that was "outfitted with wireless technology so the bloggers can post from mobile devices." [26] From the *Journal*'s perspective, bloggers "aren't there to cover the convention" so much as they are "there to cover the journalists" [27]—an interesting observation from a journalist who was at the convention to cover bloggers and an indication of how much the blogosphere had penetrated the mainstream media by the summer of 2004.

Another sign of mainstream acceptance was the attention paid to the tattletale vendors on Bloggers Boulevard. The *Journal* couldn't pass up the opportunity to give some free publicity to Ana Marie Cox, the voice behind "the risqué, inside-the-Beltway gossip blog Wonkette.com," [28] whose emphasis on sexual escapades recounted in frank language, according to a piece in the *Christian Science Monitor,* is "a quiet victory for creeping National Enquirer values." [29] The telling point about the *Journal* story was its emphasis on how Cox had rapidly converted her blogging credentials into a job covering the Democratic Convention for the mainstream MTV cable channel.

Such intermingling of new and mainstream media was furthered by the introduction of campaign blogs as Internet counterparts to traditional television programs, such as the awkwardly named "Hardblogger"—the on-line journal of the MSNBC television program *Hardball*—launched in summer 2004. Although Hardblogger is not an interactive blog—readers cannot post comments on the threads—it provides an up-to-the-minute chronicle of all things political from the panelists who regularly grace the *Hardball* set, making it a source of instantaneous information for those who seek the insights of program host Chris Matthews ("It's been an amazing couple of days out here in Tempe. We've had some great debates")[30] and his regular guests.

Journalists Debate the Internet

"The line between pure political bloggers and 'Big Journalism,' " said the *American Journalism Review,* "is fading." [31] Blogs were "definitely having an impact on political journalism," [32] admitted *USA Today* political columnist Walter Shapiro. But in summer 2004, the nature of that impact was still up for discussion. There was even disagreement over the seemingly obvious observation by the *Washington Post* that blogs are "a way to connect" that creates "a sense of community." [33] Some observers said blogs were simply echo chambers for the overly involved that served mainly to splinter political discourse and isolate people into small groups. The *New York Times* for example, raised the possibility that "online discussion has become so fragmented" that "the Internet is in danger of narrowing the spectrum of debate even as it attracts more participants to it." [34] And the *Boston Globe* reported that "even among the wired, there is a debate over whether blogs are a new form of discourse or simply an endless feedback loop, a self-enclosed circle of political junkies echoing and challenging one another." [35]

The discussion is meaningful, particularly because the same questions could be raised about conventional election coverage. For instance, it has long been an accepted practice that presidential debates are discussed in the press through the simple narrative of winners and losers. In the less-frenzied 1980s, the terms of these discussions invariably would be framed by the relative effectiveness of the spin emanating from the two campaigns. By the 1990s, television reporters began talking about the spin itself, inviting viewers to join them figuratively behind the scenes.[36] By 2004, the media's connection to the spin room was no longer figurative. With a perpetual news hole to fill, cable coverage of the 2004 debates revolved around the spin process, to the point that CNN and MSNBC broadcast footage of journalists "being spun" by campaign operatives, inviting viewers to join them in the insular world of campaign reporters.

Opening the cynical process of message manipulation to a broader audience is a way of inviting spectators into a self-enclosed circle of sorts, in a fashion that stunts political discussion. The key difference between mainstream coverage of the insular world of spin and the insularity of weblogs is that television is a passive medium, its viewers beholden to the scripts written by producers and reporters. Although it is reasonable to raise questions about the narrowness of the blogosphere, it is equally reasonable to ask whether, far from simply talking to each other, bloggers have begun to assume the role of opinion leaders, with influence extending beyond their immediate circle, a position traditionally associated with newspaper columnists rather than self-appointed folks with a keyboard.

The *Chicago Tribune* suggested that bloggers might have just this kind of high-speed access to people beyond their immediate readership, speculating that blog readers are political junkies who are motivated to reach people off-line. The *Tribune* cited the case of Markos Moulitsas Zuniga, of Daily Kos. Moulitsas helped raise awareness of—and money for—little-known congressional candidates who were being overlooked by the Democratic Party because they were running in races considered hopeless by professionals.[37] The influence chain went from Moulitsas to his active readers, then—through more conventional means—to the broader community. "While scores of political blogs don't go beyond gossip and bickering," reported the *Tribune*, "many are quite influential." [38]

The extent of this influence was documented by a George Washington University study and reported in the *New York Times*. Although the study found that only 7 percent of Americans use the Internet regularly for political news, 69 percent of those who do are opinion leaders, at least among their friends, family, and associates. According to the study, opinion leaders are seven times more likely than average citizens to influence the voting habits of their peers, meaning that the Internet is the place to reach the people "who are reaching everyone else." [39]

To the degree that this is so, bloggers are becoming self-appointed managers of information capable of setting an agenda that is different from the agenda of political reporters—another point not lost on journalists. The *Wall Street Journal* saw blogs creating

> an alternative-news universe, giving everyone with a PC and a Web connection access to the sorts of gossip that was once available only to reporters on the press bus. At a site like Feedster, which is to blogs what Google is to Web sites, you can trace the rumor du jour. And what Napster did for MP3s, blogs are doing for news—or, at least for rumors. They are eliminating the gatekeepers and all barriers to entry.[40]

What does it mean to journalists to have self-appointed on-line gatekeepers determined, as one trade publication put it, to "pok[e] at the performance of mainstream journalism more than any other alternative media ever have"? [41] One possibility is that blogs will broaden the scope of the election agenda, introducing new story lines to political coverage. Bloggers on the left like to point to the role that they played in keeping alive the story of Senate Republican leader Trent Lott's wistful remarks about Strom Thurmond's racist past until mainstream reporters picked them up and brought Lott down.[42] But if the Lott story is an example of bloggers' broadening the news agenda, their success elicits the obvious point that blogs are political in a way that reporters are not supposed to be.

Blogs do not pretend to be anything other than highly partisan, a high-tech throwback to the party press of the early nineteenth century. As they begin to influence the news agenda bloggers mix freely with reporters schooled in the tradition of journalistic objectivity. Yet to the degree that political journalists have departed in recent years from their mid-twentieth-century role as neutral observers and become more like participant observers in the political process, the fact that bloggers maintain a point of view may be a cause more for symbiosis than for conflict. In mid-2004, *Mother Jones* noted,

> The modern American idea of journalism as objectivity, with news and editorial pages strictly separated, emerged in the Progressive Era with books like Walter Lippmann's classic *Public Opinion*. For most of the last century, this idea anointed political journalists as a mandarin class of insiders with serious responsibilities; access was everything. At some point during the Reagan years, this mandarinate lost interest in politics as a contest of beliefs and policies with some bearing on the experience of people unlike themselves. Instead, elite Washington reporters turned their coverage into an account of a closed system, an intricate process, in which perceptions were the only real things and the journalists themselves were intimately involved. The machinations of Michael Deaver and Roger Ailes, followed by Lee Atwater and James Carville, became the central drama. We've grown so familiar with this approach today that you can open *The New York Times* and be unsurprised to find its chief political correspondent, Adam Nagourney, writing about polls and campaign strategies day after day.[43]

Indeed, it is quite possible that blogs will accelerate the personalization of political journalism, while broadening the scope of political news to include topics that matter to people who do not live inside the campaign bubble. There is anecdotal evidence that this is already happening. Andrew Sullivan's detailed attention to the prosecution of the Iraq war moved well beyond the question of how the war might influence the president's political fortunes. Joshua Micah Marshall (talkingpointsmemo.com) regularly blogged about his investigation into forged documents that purported to show that Iraq had purchased uranium for nuclear weapons, a claim President Bush used to bolster the case for war. Both presented their observations in the first-person style emblematic of weblogs. However, where traditional reporters frequently offer firsthand impressions of the political process, Sullivan and Marshall addressed matters of *substance* that were lost in the fog of mainstream election coverage of polls and strategies. Their writing offers a different type of firsthand account of history, based on a different set of criteria for what constitutes a political story. What they do is not far removed from what political journalists have been doing for some time, but it has the virtue of being worthwhile.

What Dean Did Not Do

As the Dean campaign began its roll down the runway in June 2003, its blog hosted a discussion on one of its favorite topics: how the mainstream media don't get what the Dean campaign is all about:

> You hear it everywhere. The pundits discuss Howard Dean. They discuss the 33,100 people signed up for Dean Meetups. They discuss the blog, sometimes, and the netroots momentum behind Howard Dean. And then they say, "It remains to be seen whether this Internet activism will make any difference in the real world, or on election day."
>
> What they miss is that it is making a difference, today, in the real world. Last night, 3,200 people showed up in Austin, Texas to hear Howard Dean speak for 20 minutes. The event was organized on-line in less than ten days by local volunteers.[44]

One month later, Joe Trippi echoed this theme and elaborated,

> I am thinking that many of the people who still do not understand our grassroots campaign are now grasping at straws . . . . Not getting it is to now spin that we are not reaching everyone—well we are reaching a lot more people than anyone else.
>
> Not getting it is to see our campaign as Internet driven—and miss completely that we are message driven. And that the Internet is just one more way to reach people with that message.
>
> Not getting it is to miss the fact that in Austin, Texas volunteers leafleted the Latino community, made phone calls, and had 3200 people turn out to a rally for Governor Dean.
>
> Not getting it is to underestimate what a small but growing group of Americans can accomplish when they work for the common good.
>
> Getting it is continuing to reach out, continuing to build the strongest grassroots campaign in history. And yes that means reaching out to everyone, and using every approach, old or new, to do so.
>
> We are the great grassroots campaign of the modern era. Yes that campaign is built from mouse pads—but also shoe leather—and more importantly it is built on the hope of people willing to sacrifice some of their time, and money to strengthen our democracy and to reach out to all Americans to join in that great cause.[45]

It can be argued that the mainstream press was slow to recognize what Trippi was doing with the Dean campaign. It can be argued that the Dean campaign shaped the discourse of the Democratic primary season, gave Democrats a voice that had been absent from their party, and laid the groundwork for the Democrats' approach to the fall contest. It can even be argued that Dean's Internet efforts empowered ordinary people who never before had been involved in politics. But it cannot be argued that Dean had a winning formula. Not in 2004.

The prima facie case that can be made about the limits of Internet politics is that Howard Dean failed to win the Democratic nomination. Throughout spring and summer 2003, Dean's e-mail membership list grew as if there was no limit to the number of new people who would connect to his on-line campaign. Then, after the campaign's third-quarter fund-raising triumph, when reporters started to take Dean seriously, the growth curve flattened: 226,000 members on July 31, became 342,000 on August 31, and 442,000 one month later, but the growth rate of August was not equaled for another three months. Dean had hit the "digital divide," the boundary between those with the fast Internet access necessary to participate in an on-line community and those without. The multiplier effect that had contributed to Dean's swift emergence and expansion diminished when the campaign reached the fringes of the Internet's potential for exponential growth. Dean was an on-line phenomenon at a time when not enough people were wired.

It would be a mistake, however, to conclude that Dean's failure to become his party's nominee is reason to dismiss the political importance of the Internet. The Dean campaign failed not because the Internet is a flawed medium but because Joe Trippi banked on 2004 being for the Internet what 1960 had been for television: the year that a new medium came of age and changed the paradigm for winning elections. In 1960, not only did John Kennedy's handlers understand how to present their candidate on television to maximum effect, but television had penetrated deep enough into American life for their efforts to make the difference. Internet politics in 2004 more closely resembled television politics in 1952. That year, Dwight Eisenhower was packaged for television by advertising agents who sold him like aspirin or soap.[46] It was a startling shift from the campaigns of the past and one that in hindsight foreshadowed the coming era of television politics. But it was not decisive.

If 2004 was for the Internet what 1952 was for television, then Dean's failings as a candidate are more readily attributable to the difficulty he had communicating through conventional means. A "hot" candidate on the "cool" medium of television, Dean was soon labeled by the mainstream press as "angry" because of the way he presented himself to the mass public (and because his opponents successfully promoted the label). His on-line supporters did not regard him that way, finding him instead commendably passionate about his policies and his campaign. What looks like anger on television can feel like passion on the Internet, where people engage rather than watch. But under the prevailing rules of political campaigning, most voters still see the candidate on television, where a little discipline goes a long way.

Although the Internet remains a supplementary medium, it can give a candidate crucial advantages. The 2004 campaign offers evidence that the

Internet can help to shift the balance of political power in a long contest by organizing volunteers, boosting morale, influencing the spin in mainstream media, and of course raising money. Howard Dean did not ride the Internet to the White House, but it is difficult to envision what his campaign would have been without it. Successful candidates still need television skills and a ground game, but if they run a good traditional campaign, the Internet can give them an important, nontraditional edge.

Perhaps more important is the Internet's value as a vehicle for engagement in the political process. On this score Dean posted a huge victory and perhaps foreshadowed the greatest potential contribution of the new medium. Browsing through the comment threads on Blog for America, it is hard not to notice the hopeful tone and the absence of cynicism in what people wrote. One supporter blogged,

> Gov. Dean, Thank you. Thank you for inspiring all of us to take action and bring politics back to the people. I am utterly speechless as to what to say about what has been accomplished this past week. Can it really be that my fellow Americans, my neighbors, my family and my friends are all waking up and willing to WORK TOGETHER to take this country back? [47]

This is not the sort of reaction one gets from watching television news, which is more likely to generate feelings of detachment than engagement.[48] After decades of being sedated by television, many people have come to regard politics as a spectator sport. To blog about the accomplishments of political action, to feel inspired by a politician, or to actually do something to further a campaign is out of step with how politics is portrayed on television, but it is a perfectly natural reaction on-line. The sentiments that the blogger cited above expressed were repeated countless times on Blog for America. There was a Frank Capra movie going on there.

There is a reason why television portrays campaigns as spectator sport: the horse race sells. According to the Project for Excellence in Journalism, people respond to stylized and entertaining news, which news organizations are happy to provide. Moreover, shallower is cheaper, and given the fragmentation of media that characterizes our time, news organizations faced with shrinking audiences are eager to produce news that is less expensive. But the public's preference for entertaining news masks a deeper conflict: it cheapens the people demanding it. And after asking for fluffy news, the public "feels repulsed and derides the messenger for delivering it." [49]

The public's desire to be amused by television, then, appears to conflict directly with its desire to be engaged, and that desire can be satisfied by Internet politics. As the reach of the Internet increases, this latter desire bodes well for the potential of on-line politics to compete with and reshape a news environment long dominated by television. In 2004, the blogosphere broke through to the mainstream. Going forward, it has the potential to redefine the mainstream.

Certainly there is room for redefinition. In a telling and unscripted moment near the end of the seemingly endless campaign season, an honest exchange took place on CNN that captured—perhaps better than any commentary or blog posting—the state of political coverage during this critically important election. The participants were two CNN hosts—and a comedian. Jon Stewart, the star of Comedy Central's news parody *The Daily Show,* appeared on *Crossfire* with hosts Tucker Carlson and Paul Begala.

The relationship between the talk show hosts and the comedian was complex. Stewart's program, which he openly calls "fake news"—although it is really more a parody of television than of the news itself—is viewed by people who, according to the National Annenberg Election Survey, knew more about the campaign than the people who relied on newspapers or network television news.[50] *Crossfire,* supposedly a hard news program, follows a more-heat-than-light formula, designed to entertain. Stewart was not shy about pointing out the irony, then condemning the consequences:

> STEWART: I made a special effort to come on the show today because I have privately, amongst my friends and also in occasional newspapers and television shows, mentioned this show as being bad. And I wanted to—I felt that wasn't fair and I should come here and tell you that I don't—it's not so much that it's bad, as it's hurting America. So I wanted to come here and say . . . here's just what I wanted to tell you guys: stop. Stop, stop, stop, stop hurting America. And come work for us, because we, as the people . . . .
> CARLSON: How do you pay?
> STEWART: Not well.
> BEGALA: Better than CNN, I'm sure.
> STEWART: But you can sleep at night.[51]

Stewart accused Carlson and Begala of being partisan hacks, of enabling politicians to obscure and diminish political discourse, of doing the bidding of media corporations that relish conflict even if it makes people feel, as the Project for Excellence in Journalism puts it, repulsed by politics. The hosts pushed back. Stewart has politicians on his show, and Carlson challenged him on why he refuses to ask them difficult questions. "You know, it's interesting to hear you talk about my responsibility," Stewart responded. "You're on CNN. The show that leads into me is puppets making crank phone calls."

> CARLSON: Well, I'm just saying, there's no reason for you—when you have this marvelous opportunity to [ask political figures tough questions]. Come on. It's embarrassing.
> STEWART: You know, the interesting thing I have is, you have a responsibility to the public discourse, and you fail miserably.
> CARLSON: You need to get a job at a journalism school, I think.
> STEWART: You need to go to one.[52]

It was great television.

And it happened less than three weeks before an election that many news reporters considered to be the most important of their lifetime. In 2004, mainstream journalists still drove the political agenda. But after a campaign that witnessed the emergence of an interactive medium and the promise of a new form of citizen politics, it was intriguing to wonder whether Carlson and Begala were defending a media system that was on the verge of passing away.

Notes

1. Blog for America, "1 AM People-Powered Howard Update" and "Dean Raises $7.5 Million in Second Quarter," July 1, 2003.
2. Matthew Robert Kerbel, "The Media: Old Frames in a Time of Transition," in *The Elections of 2000,* ed. Michael Nelson (Washington, D.C.: CQ Press, 2001), 130.
3. "The State of the News Media 2004: An Annual Report on American Journalism," Project for Excellence in Journalism, March 15, 2004, 59; www.stateofthenewsmedia.org.
4. Ibid., 4.
5. For instance, the Project for Excellence in Journalism reports that during the fall presidential debates, mainstream news reports emphasized electoral tactics, strategy, and the horse race and were generally negative in tone, especially with respect to President Bush. Such coverage occurred at the expense of reports on the substance and ramifications of the candidates' policy positions ("The Debate Effect: How the Press Covered the Pivotal Period of the 2004 Presidential Campaign," Project for Excellence in Journalism, October 27, 2004; www.journalism.org/resources/research/reports/debateeffect/thedebates.asp). This is not a new phenomenon. Mainstream media have covered elections as a horse race for years, discussing candidate behavior in strategic terms and regarding candidate issue positions as tactical devices designed to win political support. See, for instance, Thomas E. Patterson, *Out of Order* (New York: Knopf, 1993). Portraying elections in this manner is a form of framing the news—that is, offering a context to make sense of disparate facts. Although scholars vary in their definitions of framing, the existence of framing is broadly accepted as a device used by producers, editors, and reporters for making news. For an overview, see Robert M. Entman, "Framing: Toward Clarification of a Fractured Paradigm," *Journal of Communication* 43 (Autumn 1993): 51–58.
6. Matthew Klam, "Fear and Laptops on the Campaign Trail," *New York Times Magazine,* September 26, 2004. Although considered a liberal blog by journalists, Daily Kos describes itself as a reformist blog, dedicated to bringing about change in the Democratic Party.
7. Ibid., 45–46.
8. Joe Trippi, "Call for Action" Blog, March 15, 2003.
9. Such process or self-referential coverage has been a key characteristic of political reporting for several election cycles. See Matthew R. Kerbel, *Edited for Television: CNN, ABC and American Presidential Elections* (Boulder, Colo.: Westview Press, 1998).
10. Blog for America, November 4, 2003, posted by Tracker at 1:32 p.m.
11. Ibid., September 4, 2003, posted by marnie in pdx at 9:44 p.m.
12. Ibid., January 13, 2004, posted by Pat from North Beach at 3:02 a.m.
13. Ibid., January 9, 2004, posted by Barbara VA at 4:06 p.m.
14. Kenneth S. Baer, "Dean Campaign Empowers His Supporters via Internet," *Baltimore Sun,* November 9, 2003.

15. See, for instance, Jeanne Cummings, "Behind Dean's Surge," *Wall Street Journal,* October 14, 2003.
16. Ibid.
17. Dan Gillmore, "Dean Campaign's Net Savvy Shows," *San Jose Mercury News,* August 10, 2003.
18. Edward Cone, "The Marketing of the President 2004," *Baseline,* December 1, 2003.
19. Alan M. Webber, "Super Web Site Helps Dean Surge Ahead," *USA Today,* December 7, 2003.
20. Gary Wolf, "How the Internet Invented Howard Dean," *Wired Magazine,* January 2004.
21. Ibid.
22. Cummings, "Behind Dean's Surge."
23. Kathy Kiely, "Freewheeling 'Bloggers' Are Rewriting Rules of Journalism," *USA Today,* December 20, 2003.
24. Ellen McCarthy, "Beltway Bloggers," *Washington Post,* February 7, 2004.
25. Lev Grossman and Anita Hamilton, "Meet Joe Blog," *Time,* June 21, 2004.
26. Christopher Conkey, "The Democratic Convention: Bloggers Enter Big-Media Tent," *Wall Street Journal,* July 27, 2004.
27. Ibid.
28. Ibid.
29. Danna Harmon, "A Blogger, Untamed, Rattles Cages in D.C.," *Christian Science Monitor,* April 2, 2004.
30. Hardblogger, October 14, 2004, posted by Chris Matthews at 2:39 a.m.
31. Rachel Smolkin, "The Expanding Blogosphere," *American Journalism Review,* June/July 2004.
32. Ibid.
33. McCarthy, "Beltway Bloggers."
34. Amy Harmon, "Politics of the Web: Meet, Greet, Segregate, Meet Again," *New York Times,* January 25, 2004.
35. Joanna Weiss, " 'Blogs' Shake the Political Discourse," *Boston Globe,* July 23, 2003.
36. Kerbel, *Edited For Television.*
37. Anastasia Ustinova, "Political Blogs Catching On," *Chicago Tribune,* July 18, 2004.
38. Ibid.
39. Amy Harmon, "Survey Finds 'Opinion Leaders' Logging On for Political Content," *New York Times,* February 5, 2004.
40. Lee Gomes, "Portals: Blogs Have Become Part of Media Machine That Shapes Politics," *Wall Street Journal,* February 23, 2004.
41. Matthew Creamer, "Media Brands," *PR Week,* August 2, 2004.
42. See Julie Kosterlitz, "The Internet Shows Its Muscles," *National Journal,* October 4, 2003.
43. George Packer, "The Revolution Will Not Be Blogged," *Mother Jones,* May/June 2004.
44. Mathew Gross, "Blog for America," June 10, 2003.
45. Joe Trippi, "Blog for America," July 6, 2003.
46. Edwin Diamond and Stephen Bates, *The Spot: The Rise of Political Advertising on Television* (Cambridge, Mass.: MIT Press, 1988).
47. Blog for America, June 30, 2003, posted by Shane Southard, SF at 9:23 p.m.
48. Roderick Hart, *Seducing America: How Television Charms the Modern Voter* (Thousand Oaks, Calif.: Sage Publications, 1999).
49. "The State of the News Media 2004," 13.

50. *The Daily Show* has a particularly avid following among young people, and the study found, "Young people who watched *The Daily Show* scored 48 percent correct on the campaign knowledge test while young people who did not watch any late-night comedy scored 39 percent correct. Meanwhile, young people who watched four or more days of network news scored 40 percent correct, equally frequent cable news viewers 48 percent correct and newspaper readers 46 percent correct." See "Daily Show Viewers Knowledgeable about Presidential Campaign," National Annenberg Election Survey, September 21, 2004.
51. *Crossfire,* CNN Transcripts, October 15, 2004.
52. Ibid.

6

Campaign Finance: Funding the Presidential and Congressional Elections

Marian Currinder

The 2004 elections present a remarkable irony. They cost a record-breaking $4 billion and were the first to take place under the new campaign finance law known as the Bipartisan Campaign Reform Act of 2002 (BCRA). That law's primary goals were to ban unlimited soft money contributions to the national political parties and to regulate preelection issue advertising by independent groups. Even though both provisions were intended to curtail campaign spending, candidates for federal office spent $1 billion more in 2004 than in 2000. President George Bush and Sen. John Kerry raised a combined total of $700 million—more than double the amount that was raised by the two major-party candidates just four years earlier. The close partisan division in both the Senate and House led to record spending on congressional elections, as well. House and Senate candidates raised $872.5 million, 20 percent more than candidates raised in 2002.

Although it is axiomatic that each election costs more than the last, the 2004 elections were exceptional in that new spending records were set *despite* the ban on soft money. This unexpected outcome has raised numerous questions about the BCRA's ability to change the way campaigns are financed. By increasing the contribution limits for individuals and ignoring spending by independent "527" groups, the new law fueled tremendous growth in campaign receipts and expenditures. Predictions that the ban on soft money would diminish the fund-raising role of the parties also turned out to be largely overstated. The parties brought more small contributors into the process and managed to raise more money in 2004 than they raised four years earlier. And although 527 groups—named after the section of the federal tax code that defines them—did not take the place of the parties, they did play a central role in the 2004 elections. Groups such as the Swift Boat Veterans for Truth, MoveOn.org, Americans Coming Together, Progress for America, and the Media Fund raised and spent millions of dollars on campaign advertising and voter mobilization efforts.

The story of money in the 2004 elections is best understood by examining the history of campaign finance. Events leading up to the passage of BCRA shed light on how the law's central objectives were established and why it finally won majority support in Congress. History also helps to explain the challenges and criticisms that the BCRA has faced since the elections. In this chapter I examine money in the 2004 elections, in the context of campaign finance reform, and consider patterns of both continuity and change in the financing of federal elections.

The Evolution of Campaign Finance

The current campaign finance system has its roots in post–Civil War America, when laborers and farmers organized to challenge the extraordinary command that wealthy interests held over the federal government. The wealthy met the challenge by banding together, so that they would not undercut one another by financing rival candidates. The first campaign embodying this strategy was in 1896, when Republican presidential candidate William McKinley beat Democrat William Jennings Bryan. McKinley's campaign manager, Mark Hanna, devised a fund-raising strategy that assessed corporations a percentage of what he determined was their "stake in the general prosperity." The yield for McKinley was $6 million—almost ten times the $650,000 in campaign contributions that Bryan raised and spent.[1]

Later excesses led to sporadic reform efforts, beginning in 1907 with Congress's passage of the Tillman Act, which banned corporations and banks from making direct contributions to federal candidates. Further limits on contributions, along with requirements for the disclosure of receipts and expenditures by federal candidates and party organizations, came with passage of the Corrupt Practices Act of 1925. But because these laws were easily circumvented and poorly enforced, they had only a limited effect on controversial campaign activities. In 1926, political scientist James K. Pollock wrote that the campaign disclosure statements that the Justice Department required the political parties to file were "sad commentaries on public accounting. . . . No two statements are alike; there is no uniform system, and hence one must spend weary hours learning the methods of accounting used by each committee. . . . The accounts are worse for some years than for others, but in no year do they measure up to even low standards; and therefore to a very considerable extent they defeat the very purpose of the law."[2]

The extent to which the Justice Department's unofficial policy of nonenforcement prevailed became acutely evident shortly after President Nixon took office in 1969, when Clerk of the House W. Pat Jennings forwarded to Attorney General John Mitchell a list of twenty Nixon fund-raising committees that had failed to file a single report for the 1968 election. The list also included the names of 107 congressional candidates who had violated disclosure requirements. In spring 1970, a Justice Department spokesman announced that none of the violators would be prosecuted; in view of the history of the Corrupt Practices Act, he explained, "fair play demands that before prosecutions are undertaken, the Department of Justice has an obligation to notify all candidates and committees that henceforth violators will be proceeded against." [3] History, in other words, offered those who broke the law no reason to expect that they actually would be held accountable.

Public concern about the lack of either strict reporting requirements or meaningful enforcement of contribution limits fueled passage of the 1971 Federal Election Campaign Act (FECA). FECA established new contribution and expenditure limits and new disclosure requirements for federal candidates. The Revenue Act, also passed in 1971, established a public funding system for presidential general elections. Presidential candidates who accept public funding, as George Bush and John Kerry did in 2004, must abide by fund-raising limits required by the law. These initial attempts at reforming the campaign finance system would, however, prove only mildly effective.

During the 1972 presidential campaign, Washington was rife with rumors that President Nixon had used the period prior to April 7, 1972—the date FECA went into effect—to collect large campaign contributions by promising anonymity to the donors. Common Cause, a "good government" nonprofit group, sued Nixon's reelection committee for access to the list of donors. When it became clear that the case would go to trial prior to election day, the committee turned over the names of more than 1,500 people who together had contributed more than $5 million to the Nixon campaign. By mid-1973, nearly $20 million in individual and corporate contributions that had been donated in the fifteen months prior to the FECA's taking effect were revealed. News media coverage of the case was intense, and as a consequence members of Congress saw a sharp increase in constituent mail urging more stringent campaign finance reform.[4] Thus, just two years after passing FECA, Congress began working on amendments to toughen up the new law.

Although legislators generally agreed on the need to further restrict how campaign money could be raised and spent and on the need to create an independent agency to oversee campaign finance law, serious disagreement arose over providing public funding for presidential nominating campaigns. The 1971 law provided public funding only for presidential general campaigns. President Nixon's threat to veto any bill containing a public finance provision never materialized because he was forced out of office before Congress could send him the bill. President Ford also opposed the new public financing provisions, but public sentiment was such that rejecting the bill would have been politically disastrous. The 1974 FECA amendments, which replaced most of the 1971 law, restored ceilings on contributions and expenditures in congressional campaigns, created the Federal Elections Commission (FEC), and provided for public funding of presidential nominating campaigns. To receive public funds, a primary candidate must first raise $100,000 in contributions from individuals.[5] Each individual contribution to candidates who qualify is then matched, dollar-for-dollar, up to $250. Like general election candidates, primary candidates who accept public funding must abide by spending limits.

Under the new 1974 act, individuals were permitted to give $1,000 per candidate, per election. Thus, the maximum amount an individual donor could contribute to any candidate was $3,000 (if the candidate ran in a primary, runoff, and general election). The act also placed an annual limit of $25,000 on an individual's total contributions to federal candidates, political action committees (PACs), and national party committees. Although the act banned corporations, labor unions, and other organized groups from contributing directly to candidates, it did allow these organizations to establish "multi-candidate committees." These committees—more commonly known as political action committees, or PACs—had to have a donor list of at least fifty contributors and give to at least five candidates for federal office. In its 1975 SUN PAC decision, the FEC determined that the Sun Oil company could use its own money to raise funds for use in federal elections, as long as those funds were kept in a segregated account. The commission also ruled that contributions from employees and shareholders had to be voluntary. By clarifying the law, the SUN PAC decision paved the way for corporations, associations, and other organized groups to establish PACs for the purpose of participating in the federal elections process. The number of registered PACs exploded from just over 600 in 1974 to more than 4,000 in 1984.[6] In 2001, the FEC counted approximately 4,500 registered and active PACs.[7]

About two months after the 1974 FECA was enacted, its constitutionality was challenged in court. In *Buckley v. Valeo,* the Supreme Court considered the new regulatory apparatus and, invoking the First Amendment, invalidated the law's restrictions on candidates' financing their own campaigns with personal funds, on independent expenditures, and on overall campaign expenditures. FECA's contribution limits were upheld, however, because the Court viewed them as appropriate means for preventing improper influence. In 1976, Congress responded to the Court's ruling by amending those portions of the law that had been deemed unconstitutional.

FECA was amended again in 1979 to allow state and local parties to participate more actively in federal campaigns by using soft money for grassroots activities. Soft money, also referred to as "nonfederal money," was not subject to FECA rules on the size and source of contributions because it is raised and spent to support party-building activities. Funds raised and spent in accordance with FECA regulations are known as "hard money." Although the soft money loophole did not draw much attention in 1979, it later became the most controversial provision in the campaign finance law.

The Rise of Soft Money and Issue Advocacy Spending

The amount of money spent on federal elections increased dramatically throughout the 1980s and 1990s. In 1976, spending on House and Senate campaigns totaled $115.5 million; by 2000, the amount had risen above $1 billion. Over that time, the cost of living increased threefold, but the cost of running a federal campaign increased approximately eightfold.[8] The marked rise in campaign spending has not, however, corresponded with more electoral competition. Since 1976, 93 percent of House incumbents and

80 percent of Senate incumbents have won reelection—more than before the 1974 FECA was passed.

The 1996 elections marked another sharp turning point in the debate over campaign financing. For the first time, the focus turned from whether and how to further restrict already regulated spending and funding sources, to the growing influence of soft money in federal elections.[9] During the 1992 election, the parties raised a combined total of $86 million in soft money. Four years later, that figure more than tripled to $262 million. Soft money provided the parties with a way to pay for so-called issue advertising—expenditures that they claimed were not subject to the FECA rules because the ads did not contain language that specifically urged viewers to vote for or against a candidate. Court decisions had allowed such ads to be financed with soft money, as long as they did not contain phrases such as "vote for" or "vote against." [10] As a result of the 1996 elections, issue advertising was increasingly perceived as an effective means to promote a party's agenda and candidates; the parties responded by raising even more soft money to pay for issue ads.

The contemporaneous surges in soft money fund raising and issue ad spending prompted federal regulators to reconsider their ability to control campaign spending. Under the system that was beginning to take shape, candidates could rely on their party's soft money expenditures to supplement their campaigns, and the parties could rely on their candidates to help them raise soft money. Because the FECA provisions regarding this kind of fund raising and spending were unclear, the parties could claim that they were acting within the law's guidelines. Despite several recommendations to penalize the Clinton and Dole campaigns for exceeding spending limits in 1996, the FEC did not act. Congress and the Department of Justice also investigated campaign spending in the 1996 elections, but neither took any action. By failing to issue new guidelines, the FEC let confusion reign.[11] Four years later, during the 2000 election, the parties raised a combined total of $495 million in soft money. Approximately $300 million of this came from 800 donors, each of whom contributed a minimum of $120,000. Soft money represented 42 percent of total party receipts in 2000, up from just 5 percent in 1984.[12]

As the emphasis on soft money increased, so did uncertainty among candidates, who could not predict how much unregulated money might flow into their opponents' campaigns. The stakes were made even higher when independent groups began taking their cues from the parties and climbed aboard the soft money bandwagon. Regulatory guidelines did nothing to prevent such groups from spending soft money on issue ads; before long, they were registering under Section 527 of the Internal Revenue Code, which allows a political organization to engage in federal election activities without being subject to FECA rules and disclosure requirements, as long as the organization does not expressly advocate the election or defeat of a candidate.[13] Furthermore, 527s are not required to pay federal taxes and can accept contributions of more than $10,000 without being subject to the federal gift tax. Section 527 also exempts these organizations from having to disclose the names of their contributors. In July 2000, Congress passed legislation that placed minimal reporting requirements on 527s, but it did nothing to restrict their fund raising or spending.[14] Four years later, in the 2004 elections, 527s proved to be powerful players in the campaign finance game.

In addition to 527 organizations, several kinds of nonprofit, tax-exempt groups organized under section 501(c) of the Internal Revenue Code can also participate in various political activities. Groups existing for religious, charitable, scientific, or educational purposes, called 501(c)(3) organizations, may engage in voter registration activities. "Social welfare" groups are organized under section 501(c)(4) and may engage in a range of political activities, as long as those activities are not their primary focus. Section 501(c)(5) labor and agricultural groups and section 501(c)(6) business leagues, chambers of commerce, real estate boards, and boards of trade also can engage in, but not focus primarily on, political activities.[15] Various 501(c) groups participated in the 2004 elections, but they were not nearly as active as the 527 groups.

The Bipartisan Campaign Reform Act of 2002

Although reform advocates had long expressed concern over the soft money loophole in federal campaign finance law, it was the extensive use of soft money in the 1996 elections that attracted the attention of regulators and lawmakers. In the 105th Congress, the first Congress after the 1996 elections, a reform bill sponsored by Reps. Christopher Shays, R-Conn., and Martin Meehan, D-Mass., passed the House. The bill's primary goals were to prohibit the use of soft money in federal elections and to regulate issue advertising more closely. The bill's Senate companion, sponsored by Sens. John McCain, R-Ariz., and Russ Feingold, D-Wis., was debated but not brought to a vote. Again in the 106th Congress, Shays-Meehan passed the House and McCain-Feingold stalled in the Senate.

After the 2000 elections, in which campaign spending in federal elections reached an all-time high, the Senate was ready to follow the House's lead.[16] In the 107th Congress, the Senate passed McCain-Feingold and the House passed Shays-Meehan. The Senate then voted to accept the House version (there were minor differences between the two bills), and President Bush signed it into law on March 27, 2002. BCRA became effective on November 6, 2002—right after the 2002 elections and just in time for the 2004 elections.

BCRA's central goals are to ban the national parties and congressional campaign committees from raising and spending soft money and to prevent other organized groups from running issue ads that mention candidates by name just prior to an election. The new law also doubles the hard money contribution limits for individuals, from $1,000 per candidate, per election, to $2,000 per candidate, per election. The law placed new limits on individual contributions to national, state, and local party committees. Individuals can give an annual maximum of $25,000 per national party committee. Individual contributions to national party committees, however, may not total more than $57,500 to all national party committees and PACs in any two-year election cycle. The total amount an individual can give also was adjusted. One result of the new limits was a marked increase in the number and overall amount of individual contributions in the 2004 elections over all previous elections. Table 6-1 lists the old and new contribution limits.

The new law still permits federal politicians to give campaign contributions to each other and to other candidates. Federal officeholders can give a candidate up to $1,000 per election out of their personal campaign accounts and up to $5,000 per election out of their leadership PACs. Most leadership

Table 6-1 New and Old Campaign Contribution Limits

	To any candidate committee (per election)[1]	To any national party committee (per year)	To any PAC, state/local party, or other political committee (per year)	Aggregate total
Individual can give[2]	Old law: $1,000 New law: $2,000, subject to aggregate limit[3]	Old law: $20,000 New law: $25,000 per party committee, subject to aggregate limit	Old law: $5,000 New law: $10,000 to each state or local party committee (Levin funds)[4] $5,000 to each PAC or other political committee, subject to aggregate limit	Old law: $25,000 per year New law: $95,000 per two-year election cycle as follows: $37,500 per cycle to candidates and $57,500 per cycle to all national party committees and PACs (of which no more than $37,500 per cycle can go to PACs)
Multicandidate committee can give[5]	Old law: $5,000 New law: same	Old law: $15,000 New law: same	Old law: $5,000 New law: same	Old law: no limit New law: same
Other political committee can give	Old law: $1,000 New law: same	Old law: $20,000 New law: same	Old law: $5,000 New law: same	Old law: no limit New law: same

Source: The Center for Responsive Politics.

[1]Primary and general elections count as separate elections.

[2]Individual contribution limits under the new law will be indexed for inflation.

[3]Individual contribution limits under the new law are higher to candidates facing wealthy opponents financing their own election campaign.

[4]Levin funds also can come from corporations and labor unions if allowed by state law.

[5]Multicandidate committees are those with more than 50 contributors that have been registered for at least six months and (with the exception of state party committees) have made contributions to five or more federal candidates.

PACs are connected to members of Congress and are typically used to support both personal and party goals. Like other kinds of PACs, leadership PACs receive donations from individuals and groups, and they make contributions to political candidates, party committees, and other PACs.

BCRA prohibits members of Congress, federal officials, and federal candidates from raising soft money for their parties. Officeholders and candidates can, however, raise up to $20,000 for 527 and 501(c) groups, as long as the money is used specifically for voter registration or get-out-the-vote efforts. BCRA also requires that state, local, and district party committees fund federal election activities only with hard money. An exception—known as the "Levin Amendment"—was made to allow state and local parties to fund voter registration and voter turnout efforts with soft money (contributions are limited to $10,000 per party organization), as long as state law permits. Federal officeholders and national parties, however, cannot raise Levin Amendment funds, and all receipts and disbursements of these funds must be disclosed.

Under the new law, "electioneering communication" is defined to include broadcast, cable, or satellite advertisements that clearly refer to a candidate within sixty days of a general election or thirty days of a primary. The national parties may spend only hard money on electioneering communications; state and local parties must spend hard money for any communications that attack or promote a federal candidate. Federal and state candidates are permitted to raise and spend hard money for advertising that attacks or promotes a federal candidate.[17]

BCRA prohibits corporations and unions from making targeted electioneering communications, except through a PAC.[18] Because PACs raise and spend money in accordance with federal regulations, their expenditures are considered hard money. Individuals and unincorporated groups may also make electioneering communications, but they must disclose who is funding the ad, as well as the names of large donors.

BCRA also contains new provisions regarding party expenditures on behalf of federal candidates. National, congressional, and state party committees may contribute a maximum of $5,000 apiece to a House candidate, per election. The national and senatorial party committees may give a combined total of $17,500 to a Senate candidate, per election. State parties may contribute a maximum of $5,000 per election to a Senate candidate. In addition, BCRA establishes new guidelines regulating coordinated and independent expenditures. "Coordinated expenditures" are funds a party spends for services such as polling or buying news media time or space on behalf of a candidate who has requested it. For Senate races, party committees may spend two cents for every person of voting age in the state; for House races, they may spend no more than $33,780 per candidate, per race.[19] Coordinated funds may only be used in general elections. The national parties also are allowed to make coordinated expenditures of up to $16.2 million on behalf of their presidential candidates. As originally enacted, BCRA did not allow the parties to make unlimited independent expenditures on behalf of candidates. "Independent expenditures" are funds spent on behalf of a candidate but not coordinated with the candidate's campaign. The Supreme Court endorsed the parties' right to do so, however, by overturning that provision in December 2003.

BCRA Goes to Court

Shortly after BCRA became law, Sen. Mitch McConnell, R-Ky., and several groups filed suit challenging the law's constitutionality on First Amendment grounds (*McConnell v. FEC*). On May 2, 2003, the U.S. District Court for the District of Columbia struck down the law's prohibition on soft money but retained the ban for electioneering communications that clearly identify a federal candidate. The court also approved the BCRA provisions that prohibit federal officials and candidates from raising soft money. The district court issued a stay of its ruling on May 19, 2003, which kept BCRA in effect as enacted pending review by the Supreme Court.[20]

On September 8, 2003, the Supreme Court heard oral arguments in *McConnell v. FEC*. The Court faced a complex task: The lower court's decision was 1,600 pages long and involved approximately eighty plaintiffs, as well as numerous lawyers. On December 10, 2003, in its most far-reaching campaign finance ruling since *Buckley v. Valeo* in 1976, the Supreme Court upheld the constitutionality of BCRA's key provisions. In a 5–4 decision, the Court validated the law's restrictions on the raising and spending of soft money and on electioneering communications. The only provisions the Court invalidated were BCRA's requirement that parties choose between making "independent expenditures" or "coordinated expenditures" on behalf of candidates and its prohibition on persons aged seventeen and under making campaign contributions.[21]

Because the Supreme Court's decision to uphold the key provisions of BCRA was unexpected, campaign finance experts are still sorting out the implications. One remarkable aspect of the Court's ruling is the extent to which the majority deferred to Congress and adopted a pragmatic approach in reaching its decision. The Court remarked on the appropriateness of showing "proper deference" to Congress's judgment "in an area in which it enjoys particular expertise." The Court also remarked that "Congress is fully entitled to consider the real-world" as it determines how to best regulate in the political realm.[22]

The 2004 Presidential Primaries

The presidential race of 2000 was by far the most expensive one in history. The eighteen candidates who sought the Republican or Democratic nomination raised a total of $343 million during the primaries alone—$100 million more than seventeen candidates raised in the 1996 nominating contests.

George Bush alone raised $96 million, or 28 percent of the total.[23] From the time he entered the presidential race in March 1999 until he was nominated in July 2000, Bush spent money at a rate of $6.1 million a month, shattering previous records in both fund raising and spending.[24] When the 2000 presidential race finally ended, Bush had raised approximately $193 million, and Albert Gore, the Democratic nominee, had raised approximately $133 million.

During his first term in office, Bush had to contend with the September 11, 2001, terrorist attacks and their aftermath: wars waged in Afghanistan and Iraq, expanding budget deficits, and a faltering economy. Apprehension over job losses added to public uncertainty. It was clear that issues of war and economics would define the 2004 presidential primaries, and ten Democrats rose to the challenge. Bush ran unopposed for the Republican nomination.[25]

The 2004 nominating contests shattered previous fund-raising records (see Table 6-2). A total of $662 million was raised by the candidates—$259 million of it by an incumbent president with no challenger. The Democratic

Table 6-2 2004 Presidential Primary Receipts and Expenditures Through August 31, 2004

Candidate	Total adjusted receipts	Individual contributions	Political committee contributions	Federal matching funds	Other receipts[1]	Total expenditures[2]
Republicans						
Bush	258,939,099	254,817,068	2,633,400	0	1,488,631	219,342,110
Democrats						
Clark	25,073,530	17,321,849	45,950	7,615,360	90,371	24,650,135
Dean	51,126,828	51,083,674	15,300	0	27,854	49,964,901
Edwards	29,206,170	21,636,492	2,000	6,604,769	962,908	29,071,211
Gephardt	21,203,139	14,263,715	406,462	4,104,320	2,428,641	20,640,327
Kerry	233,985,144	214,898,596	146,269	0	18,940,279	175,865,579
Kucinich	10,669,287	7,803,394	16,000	2,847,080	2,813	10,493,632
LaRouche	9,606,640	8,193,775	2,798	1,408,993	1,074	9,601,073
Lieberman	18,536,930	14,052,813	214,320	4,267,797	2,000	18,319,261
Moseley Braun	582,547	526,426	41,273	0	14,848	582,425
Sharpton	589,866	512,736	4,200	0	72,931	686,888
Other						
Nader	2,373,338	1,445,069	0	547,097	381,172	2,669,513
Subtotals						
Republicans	258,939,099	254,817,068	2,633,400	0	1,488,631	219,342,110
Democrats	400,580,081	350,293,470	894,572	26,848,319	22,543,720	339,875,432
Other	2,373,338	1,445,069	0	547,097	381,172	2,669,513
Grand total	661,892,518	606,555,607	3,527,972	27,395,416	24,413,523	561,887,056

Source: Federal Election Commission.

Note: Receipts and expenditures are in dollars.

[1]Includes contributions and loans from candidates minus repayments, other loans minus repayments, and transfers from previous campaigns.

[2]Includes operating expenditures, fund-raising disbursements, and legal and accounting disbursements.

candidates raised a total of $400.5 million, and independent candidate Ralph Nader raised approximately $2.4 million.[26] In November 2003, Howard Dean became the first Democratic candidate in history to decline public matching funds in order to avoid the accompanying $45 million spending limit required by the 1974 FECA. Democratic candidate John Kerry followed Dean's lead and also declined matching funds. As in 2000, Bush did too.

In addition to raising money, some of the Democratic candidates strategically donated money early in the campaign. Believing that their chances of winning the nomination hinged on doing well in Iowa and New Hampshire, John Edwards, Richard Gephardt, and John Kerry began seeking support early in those states. Edwards contributed nearly half a million dollars in soft money to party committees in Iowa and New Hampshire in 2002 and nearly $69,000 to party committees in South Carolina. Gephardt contributed more than $360,000 in soft money to Iowa and New Hampshire in 2002, most of it to local candidates. (He also donated $132,000 to candidates in South Carolina.) Kerry contributed more than $137,000 in soft money to party committees in Iowa and New Hampshire in 2002.[27]

By the end of March 2003, the Democratic candidates had raised approximately $34.5 million for their races. Kerry led with $10 million, Edwards was second with $7.4 million, and Gephardt was third with just under $6 million. Within a few months, however, the fund-raising picture shifted dramatically. Dean surged ahead, raising more than $25 million by September 30, 2003. Kerry was next with approximately $20 million, Edwards was third with $14.5 million, and Gephardt was a close fourth with $13.5 million. By the end of 2003, Dean was the Democratic fund-raising front-runner by far, having raised approximately $41 million. Kerry trailed with $25 million, and Edwards and Gephardt each finished the year with about $16 million. Candidates Wesley Clark and Joe Lieberman were not far behind, with just under $14 million each. These numbers, although substantial, pale in comparison to the $132 million that Bush had raised by the end of 2003.[28]

Dean's quick transition to the best-financed Democratic candidate was due in large part to his success at using the Internet to raise money. Although Internet fund raising was not entirely new in the 2004 election, the Dean campaign recast the way candidates and consultants thought about fund raising. Using the Internet as its primary tool, the campaign built a base of over 300,000 donors and raised more than $40 million. The national news media were fascinated by this campaign innovation, and their focus worked to Dean's advantage, at least in the short term. When Dean fared poorly in the early primaries, however, questions were raised about whether on-line political organizing, for all of its financial benefits, was enough to sustain a campaign. The Internet provided Dean with an army of willing volunteers, but most of them were politically inexperienced and did not know how to organize at the grassroots or to plan campaign events.[29]

Despite its organizational problems, the Dean campaign's remarkable success in Internet fund raising left a mark on the political fund-raising community. Clark's supporters solicited almost $2 million in on-line pledges in the effort to convince him to join the presidential race. Kerry, Edwards, and other Democratic hopefuls significantly expanded their Internet efforts after witnessing Dean's success. Kerry was particularly successful in using on-line organizing to bring together networks of experienced state and local government officials in both Iowa and New Hampshire.[30]

By the end of 2003, the media had awarded Dean front-runner status, primarily because of the huge fund-raising lead he had opened over the other Democratic candidates. Dean's good fortune, however, was short-lived. The campaign lost momentum after his poor showing in Iowa, where he finished a distant third behind Kerry and Edwards. The Iowa effort had cost the campaign millions of dollars. When Dean lost to Kerry in New Hampshire, the campaign faced even greater fund-raising challenges. Unable to reenergize his campaign and fund-raising operation, Dean pulled out of the race in mid-February. He had spent about $50 million campaigning for his party's nomination—a record for a Democratic primary candidate.

Meanwhile, Kerry's campaign continued to gather support. Heading into the March 2 Super Tuesday primaries, Kerry and Edwards were the only two major candidates still competing for the Democratic nomination.[31] In the month after the January 19 Iowa caucuses, Kerry had raised about $6 million and Edwards about $3.5 million. While Kerry relied largely on the Internet, Edwards focused on raising money at events in places such as Los Angeles and New York, where he attracted generous support. Edwards also counted on federal matching funds, lower overhead costs, free media exposure, and Dean's departure to keep him competitive.[32] By the end of February 2004, Kerry had raised a total of $40.5 million, and Edwards had raised $27.5 million. Meanwhile, Bush had raised an imposing $158 million.[33]

The General Election

Kerry's solid performance on Super Tuesday forced Edwards to end his candidacy. Kerry won nine of the ten primaries, losing only Vermont to Dean, its former governor. Bush started March with $110 million in the bank, and Kerry had about $2 million on hand. Because both candidates had refused public financing during the primaries, both were permitted to raise and spend without limit until they were officially nominated at their party conventions. On March 4, one day after Kerry became the presumptive Democratic nominee, Bush began spending millions on television ads to boost his approval ratings and paint Kerry as a liberal. The ads aired in seventeen likely battleground states and cost the Bush campaign $17.5 million in March alone. The biggest Bush ad buy was in Florida, followed by Pennsylvania, Michigan, and Ohio. Although each party is permitted to spend approximately $16 million in coordinated expenditures on behalf of its nominee, the law prevented the Democrats from coming anywhere near what the Bush campaign was spending. Kerry's campaign, however, received a boost when several 527 organizations countered the Bush advertising blitz by running millions of dollars worth of anti-Bush ads in battleground states. MoveOn.org and the Media Fund, both pro-Democratic groups, spent $4.5 million and $50 million, respectively, in twenty-one states.[34]

Kerry began a twenty-city fund-raising tour just after Super Tuesday, with a goal of raising at least $20 million by early May. Kerry also continued to pursue contributions over the Internet, where he averaged almost $1 million a day in the weeks following Super Tuesday. Democrats believed that Kerry was well positioned to capitalize on his primary victories, but they also were resigned to being outspent by the Bush campaign in the months leading up to the party conventions. In the short term, Kerry would have to rely on ads sponsored by the Democratic Party and by independent groups—a somewhat risky prospect because of laws preventing these groups from coordinating their messages with the Kerry campaign. The Democratic National Committee (DNC) also launched an effort to raise money jointly with Kerry. Individual donors were encouraged to contribute $25,000, the maximum amount one may donate to a national party committee under BCRA.[35]

The campaign finance reports that Bush and Kerry filed in March 2004 revealed that both were setting new fund-raising records. Kerry raised roughly $60 million in the first quarter of 2004, about $7 million more than Bush raised during the same period. Kerry broke the previous quarterly record of $50 million, which Bush had set in summer 2003. In March alone, Kerry raised a remarkable $44 million from on-line donors and from Democrats who had waited until after the primaries to give or who had previously given to his primary rivals. Kerry spent about $15 million in March and continued to benefit from at least $28 million in ads by independent groups, including MoveOn.org and the AFL-CIO.[36] At the beginning of April, Kerry had about $32 million in the bank. Bush raised $26.2 million in March and began April with $86.6 million on hand.[37] As the summer conventions approached, neither Bush nor Kerry showed any sign of slowing down fund-raising efforts.

By the end of June, Kerry reported total campaign receipts of $182 million, and Bush reported total receipts of $226.5 million. Because the nominating campaign officially ends when a candidate accepts his party's nomination, Kerry was at a fund-raising disadvantage. Both candidates had agreed to participate in the public funding program (established by the 1971 FECA) during the general election, which meant abiding by the fund-raising limits the law required. The Democratic convention, where Kerry was set to accept his party's nomination, was scheduled for the end of July. The Republican convention would be five weeks later, in early September. This meant that Bush had an additional five weeks to raise money before entering the public funding phase of the campaign. Kerry flirted with the idea of delaying his acceptance of the nomination so that he could keep raising money, but tradition won out and he accepted at the convention in July. By the end of August, when the general campaign officially got under way, Kerry's receipts for the entire nominating process totaled $234 million, and Bush's totaled $259 million.[38]

Bush and Kerry each received $75 million in public funding for the general election when they accepted their parties' nominations.

Individual Donors. About 75 percent of Bush's total contributions came from individual donors, compared with about 67 percent of Kerry's. In the 2000 race, individual contributions made up about 55 percent of Bush's total contributions and about 25 percent of Gore's. Because the new campaign finance law doubled the contribution limits for individual donors from $1,000 to $2,000, the jump in individual contributions is not surprising.

As in 2000, Bush relied heavily in 2004 on his network of Pioneers and Rangers—individuals who raised at least $100,000 and $200,000, respectively. In 2004, Bush doubled his network of six-figure fund-raisers to about 550. Since 1999, 350 of these individuals have contributed close to $40 million to federal candidates, leadership PACs, and party committees, and Bush was by far their biggest beneficiary. In 2003, he received more than $1 million from the Pioneers and Rangers themselves, and during the first nine months of the 2004 election cycle they gave more than $5 million, 36 percent of which went to the Republican National Committee (RNC). David Brennan, the CEO of the Brennan Industrial Group, and his wife topped Bush's 2004 fund-raising list, giving a combined total of $132,000. About one-quarter of Bush's fund-raisers have given more than $100,000 each since 1999, and six have given more than $1 million. American Financial Group CEO Carl H. Lindner Jr. was the most generous of all, giving more than $2.6 million from 1999 to 2004. Bush was predictably popular among contributors from his home state. Texans contributed over $21 million to Bush's 2004 campaign—about $4.5 million more than they gave him in 2000.

Raising money for the president can be a rewarding endeavor. After the 2000 elections, one-third of Bush's leading fund-raisers were appointed to high-level government positions. During his first term in office, Bush named at least fifty-seven contributors or their spouses to agency positions, advisory committees, or U.S. delegations. Three of Bush's top fund-raisers in 2000 became cabinet secretaries: Don Evans at Commerce, Elaine Chao at Labor, and Tom Ridge at Homeland Security. Because Bush has fewer jobs to fill during his second term, and because the number of Pioneers and Rangers doubled from his election to his reelection, competition among his 2004 fund-raisers for plum administration jobs will likely be tougher than in 2000.[39]

Kerry also relied heavily on a base of wealthy donors. Starting in 1999, thirty-two individuals and couples raised more than $100,000 apiece for Kerry, for a total of about $4 million. An additional eighty-seven individuals raised between $50,000 and $100,000 each for Kerry. In the first nine months of 2003, Kerry's top fund-raisers and their families gave more than $750,000, with about 21 percent going to the Democratic National Committee. Investment banker Orin Kramer topped Kerry's 2004 list, giving $106,000 to Democratic candidates, leadership PACs, and party committees.

Kerry's campaign also received a financial boost when he chose Edwards as his running mate. Edwards, a former trial lawyer, had raised far more money for his own campaigns from lawyers and law firms than from any other sector. Beginning in 1998, when he was elected to the Senate, Edwards collected about $11.6 million from the legal profession. Sixteen of Edwards's top twenty contributors were law firms. The Los Angeles firm of Girardi and Keese, whose associates gave Edwards close to $158,000, was at the top of the list. Another big Edwards supporter, Fred Baron, of Baron and Budd, a Dallas law firm, began raising money for Kerry when Edwards dropped out of the race.

PAC Contributions. Neither the Bush nor the Kerry campaign received more than 1 percent of its contributions from PACs, but both benefited from PAC spending, particularly in the final weeks of the general election campaign. PACs spent more than $25 million between Labor Day and election day. Although PAC spending paled in comparison to spending by 527 groups, PACs were able to use "express" language that asked the public to support or oppose candidates—a powerful advantage that the 527s did not enjoy. PACs supporting Kerry outspent those backing Bush by more than four to one, with most of the spending going toward television and radio ads, hats, T-shirts, mass mailings, yard signs, and phone calls. Labor union PACs spent close to $9 million promoting Kerry, and environmental PACs spent about $4 million on his behalf. The National Rifle Association's PAC spent more than $3 million to promote Bush, and antiabortion PACs spent more than $1 million supporting him.[40]

The 527 Groups. The major "outside money" story of the 2004 elections involved spending by 527 groups. Although BCRA cracked down on soft money spending by the political parties, it did nothing to constrain spending by outside groups. In late 2002, a number of pro-Democratic groups began organizing around a common goal of raising at least $300 million to spend in the 2004 elections. Most of them organized under section 527 of the tax code so that they could collect unregulated contributions. Bush's campaign committee responded by filing a complaint against a number of the pro-Democratic 527 groups, claiming that they were violating BCRA's restrictions on soft money fund raising. After delaying action and deadlocking for several months, the FEC approved rules in August 2004 to make it more difficult for 527 groups to spend millions in unrestricted contributions. The commission also decided, however, that the new rules would not take effect until 2005. As a result, 527 groups were allowed to continue raising and spending millions of dollars in unregulated money over the course of the 2004 elections.[41]

Although 527 groups are supposed to be independent of the parties, in reality the overlaps are quite obvious. Many of the groups use the same consultants and lawyers as the parties, and the parties, especially the Democrats, have outsourced many of their traditional campaign jobs to the groups. For example, a number of pro-Democrat 527s used sophisticated technology to gather information that their paid canvassers had collected about voters' issue positions. The information was then shared with Democrats, who used it to target campaign messages to voters. Pro-Democratic 527 groups attracted huge donations from some of the country's wealthiest individuals. Steve Rosenthal, the former political director of the AFL-CIO, joined forces with Harold Ickes, President Clinton's former chief of staff, Emily Malcolm, the founder of EMILY's List, and other well-placed Democrats to form Americans Coming Together (ACT). Billionaire investor George Soros and insurance executive Peter Lewis each pledged $10 million in seed money to ACT. Soros and Lewis gave more than $23 million apiece to pro-Democrat 527s during the 2004 elections. Rob McKay, an heir to the Taco Bell fortune, Robert Glaser, the CEO of RealNetworks Inc., and others pledged several million more to ACT. Ninety-one percent of the contributions to ACT came from donors giving at least $100,000. After forming in 2003, ACT raised more than $125 million. Ickes also helped establish the Media Fund, a 527 group that raised $50 million for pro-Democrat television ads. Hollywood executive Stephen Bing, who gave $13.6 million to various pro-Democrat 527 groups, provided substantial seed money for the Media Fund.

Republicans initially put their efforts into challenging the laws regulating 527s because they (correctly) worried that Democrats would gain an advantage from them. But when that approach failed, they jumped into the fray themselves. The fastest-growing pro-Bush 527 group was Progress for America, which was set up by Bush campaign consultant Tom Synhorst. Progress for America raised around $50 million from donors such as Amway founders Richard DeVos and Jay Van Andel, Missouri financier Sam Fox, and Harlan Crow, a Dallas real estate magnate. Crow also provided seed money to the Swift Boat Veterans for Truth, another pro-Bush 527 group, which ran ads smearing Kerry's military record. The Swift Boat Veterans raised about $7 million from big donors such as Texas oilman T. Boone Pickens, who gave the group $500,000. Pickens gave a total of $4 million to pro-Republican 527s during the 2004 election. Ben Ginsburg, the Bush campaign's attorney, resigned from the campaign when it was revealed that he had also advised the Swift Boat Veterans.

Nowhere was 527 spending more evident than on television. Between March 3 and October 28, 2004, the candidates and the outside groups supporting them spent approximately $575 million on television ads. More than half was spent in the five battleground states of Florida, Iowa, Ohio, Pennsylvania, and Wisconsin. Kerry and the groups supporting him spent $70.2 million in Florida, and Bush and his supporters spent $46 million. In Iowa, the Kerry forces spent $11.2 million, and the Bush camp spent $8.4 million. Kerry and his allies spent $68 million in Ohio, while Bush and his allies spent $36 million. In Pennsylvania, Kerry and his supporters spent $46.2 million, and Bush and his backers spent $29.4 million. The pro-Kerry forces spent just under $20 million in Wisconsin and the pro-Bush forces spent $13 million.[42]

Overall spending by advocacy groups during the 2004 election topped $435 million. Most of the Republican 527s formed to react to the Democratic groups and planned to disband after the election. The Democrats, however, see a broader mission in building a progressive infrastructure to promote issues and influence elections. ACT registered more than 450,000 new voters and on election day put close to 50,000 of its employees on the streets to get people to the polls in crucial cities. Soros has described ACT's extensive voter files as "intellectual property" that should be invested and built up. As testament to this longer-term goal, America Votes, another 527 group, was formed to coordinate the future activities of thirty-two pro-Democratic groups.[43]

Political Party Financing. Despite predictions that BCRA's ban on soft money would squeeze the parties out of the campaign finance game, they played a significant role in 2004. The national parties were allowed to make unlimited independent expenditures on behalf of their presidential candidates and coordinated expenditures of up to $16.2 million. Between January 1, 2003, and October 13, 2004, the national party committees raised a combined total of over $1 billion, of which they spent more than $875 million. Republican committees, including the Republican National Committee, the National Republican Senatorial Committee (NRSC), and the National Republican Congressional Committee (NRCC), raised $554.7 million in hard money from individuals and PACs. Democratic committees, including the Democratic National Committee, the Democratic Senatorial Campaign Committee (DSCC), and the Democratic Congressional Campaign Committee (DCCC), raised $451.8 million in hard money. Remarkably, the hard money totals for both parties were greater than the combined hard and soft money totals they had raised in any previous campaign.[44] In addition, the national Democratic committees together transferred about $35 million to state and local parties, and the national Republican committees transferred about $27.5 million. State and local parties in the battleground states of Florida, Ohio, Pennsylvania, Michigan, Colorado, and California received the most money from their national counterparts.

The DNC reported making independent expenditures of $79.4 million on the presidential race through October 13, 2004, and the RNC reported $5 million in independent expenditures. The RNC also reported $45.8 million in "generic media expenses," including television and radio ads that it financed jointly with the Bush campaign. Sticking with tradition, the parties dramatically increased their spending as the election approached. In September and October alone, the DNC spent $87.8 million to oppose Bush and $4.5 million to support Kerry. The RNC spent $4 million to support Bush and $11.5 million to oppose Kerry.[45]

Three weeks prior to election day, Bush reported total receipts of $365.5 million and Kerry reported a total of $334 million for the entire election process. Bush spent $306.3 million in private and federal funds from January 2003 to election day, and Kerry spent $260.5 million. Combining candidate, party, and advocacy group expenditures, the Center for Responsive Politics conservatively estimates that total spending in the 2004 presidential race exceeded $1.2 billion.[46]

The 2004 Congressional Races

The 2004 congressional election campaign also broke the record for spending. The battle for control of the Senate came down to about nine close races; in the House, only about thirty races were considered competitive. Senate candidates spent a total of about $280 million during the 2004 election cycle, and House candidates spent about $435 million (see Table 6-3). These figures represent spending increases of 22 percent for Senate races and 11 percent for House races since 2002. In the House, Republican candidates were responsible for most of the growth in spending. Republican House candidates increased their spending by about 21 percent over 2002, while spending by Democrats rose only 1 percent. About 64 percent of the donations to congressional candidates in 2004 came from individuals, and PAC contributions represented about 29 percent. In the Senate, Republican candidates struggled

Table 6-3 Financing of 2004 Senate and House General Election Campaigns

	Number of candidates	Receipts	Contributions from individuals	Contributions from other committees	Candidate contributions and loans	Other loans	Disbursements
SENATE	113	$327,722,649	$240,165,355	$56,579,071	$9,859,798	$811,829	$278,020,768
Democrats	36	$172,144,496	$134,553,849	$26,188,610	$2,806,219	$791,267	$148,616,813
Incumbents	14	$97,620,122	$75,027,573	$18,165,980	$0	$0	$83,414,475
Challengers	11	$15,566,426	$12,213,808	$1,896,530	$811,902	$91,267	$14,154,713
Open seats	11	$58,957,948	$47,312,468	$6,126,100	$1,994,317	$700,000	$51,047,625
Republicans	34	$154,417,655	$105,264,263	$30,378,909	$6,275,369	$20,562	$128,989,139
Incumbents	12	$61,859,905	$40,621,954	$17,745,519	$0	$0	$52,323,340
Challengers	14	$39,117,723	$29,108,247	$2,905,770	$5,230,369	$20,562	$32,866,851
Open seats	8	$53,440,027	$35,534,062	$9,727,620	$1,045,000	$0	$43,798,948
Other party	43	$1,160,498	$347,243	$11,552	$778,210	$0	$414,816
Challengers	28	$1,103,439	$329,292	$10,000	$755,172	$0	$367,761
Open seats	15	$57,059	$17,951	$1,552	$23,038	$0	$47,055
HOUSE	1,067	$544,765,321	$313,026,079	$194,309,877	$21,839,556	$1,795,397	$433,622,979
Democrats	408	$242,824,033	$140,726,080	$85,287,890	$10,754,987	$682,155	$198,907,024
Incumbents	191	$173,284,571	$96,469,192	$72,068,368	$63,453	$225,486	$140,078,920
Challengers	185	$45,064,455	$27,460,500	$7,698,449	$8,808,602	$451,277	$38,262,729
Open seats	32	$24,475,007	$16,796,388	$5,521,073	$1,882,932	$5,392	$20,565,375
Republicans	416	$300,907,616	$171,523,596	$108,903,507	$10,967,942	$1,113,242	$233,770,870
Incumbents	210	$227,102,827	$123,041,004	$95,881,355	$942,317	$1,014,342	$171,376,215
Challengers	169	$37,157,201	$26,780,987	$5,100,381	$4,173,296	$98,800	$31,414,096
Open seats	37	$36,647,588	$21,701,605	$7,921,771	$5,852,329	$100	$30,980,559
Other party	243	$1,033,672	$776,403	$118,480	$116,627	$0	$945,085
Incumbents	1	$790,216	$658,712	$111,650	$0	$0	$735,243
Challengers	228	$229,749	$109,572	$6,830	$111,039	$0	$199,029
Open seats	14	$13,707	$8,119	$0	$5,588	$0	$10,813

Source: Federal Election Commission, as of October 28, 2004.

to keep seats in Colorado, Oklahoma, and Alaska, while Democrats fought to hold five open seats in the South. The most expensive Senate race was in South Dakota, where Democratic leader Tom Daschle and former representative John Thune spent about $30 million contesting the seat that Daschle had held for eighteen years.[47]

In 96 percent of the 2004 House races, the candidate who spent the most money won. Close to one-third of House races (127) involved a candidate with no financial opposition. In thirty of those races, the incumbent faced no opponent at all. Ninety-seven House candidates faced opponents who spent either no money or less than $5,000.[48] Big spenders fared well in open seat races, 84 percent of which were won by the candidate who spent the most money. One major exception was Democratic representative Martin Frost, a thirteen-term member, who lost to Republican representative Pete Sessions. Frost, whose Texas district was redrawn, spent $3.9 million in his losing battle against Sessions, who spent $2.8 million.[49]

According to the FEC reports filed through mid-October, House incumbents raised a record average of just over $1 million each. As is typically the case, spending was higher in closer races. The 343 "safe" incumbents—those who were reelected with at least 60 percent of the vote—raised an average of $900,679, while their challengers raised an average of $169,559. The forty-nine incumbents who won competitive races (that is, won with less than 60 percent of the vote) raised an average of $1.6 million, while their challengers collected an average of $685,063. The five incumbents who lost their seats to challengers raised an average of $1.8, million while their competitors raised an average of $1.4 million. The winners of open seat races spent an average of $1.3 million and the losers an average of $584,875. Because spending typically skyrockets during the last few weeks of the campaign, the funds House candidates raised through election day are likely to be much higher than the mid-October figures.[50]

In 91 percent of the thirty-four Senate races, the candidate who spent the most money was elected. The average cost of winning a Senate seat in 2004 was $6.5 million, up 47 percent from 2002 and up 57 percent from 1998, when the same thirty-four seats were last contested. Senate incumbents who won with more than 60 percent of the vote raised an average of $5.0 million, while their challengers raised an average of $900,000. Incumbents who won with less than 60 percent of the vote raised an average of $7.8 million, while their challengers collected an average of $3.6 million. Daschle, the only incumbent Senator to lose, earned the dubious distinction of spending the most money on a losing race. Daschle spent $17.4 million but was beaten by Thune, who spent $10.3 million. Thune's campaign also benefited, however, from outside groups' spending of close to $10 million in the effort to defeat Daschle. Winners in the eight open seat Senate races raised an average of $8.5 million, while the losing candidates raised an average of $5.5 million.[51]

Self-financed candidates did not fare well in 2004. Of the twenty-one House and Senate candidates who spent more than $1 million of their own money, only one—Michael McCaul—won. McCaul, a Republican, spent almost $2 million of his own money to win a Texas seat. Only seven of the twenty-one candidates who spent $1 million or more in personal funds even made it to the general election; the other fourteen were defeated in primaries. Erskine Bowles, a former chief of staff to President Clinton, spent $1.5 million on his unsuccessful run for the North Carolina Senate seat vacated by John Edwards. In 2002, Bowles had spent $6.8 million of his own money in a race for North Carolina's other Senate seat but lost to Republican Elizabeth Dole. The biggest personal spender by far was Illinois Senate candidate Blair Hull, who invested $28.7 million in the Democratic primary but lost to Barack Obama, who went on to be elected.[52]

PAC Spending. Although the presidential race attracted most of the independent expenditures by PACs in 2004, PAC money also found its way into a few high-profile congressional races. The You're Fired PAC focused all of its efforts in South Dakota and spent $250,000 on ads opposing Sen. Tom Daschle. A number of PACs, led by the American Medical Association, spent more than $1.5 million backing Republican Richard Burr's bid for a North Carolina Senate seat. The National Rifle Association's Victory Fund invested in about two dozen congressional races, including $270,000 in Burr's campaign, and $4,700 in Florida Republican Katherine Harris's bid for reelection. (As Florida's secretary of state, Harris had presided over the state's 2000 presidential recount.) The National Association of Realtors PAC spent more than $350,000 on behalf of Republican Anne Northup of Kentucky. Northup, whose seat was targeted by the Democrats, won the realtors' backing after she supported them in a dispute with banks over home sales. Some PACs chose to invest in their own members. The National Beer Wholesalers PAC spent about $72,000 on mailings supporting Republican Pete Coors's bid for a Colorado Senate seat, and the American Dental PAC spent about $93,000 on radio ads to promote dentist and Democratic House candidate Jim Harrell of North Carolina.[53]

Political Party Financing. Party spending on behalf of federal candidates increased substantially in 2004. The two House campaign committees—the NRCC and the DCCC—were particularly aggressive in their fundraising efforts. Although the DCCC met its goal of raising $75 million, that total paled in comparison to the $169 million that the NRCC raised. During the 2004 election, the NRCC paid $85 million to Infocision, an Ohio-based telemarketing and direct-mail company, to work with the committee to build a new hard money donor list.[54] The DNC also undertook a major effort to restructure its fund-raising and voter outreach programs and invested millions of dollars in new technology.

In addition to raising money from donors, both House campaign committees collected money from incumbent members of Congress. The NRCC raised more than $16 million from Republican members. The DCCC had hoped to raise $25 million from Democratic members but came up short by about $5 million.[55] House members were more generous than their Senate counterparts when it came to giving money to each other and to other candidates. Members can give candidates a maximum of $1,000 per election out of their campaign accounts, and $5,000 per election out of their leadership PACs. The top five candidate-to-candidate contributors were House Majority Leader Tom DeLay, who gave Republican candidates $846,278; House Minority Whip Steny Hoyer, who gave Democrat candidates $709,000; House Speaker Dennis Hastert, who gave Republicans $643,000; Republican John Boehner, who gave $552,077 to fellow partisans; and Republican Ralph Regula, who gave $535,500 to his party's candidates.[56] In the closing weeks of the campaign, candidates in close races received a deluge of contributions from candidates in safe races. Illinois Senate candidate Democrat Barack Obama, who was way ahead of his Republican opponent, gave hundreds of thousands of dollars from his campaign treasury to Democratic candidates and party committees.

Most of both party committees' spending went toward television advertising in competitive races. Between September 1 and October 28, 2004, the DCCC spent $34.2 million and the NRCC spent $48.2 million. In all, the parties invested money in forty-seven House races and six Senate races. Spending by independent groups was largely concentrated in a few of these races, including Colorado's third district, where the DCCC spent $2.1 million to support John Salazar, and the NRCC spent $2.6 million opposing him and $1.8 million supporting his opponent, Gregory Walcher. The NRCC also helped vulnerable Republican incumbents, including Rick Renzi, Ariz., Bob Beauprez, Colo., and Anne Northup, Ky. The DCCC provided financial assistance to vulnerable Democratic incumbents such as Tim Bishop, N.Y., and Chet Edwards, Texas.[57] Because of the partisan battle over redistricting in Texas, the House races in the state were important to both party committees. The NRCC spent more than $8 million on five Texas races and also established "Team Texas," a joint fund-raising committee to help the Republican candidates in these districts. Republican House members also gave generously to their Texas colleagues. The DCCC invested heavily in the Texas races as well and helped set up the "Texas Fund," its own joint fund-raising committee.[58]

Although the House party committees' fund-raising totals in 2004 were similar to their 2002 totals (despite the ban on soft money fund raising), the Senate party committees raised far less in the 2004 cycle than in either 2002 or 2000. Between January 1, 2003, and October 13, 2004, the DSCC raised $76.4 million and the NRSC raised $68.7 million. In the previous election, the DSCC had raised $114.6 million and the NRSC $109 million. Nonetheless, the amounts of hard money the Senate committees managed to raise in 2004 were impressive, and the committees were particularly active in spending it during the final weeks of the election. In September and October, the NRSC spent $1.3 million to support Republican Senate candidates and $16.2 million to oppose Democrats; the DSCC spent $2.5 million supporting Democrats but only $5,566 opposing Republicans. The NRSC invested in the Alaska, Oklahoma, and South Dakota races, but the DSCC did not. Both the

NRSC and the DSCC spent money on the Florida, North Carolina, and South Carolina races, but in each state the NRSC outspent its rival by a substantial margin.[59]

Conclusion

The Bipartisan Campaign Reform Act did more to change the way campaigns for federal office are financed than any legislation since the 1970s. The BCRA ended the system that for more than a decade had allowed the parties to collect millions of dollars in soft money. But the new system has been the subject of fierce debate. Most criticisms center on the loophole that allows 527 groups to raise and spend soft money in the same way that the parties did before BCRA was enacted. BCRA's sponsors, Sens. John McCain and Russ Feingold, and Reps. Christopher Shays and Martin Meehan, claim that the law's primary goal was to stop federal officeholders from soliciting corporate and union soft money and that it was never intended to reduce the total amount of money spent in elections.[60] Critics, however, claim that the change that the law brought about is virtually meaningless because 527 groups are essentially operating as "shadow parties." Most 527s are aligned with either the Democrats or the Republicans, and in 2004 they injected many millions of unregulated dollars into the federal elections.

Even BCRA's sponsors acknowledge that more reform is needed. To this end, they have proposed new legislation barring 527 groups from raising and spending unlimited amounts of money on federal campaigns. The lawmakers argue that the groups should be required to register with the FEC if their primary purpose is to influence federal campaigns,[61] and they have turned to the courts for help in establishing that 527s are already barred from participating in federal elections by the 1974 FECA. They maintain that the FEC has not enforced the 1974 law and should either be replaced by a tougher agency or ordered by a judge to better regulate 527 activity. For their part, many 527 groups are passionate about participating in electoral politics and vow to become fixtures in both federal and local elections.[62] In 2004, the connections between the parties and many of the 527s were evident, but these relationships may become more contentious in future elections. MoveOn.org, one of the most active pro-Democratic groups in the 2004 elections, sent a post–election day e-mail to its supporters saying that by raising more than $300 million from grassroots contributors, the group had proved that the Democratic Party "does not need corporate cash to be competitive. Now it's our party: we bought it, we own it, and we're going to take it back." [63]

Because spending by 527 groups was the big campaign finance story in 2004, the fact that a record number of Americans contributed to federal candidates was easy to overlook. Many first-time donors in 2004 were motivated by the ideologically polarized campaigns and the ease of giving over the Internet. The national parties also defied expectations in 2004 and raised money in record-breaking amounts. The Democrats built up their donor mailing lists, and Republicans expanded theirs in a remarkably successful effort to attract small donors.

In 2004, money was raised and spent somewhat differently than in the past, but the effects were much the same. As in previous elections, most of the money went toward candidate and issue advertising. But a good amount also went toward drives to mobilize voters and small donors, which helped bring about the highest voter turnout rate since 1968. Although the final verdict on BCRA is still pending, one effect is clear: Like its predecessors, the new reform law seems to have imparted both major change and more of the same.

Notes

1. George Thayer, *Who Shakes the Money Tree? American Campaign Practices from 1789 to the Present* (New York: Simon and Schuster, 1973), 49–50.
2. Robert E. Mutch, *Campaigns, Congress, and Courts: The Making of Federal Campaign Finance Law* (New York: Praeger, 1988), 25–26.
3. Ibid., 28.
4. Ibid., 46.
5. Candidates must raise at least $5,000 in twenty different states. Individuals can contribute up to $2,000 per candidate, but only $250 of that amount counts towards the $5,000 requirement in each state.
6. Paul S. Herrnson, "The Money Maze: Financing Congressional Elections," in *Congress Reconsidered,* 7th ed., ed. Lawrence C. Dodd and Bruce I. Oppenheimer (Washington, D.C.: CQ Press, 2001), 99; Paul S. Herrnson, *Congressional Elections: Campaigning at Home and in Washington* (Washington, D.C.: CQ Press, 2000), 122.
7. Federal Election Commission press release, May 31, 2001.
8. Ibid., 2.
9. Joseph E. Cantor, "Campaign Financing" (Congressional Research Service Issue Brief for Congress, July 16, 2004), summary.
10. Center for Responsive Politics, "The Rise of Soft Money," updated September 8, 2003, www.opensecrets.org/news/McConnell/softmoney.asp; L. Paige Whitaker, "Campaign Finance Law: A Legal Analysis of the Supreme Court Ruling in *McConnell v. FEC*" (Congressional Research Service Issue Brief for Congress, February 24, 2004), 7–9.
11. Anthony Corrado, "Financing the 2000 Elections," in *The Election of 2000,* ed. Gerald M. Pomper (New York: Chatham House, 2001), 95–96.
12. Center for Responsive Politics, "The Rise of Soft Money"; Whitaker, "Campaign Finance Law," 7–9.
13. Generally speaking, so long as 527 organizations avoid using "vote for or against" terminology, they are acting within the law.
14. Public Law 106-230.
15. Center for Responsive Politics, "Types of Advocacy Groups," www.opensecrets.org/527s/types.asp.
16. House and Senate candidates spent a total of $1,047.3 million seeking office in 1999–2000, according to an FEC summary. During the 1997–1998 election cycle, House and Senate candidates spent a total of $740.4 million.
17. The BCRA does not define "promote" or "attack."
18. Express advocacy communications specifically advocate the election or defeat of a clearly identified candidate for federal office. Electioneering communications that do not meet the "express advocacy" definition generally are considered issue advocacy.

19. These figures are adjusted for inflation. Roger H. Davidson and Walter J. Oleszek, *Congress and its Members* (Washington, D.C.: CQ Press, 2004), 71–72.
20. Cantor, "Campaign Financing," 13.
21. Whitaker, "Campaign Finance Law," summary.
22. Ibid., 18–19.
23. Federal Election Commission press release, "Receipts of 2000 Presidential Campaigns through July 31, 2000," www.fec.gov/press/bkgnd/pres_cf/pres_cf.shtml.
24. Holly Bailey, "George W's Spending Spree," *Capital Eye* (a Center for Responsive Politics publication), www.opensecrets.org/newsletter/ce71/01bush.asp.
25. As in 2000, four third-party candidates had already received or were seeking their party's nomination.
26. Federal Election Commission press release, "Presidential Pre-Nomination Campaign Receipts through August 31, 2004," www.fec.gov/press/bkgnd/pres_cf/pres_cf.shtml.
27. Steven Weiss, "Laying the Foundation," *Capital Eye* (a Center for Responsive Politics publication), January 9, 2003, www.capitaleye.org/inside.asp?ID=58.
28. Federal Election Commission, "Presidential Campaign Finance Summaries," www.fec.gov/press/bkgnd/pres_cf/pres_cf.shtml.
29. Glen Justice, "Howard Dean's Internet Push: Where Will It Lead?" *New York Times,* November 2, 2003, Sec. 4, p. 5; Michael Cudahy and Jock Gill, "The Political Is Personal—Not Web-Based," *Pittsburgh Post-Gazette,* February 1, 2004, E1; Emily Fredrix, "Trippi: Dean Campaign Changes Politics with the Internet," Associated Press, June 4, 2004.
30. Ibid.
31. Carol Moseley Braun withdrew from the race on January 15; Wesley Clark withdrew on February 11; Richard Gephardt withdrew on January 20; Bob Graham withdrew on October 7, 2003; Joe Lieberman withdrew after the February 2 primaries. Dennis Kucinich, Lyndon LaRouche, and Al Sharpton remained in the race, but none was considered a serious contender.
32. Paul Farhi, "N.C. Senator Needs Money to Remain Competitive," *Washington Post,* February 19, 2004, A8; "Election 2004; Bush Adds to War Chest, Wants No New Cliffhanger; Kerry, Edwards Raising Funds with Eye on March 2," *Houston Chronicle,* February 21, 2004, A18.
33. Federal Election Commission, "Receipts of Presidential Campaigns through February 29, 2004," www.fec.gov/press/bkgnd/pres_cf/pres_cf.shtml.
34. David Westphal, "Next Opponent: Bush's $100 million," *Minneapolis Star Tribune,* March 3, 2004, 13A; Scott Shephard, "Kerry Cements Party's Nomination," *Austin American-Statesman,* March 3, 2004, A1; Sharon Theimer, "Bush, Kerry to Spend Almost Half-Billion," Associated Press, March 20, 2004.
35. Glen Justice, "Kerry Prepares for Big Fund-Raising Tour as Bush Shifts from Money Circuit to Campaigning," *New York Times,* March 20, 2004, A11.
36. Ibid.
37. Sharon Theimer, "Bush, Kerry Set New Presidential Fund-Raising Records," Associated Press, April 21, 2004.
38. Federal Election Commission, "Presidential Pre-Nomination Campaign Receipts through June 31, 2004" and "Presidential Pre-Nomination Campaign Receipts through August 31, 2004," www.fec.gov/press/bkgnd/pres_cf/pres_cf.shtml.
39. "A Third of Top Bush Fund-Raisers for 2000 Given Appointments," Associated Press, November 19, 2004.
40. "Post-Labor Day Spending by PACs Favors Kerry," CNN.com, October 26, 2004.
41. Thomas B. Edsall, "Proposed Rules for '527' Groups Lead to Some Unusual Alliances," *Washington Post,* April 14, 2004, A23; Glen Justice, "Panel Compromises on Soft Money Rules," *New York Times,* August 20, 2004, A16.

42. Chuck Todd, "Campaign by the Numbers," *New York Times,* November 3, 2004, op-ed.
43. Mark Hosenball, Michael Isikoff, and Holly Bailey, "The Secret Money War," *Newsweek,* September 20, 2004; Katharine Q. Seelye, "Money-Rich Advocacy Groups, Formed for Bush-Kerry Race, Look Far Beyond Election Day," *New York Times,* October 14, 2004, Section 1, 31; James V. Grimaldi and Thomas B. Edsall, "Super Rich Step into Political Vacuum; McCain-Feingold Paved Way for 527s," *Washington Post,* October 17, 2004, A1; Sharon Theimer, "Cost of 2004 Elections: $4 billion and Counting," Associated Press, November 2, 2004.
44. Federal Election Commission press release, "Party Fundraising Continues to Grow," October 25, 2004.
45. Ibid.; Campaign Finance Institute, "Party Independent Spending Soars," November 5, 2004, www.cfinst.org/pr/110504b.html. Although the Democrats' nineteen to one spending ratio is remarkable, it likely will decrease once overall party expenditures are accounted for.
46. Steven Weiss, "04 Elections Expected to Cost Nearly $4 Billion," Center for Responsive Politics, October 21, 2004, www.opensecrets.org/pressreleases/2004/04spending.asp.
47. Carl Hulse and Sheryl Gay Stolberg, "Races to Determine Control of House and Senate Have Been Nasty, Expensive, and Local," *New York Times,* October 31, 2004, Sec. A.
48. The FEC requires candidates to file detailed reports only if their campaign costs exceed $5,000.
49. Steven Weiss, "2004 Election Outcome: Money Wins," Center for Responsive Politics, November 3, 2004, www.opensecrets.org/pressreleases/2004/04results.asp.
50. Steve Weissman and Michael Malbin, "CFI's Post-Election Analysis of the 2004 Battle for Congress," Campaign Finance Institute, November 5, 2004, www.cfinst.org/pr/110504b.html.
51. Ibid.
52. Weiss, "2004 Election Outcome."
53. "Post-Labor Day spending by PACs favors Kerry," CNN.com, October 26, 2004.
54. Paul Kane, "Campaign Committees Prep for Reduced Roles," *Roll Call,* December 15, 2003.
55. Chris Cillizza, "DCCC, NRCC Now Nearly Even in Cash on Hand," *Roll Call,* October 21, 2004.
56. Based on data released by the FEC on October 4, 2004.
57. Patrick O'Connor and Hans Nichols, "GOP Takes Money Edge into Sprint until the End," *The Hill,* October 20, 2004, 3.
58. Chris Cillizza, "GOP Confident of Texas Gains," *Roll Call,* October 21, 2004.
59. Campaign Finance Institute, "Party Independent Spending Soars," November 5, 2004, www.cfinst.org/pr/110504b.html.
60. Glen Justice, "Even with Campaign Finance Law, Money Talks Louder Than Ever," *New York Times,* November 8, 2004, A16.
61. Helen Dewar, "Bill Would Curb '527' Spending; No Action Expected before Elections," *Washington Post,* September 23, 2004, A27.
62. Michael Moss and Ford Fessenden, "Interest Groups Mounting Costly Push to Get Out Vote," *New York Times,* October 20, 2004.
63. "MoveOn to Democratic Party: 'We Bought It, We Own It,' " Associated Press, December 10, 2004.

7

The Presidency: The 2004 Elections and the Prospects for Leadership

Paul J. Quirk and Sean C. Matheson

Elections not only decide presidents, they also shape presidencies. Presidential elections have importance beyond whether they install a Democrat or a Republican, a liberal, a moderate, or a conservative in the Oval Office. Campaigns as well as outcomes of presidential and congressional elections play roles in defining a president's leadership capabilities, opportunities and constraints, and prospects for success. Stated broadly, how a president is elected reveals a great deal about how, and how effectively, a president will govern.[1]

Elections affect the presidency in three ways. First, a presidential election results in the appointment to office of an individual with certain skills, experience, and personality. Some presidents have been poorly suited to the office in important respects. Richard Nixon, for example, was driven by deep-seated anger and suspicion; his aggressive illegality provoked the constitutional crisis of Watergate. Jimmy Carter disdained politicians and had a hard time dealing with them. Bill Clinton's reckless mendacity led to an impeachment crisis that undermined his effectiveness and nearly ended his presidency.

Second, the rhetoric of the campaign, especially that of the winning presidential candidate, creates commitments that carry weight after the election. These commitments may help to establish a popular mandate for the president's program, but they also may bind him to an unworkable strategy for governing. After George H. W. Bush made an emphatically categorical campaign promise to oppose new taxes during his run for the presidency in 1988, having to reverse his position two years later and tell voters in effect to "re-read" his lips proved to be politically devastating.

Third, elections measure and ultimately define the extent of support for the president and his initiatives. The tenor of debate in the presidential and congressional elections, the balance of partisan and ideological power in Congress, and the president's margin of victory all affect the support for his agenda and the prospects for effective leadership. Lyndon Johnson prevailing in the 1964 presidential election in a landslide along with fellow Democrats winning lopsided majorities in both houses of Congress set the stage for the enactment of an ambitious domestic agenda. In contrast, when Bill Clinton won the 1992 presidential election with 43 percent of the popular vote in a three-way race, Senate Republican leader Bob Dole warned on election night that his party would stand up for the majority of voters who had not voted for Clinton. Dole's remark foretold the bitter partisan conflicts and limited policy achievements of the Clinton presidency. When George W. Bush won the presidency in 2000—by virtue of a highly controversial Supreme Court ruling and despite losing the popular vote—many Democrats refused even to acknowledge the legitimacy of his presidency, much less show him the respect and deference normally enjoyed by a new president.

In some ways, the circumstances of the presidency after the 2004 elections appear to be the opposite of those that existed after 2000. The prospects of Bush winning political support for his agenda, especially in Congress, have markedly improved, but he also faces huge policy problems, partly through his own doing, and has made untenable commitments for dealing with them. He has also demonstrated—and shown no inclination to change—methods of decision making that greatly increase the risk of serious mistakes.

Qualifications

Despite the adage that anyone can grow up to be president, not everyone can do the job effectively. Voters should therefore seriously consider whether a presidential candidate is reasonably qualified for the office. Primary campaigns, when there may be more than one candidate from the major parties, are the best time to do so. The answers to four questions can be used to evaluate how the 2004 election process worked in selecting appropriate qualifications: What traits are important in a president? Did the campaign reveal these traits? To the extent that it did so, did the voters pay attention and weigh the candidates' qualifications in making their decisions? In the end, how qualified were the two major parties' nominees, especially the victor?

Defining Qualifications

No simple checklist of qualifications for the presidency exists that all citizens and commentators agree on.[2] In attempting to identify the most important qualifications, the public focuses largely on traits that reflect general cultural values, preferring honesty, strength, open-mindedness, warmth, and caring, and rejects the "power hungry" among others.[3] These preferences appear to derive more from what people want in a parent, a spouse, or a professional colleague than from requirements specific to the presidency. It is doubtful, for example, that presidents should always be honest or that they should not have a taste for power. An adequate approach to assessing the qualities required by the presidency must first recognize that several kinds of specifically presidential qualifications actually exist.[4] The main determinants are skills, experience, and personality, all which shape a president's performance in office.[5]

Skills. Several skills are important to the presidency. First, a president should have a broad strategic sense—the ability to see the big picture, set a viable course for coherent, attainable policy goals, and formulate general plans for achieving them. Second, a president should have a reasonably strong grasp of major national issues and especially those in economics and foreign policy, the central arenas for presidential decision making. It is neither necessary nor clearly desirable that he be (like Bill Clinton) a "policy wonk," able to knowledgeably engage in discourse about a wide variety of issues, but the president should be sufficiently familiar with the substance of policy debates to avoid simplistic or formulaic thinking and to distinguish balanced, responsible advice from tendentious advocacy.

Third, presidents should be able to work with other policymakers, especially those in Congress, and to build coalitions to enact their policies. Doing so requires communication skills and a desire to influence others.[6] It also requires tactical shrewdness and a refined understanding of the policymaking process, although it may suffice that these skills be present among the president's staff. Because other policymakers have their own goals and independent sources of power, building coalitions often requires flexibility and a collaborative disposition. Fourth, a president should be able to speak persuasively to the public. Appealing "over the heads" of congressional representatives and the rest of the Washington establishment is a central technique of modern presidential leadership.[7] As Ronald Reagan demonstrated, the skills required for effective public appeals are much akin to those of acting. Fifth, a president should understand how to manage the White House and the executive branch to obtain the assistance needed to perform all the other tasks of leadership. Devising a broad strategy, making good policy decisions, forming coalitions to adopt policies, and persuading the public are all, in large part, a matter of getting subordinates to work effectively.

For most presidents, exercising these skills requires a large investment of personal effort.[8] With rare exceptions—Calvin Coolidge, Ronald Reagan, and George W. Bush—presidents have been energetic, if not driven, and have put in long hours on the job. It is far from certain that a president can substitute delegating tasks to subordinates for modest personal effort.[9] Certainly delegation can help enormously, but a president who relies on it too heavily will lose influence, even within his administration, and may be held responsible for serious mistakes made by others.

Experience. In parliamentary systems, rising through the party ranks—normally spending considerable time in the cabinet or shadow cabinet—prepares politicians to assume the reins of leadership. Indeed, becoming prime minister is often a matter of moving from the side of the table to the head of it at cabinet meetings. In the United States, however, no comparable training system exists. Success in waging a presidential campaign presumably guarantees some skills in mass communication, but none of the other elements of presidential leadership can be taken for granted.[10] Whether candidates have developed the necessary skills for the presidency depends on their prior careers. Most presidents have lacked relevant experience for crucial aspects of the job.

The majority of presidents have previously held one of three positions: member of Congress, governor of a state, or high official in the executive branch (including the cabinet or military). Among twentieth-century presidents, only four—William McKinley, Theodore Roosevelt, Franklin Roosevelt, and George Bush—have held two of the three positions; none has held all three.[11] From the standpoint of training presidents, each position is lacking in some respect. A member of Congress, for example, manages a staff roughly the size of a large automobile dealership. Governors, especially of small states, do not participate in national policymaking or deal with comparably complex policy processes. Some governors have limited authority under their state constitutions and, thus, few substantial tasks. Governors also typically lack experience in managing an economy and making foreign policy. Most executive branch officials have highly specialized responsibilities and only modest exposure to the public. Their involvement in the legislative process may be limited.

The only job that provides well-rounded preparation for the presidency is, perversely, the presidency. A president without relevant experience on first taking office obviously will have plenty of it by the time the campaign for a second term comes around. Incumbent presidents build a record of performance that should inform voters of their capabilities. Another training ground is the vice presidency, inasmuch as recent presidents have treated their vice presidents increasingly as partners rather than as rivals.[12]

Personality. Although personality, or character—fundamental traits of an individual—is important in presidential performance, which traits matter is hard to say. In 1972 political scientist James David Barber proposed a simple typology of psychological character in an attempt to explain important aspects of presidential performance.[13] In one of political science's most celebrated predictions, Barber used Nixon's "active-negative" personality to predict his irrational and self-destructive tendencies before the Watergate scandal dramatically revealed them to the public. As Jeffrey Tulis points out, however, Barber's scheme would also have warned against Abraham Lincoln, who was just as clearly an active-negative.[14] After reviewing research on presidential personality and performance, psychologist Dean Simonton concluded that no single personality type is clearly best suited for the presidency. Instead, various traits have advantages and disadvantages.[15]

The issue concerning "presidential personality" may not be finding the right personality type, but recognizing the dangers of specific flaws. In addition to identifying Nixon's paranoid aggression, Barber convincingly described the extreme, arguably pathological rigidity on the part of Woodrow Wilson (in the controversy over ratifying the League of Nations treaty), Herbert Hoover (in responding to the Great Depression), and Lyndon Johnson (in escalating the Vietnam War). More recently, Reagan's simplistic, categorical thinking helped produce the huge budget deficits that dominated U.S. politics in the 1980s and much of the 1990s. Reagan's case also serves as a reminder of the relevance of age and health in presidential performance. By the end of his second term, Reagan's increasingly apparent lapses of memory provoked press speculation of progressing senility. Reagan died of Alzheimer's disease fifteen years after leaving the presidency; given that the course of the disease, from onset until death, ranges up to about eighteen years and sometimes longer, these lapses may have represented the first stages of the disease.[16] Voters should want to avoid electing a president who is likely to die or suffer a disabling illness during his term of office. Bill Clinton's lack of self-discipline not only produced the sexual misconduct that ultimately led to scandal and his impeachment over the Monica Lewinsky affair, but also contributed to chaotic and inconsistent White House decision making that produced numerous gaffes, scandals, and political failures in his first two years as president.[17]

One lesson from all these cases is the impossibility of avoiding all potentially harmful personal weaknesses in a president. The U.S. political system offers no real choice but to work with flawed presidents. Even so, an adequate electoral system should ideally filter out candidates with glaring deficiencies in skills, experience, or personality. This expectation relies especially on the nominating process, in which the parties narrow the field of potential presidents from the hundreds or thousands of constitutionally eligible candidates to (usually) just two. Despite the potential benefit of continuing to debate the nominees' qualifications, by the general election campaign, ideology dominates most voters' choice in candidates.

Qualifications and the 2004 Campaign

The 2004 presidential election presented voters with a choice between two distinct styles of leadership. This contrast, however, received far less attention than a more easily understood, emotionally resonant, but almost irrelevant issue of qualification for office—the Vietnam-era military service of the major party nominees, Republican George W. Bush and Democrat John Kerry. Even when the campaign debate focused on leadership and decision making, it largely overlooked the most important issues concerning the abilities and methods of President Bush. In particular, the campaign demonstrated how highly salient information trumps realistic and informed consideration of qualifications for the presidency.

From the start of the campaign, the president's role as commander in chief dominated both parties' agendas. For the first time since 1992, the Democratic nominating contest featured serious competition, with ten candidates vying for the nomination. The field proved typical in terms of the candidates' prior experience: six members of Congress (Senators John Edwards, Bob Graham, John Kerry, and Joe Lieberman and Representatives Richard Gephardt and Dennis Kucinich), a former governor (Howard Dean), a former senator (Carol Moseley Braun), a former general (Wesley Clark), and an activist minister (Al Sharpton). Of the seven candidates with congressional experience, only Senator Graham had, in addition, relevant executive experience, having served as governor of Florida from 1979 to 1987. The two other former executives had experience far removed from the presidency: Dean had served five two-year terms as governor of Vermont, and Clark had held the position of supreme allied commander of NATO. None of the candidates had benefited from the learning experience of being a cabinet or subcabinet official or a White House staff member.

The main qualification on Democratic voters' minds, however, was simple and political: the ability to defeat George W. Bush. One in four participants in Iowa's Democratic caucus and one in three voters in the New Hampshire primary rated the ability to "beat Bush" as the most important quality for the Democratic nominee, outranking the candidate's experience, endorsements, or caring about people.[18] By the beginning of 2004, this concern had boiled the contest down to what pundits called "two candidates-Dean and anyone-but-Dean." Dean had unexpectedly rocketed to the front of the Democratic field in fall 2003 by breaking with most Democrats' strategy of accommodating the Bush administration on national security issues.

Opponents of Dean argued two points: that he was too liberal to be elected president and that he lacked the military experience that a Democrat would need to defeat an incumbent president in wartime. Only two candidates met the military service qualification: former NATO commander Clark and Senator Kerry, a decorated veteran of the Vietnam War. Both made their military records the centerpiece of their campaigns. As former Georgia senator Max Cleland put it, Kerry won the Iowa caucuses with support from " 'middle-class, white veterans' recruited at American Legion and Veterans of Foreign Wars halls where [other] Democrats have 'feared to tread.' "[19] Kerry continued to capitalize on his military record in the subsequent primaries and by early March had secured the nomination.

A twenty-year veteran of the U.S. Senate with a respectable but undistinguished legislative record, Kerry proceeded to campaign for president in large part by trumpeting his military accomplishments from a quarter-century past. Kerry had captained a navy "swift boat" on the rivers of South Vietnam for four months during 1968 and 1969. He received the Bronze Star and the Silver Star for heroism, and three Purple Hearts for wounds suffered in combat. The third Purple Heart entitled Kerry to end his tour of duty in Vietnam. Upon his return home, he became a vocal opponent of the war.

Kerry employed his Vietnam heroics in hopes of showing that he had the courage and toughness needed in a wartime president, but his antiwar activism undermined his appeal to many voters (even though the antiwar movement had ultimately "won" the argument about the conflict, and the United States withdrew its forces from Vietnam). A group of critics, loosely tied to the Bush campaign and calling themselves Swift Vets and POWs for Truth, spent $13.8 million on advertisements attacking Kerry's Vietnam record and his fitness to serve as commander in chief.[20] Playing fast and loose with alleged evidence, the group made four accusations: Kerry had exaggerated his wounds to escape further duty; he did not actually save crew members' lives under fire (the basis for his Bronze Star); he had committed a wartime atrocity (shooting a wounded enemy soldier in the back); and he had undermined the morale of U.S. troops and may have lengthened the war by his criticism of it.

These allegations by the Swift Vets for Truth were, despite the group's name, false. Investigations by major newspapers and the Political Fact Check project at the University of Pennsylvania pronounced the charges without merit. Nevertheless, because the Swift Boat ads made harsh allegations of matters that voters could easily understand, they significantly affected the election, turning the centerpiece of Kerry's campaign into, at best, a debatable subject and sowing doubts in the minds of many voters about Kerry's service and integrity. Kerry's standing in the polls sharply declined.[21] Throughout the controversy over the ads, Bush repeatedly acknowledged Kerry's war service but refused to disavow the swift boat veterans' ads or ask that they be discontinued. The ads represent one of the most successful uses of false or distorted claims in any recent presidential campaign.[22]

Bush faced similar abuse concerning his Vietnam-era military service, but to much less effect. Having led the nation to war in Afghanistan and Iraq gave Bush instant credibility as commander in chief. Crucial military decisions in both conflicts had provoked severe criticism among knowledgeable observers, including the use of proxies instead of U.S. troops in the unsuccessful effort to capture Osama bin Laden in Afghanistan and the lack of adequate troops and resources to secure control of Iraq. Nevertheless, Bush's military credentials, like Kerry's, were criticized in the campaign primarily in relation to the Vietnam War. Liberal satirist Michael Moore launched the assault by labeling Bush a deserter in his book *Stupid White Men* and then again in a campaign appearance with Wesley Clark in January 2004: "I want to see that debate," he said, "the general versus the deserter!"[23] Mainstream news organizations explored Bush's National Guard service and found grounds to doubt that he had properly completed his obligation. They also found that the relevant records were suspiciously hard to obtain. The issue exploded, however, when the CBS News program *60 Minutes II* reported that it had uncovered documents, signed by the commanding officer of Bush's Alabama National Guard unit, noting that Bush had failed to show up for mandatory duties but was protected from appropriate discipline by the state commander. When the documents, which bore telltale signs of having been typed in a recent version of Microsoft Word, were exposed as fraudulent, attention shifted to CBS's careless reporting, and the issue of Bush's actual performance in the National Guard faded.

Despite all the attention given to Bush and Kerry's military records, the issue is largely irrelevant to their qualifications to be president. Courage under fire would be a useful trait for a sheriff of Dodge City, but presidents are rarely shot at, and they are never expected to shoot back. A president's "courage" in military conflict involves sending other people into battle and facing up to the consequences. Military service has historically had no apparent effect on how presidents conduct national security policy. John Kennedy and Richard Nixon, both World War II veterans, differed sharply in their cold war foreign policies. World War II veteran George Bush and Bill Clinton, who did not serve, each pursued cautious approaches toward military interventions in the Balkans and Somalia.

Some commentators have suggested that prior military service enhances a president's credibility with the armed forces. Kerry implied as much in his acceptance speech at the Democratic National Convention:

> I know what kids go through when they are carrying an M-16 in a dangerous place and they can't tell friend from foe. I know what they go through when they're out on patrol at night and they don't know what's coming around the next bend. I know what it's like to write letters home telling your family that everything's all right when you're not sure that's true. As President, I will wage this war [in Iraq] with the lessons I learned in war.[24]

Little evidence exists that such experiences make a difference in shaping a president's national security policy or relationship with the military. Ronald Reagan, who dramatically increased defense spending, was wildly popular among the military, although the only uniform he ever wore came from central casting. Naval officer Jimmy Carter cut defense programs and struggled in his relationship with the armed forces.

Nevertheless, voters seized on the easily understandable issue of military credentials, including those decades old. More important, the attacks on Kerry and Bush's Vietnam-era conduct turned the issue into one of integrity, with each candidate's critics implying that he had violated laws or regulations and lied about it. The issue dominated the news for weeks, but the coverage consisted mostly of false or misleading claims about barely relevant ancient history.

Kerry's need to appear credible as a commander in chief also influenced the second major debate over qualifications, a debate about decision making and leadership. In October 2002 Kerry joined seventy-six other senators in voting for the bill authorizing the president to use force in Iraq.[25] A year later, however, with Howard Dean's antiwar candidacy at its zenith and Kerry facing criticism for initially supporting the war, he joined only eleven other senators (including fellow Democratic presidential candidate John Edwards) in voting against a supplemental defense appropriations bill to fund the wars in Iraq and Afghanistan.[26] Before the vote, however, Kerry cosponsored an unsuccessful amendment to the bill that would have offset the costs of the wars by repealing Bush tax cuts for persons in the highest income tax bracket.[27] After the defeat of his amendment, Kerry voted against the supplemental appropriation. From the standpoint of congressional strategy, Kerry's vote appeared perfectly sensible: vote "no" on a supplemental bill that will pass anyway in order to protest Bush's refusal to pay the cost of the war. At that time, such a move might also have helped Kerry attract votes in the Democratic primaries, but in the long haul it placed Kerry in the politically vulnerable position of having first supported the war and then opposed funding it. His attempt to explain his position made matters worse by playing into a Bush charge that he was a "flip-flopper": "I actually did vote for the $87 billion before I voted against it." The Bush campaign portrayed the vote without reference to legislative strategies: Kerry "voted . . . for military action in Iraq" and then "voted against funding our soldiers." [28] Kerry was never able to shake the flip-flopper charge. In truth, Kerry's position on the war had been consistent, but also complex. In his statement accompanying his vote to authorize the use of force, Kerry had expressed numerous caveats:

> Let me be clear, the vote I will give to the President is for one reason and one reason only: To disarm Iraq of weapons of mass destruction, if we cannot accomplish that objective through new, tough weapons inspections in joint concert with our allies. . . . If we do wind up going to war with Iraq, it is imperative that we do so with others in the international community, unless there is a showing of a grave, imminent—and I emphasize "imminent"—threat to this country which requires the president to respond in a way that protects our immediate national security needs.[29]

These nuances and Kerry's carefully reasoned position were buried in the rhetoric of the campaign. Republicans ignored his caveats, and Kerry could never explain his position effectively. Although Kerry's votes on the war took into consideration short-term political gains, taken together, his positions reflect his general approach to decision making—that of an extremely careful politician and policymaker.[30] Sympathetic observers described Kerry as highly intelligent and inquisitive, worthy traits in a president:

> Kerry has an avid appetite for consuming large amounts of information . . . gathering in the maximum number of conflicting, contrasting opinions, in a sense sort of circumscribing and circumnavigating an issue and making decisions. . . . Of course, the risks or downsides in this approach [are] that there are these periods of tremendous vagueness, or apparent vagueness, when he has decided that he doesn't actually have to have a conclusion yet. And so he appears actually to be inconclusive.[31]

Kerry read extensively and preferred to learn by debating options in an almost Socratic manner. To some observers, however, this reliance on debate and his penchant for political caution evoked the image of indecision and uncertainty rather than wisdom. In the case of the supplemental appropriation, it led to a decision too clever by half.

While focusing attention on Kerry's alleged indecisiveness, the media showed much less interest in George W. Bush's skills and methods in decision making. Bush's image of competence had fluctuated with the dramatic events of his first term. Bush had emerged from the 2000 election facing "an extraordinarily complex, unpredictable situation with respect to popular and congressional support, along with one of the most ambiguous mandates in the history of the presidency." [32] Nevertheless, he succeeded in persuading Congress to approve his two most prominent legislative initiatives, the No Child Left Behind Act and a package of aggressive tax cuts that primarily benefited wealthy Americans. The events of September 11, 2001, transformed and redefined his presidency.[33] Bush's response to the attacks and his subsequent invasion of Afghanistan received strong bipartisan and even international support. His approval rating rose to 86 percent in September and remained above 70 percent for the next eleven months. Few observers repeated the earlier criticisms that Bush lacked important qualifications to be an effective president. The aftermath of the March 2003 invasion of Iraq ended Bush's run of image-boosting developments, as his approval ratings sagged and criticism of him as inarticulate, uninformed, or even unintelligent resumed.

Although late-night comedians' ridiculing of Bush's intelligence is obviously exaggerated, his actual abilities and methods of decision making provide a great deal about which to worry. Close observers describe Bush as intelligent but unconcerned with the specifics of public policy. Admirers call these specifics "nuances," implying that they are appropriately beneath the level of presidential attention. The record, however, shows Bush often overlooking issues that experienced senior officials regard as well within his purview.[34] Andrew Card, the White House chief of staff, was quoted in the *New York Times* as saying that Bush had devoted "in the neighborhood of five hours" to budget proposal meetings, a level of attention that certainly requires overlooking more than nuance.[35] In any instance, Bush expects his staff to address the specific issues and then present big, clear questions to which he responds.

On its face, Bush's approach to decision making seems reasonable. Why should a president worry about details? As a general proposition, however, such an approach creates serious risks: that the president will fail to understand the issues on which he is making decisions; that he will be "captured" by advocates of one point of view; or that he will fail to consider relevant options, among others. A detached approach, with heavy reliance on delegation, invites mistakes.[36]

Bush's lack of intellectual investment in policymaking and his overreliance on delegation to White House staff might not be viewed as potentially serious problems were he served by senior officials who insured that he heard the full range of relevant views. Instead, as accounts from former administration insiders reveal, the White House during Bush's first term permitted policymaking processes to be dominated by groups of officials who were either ideologically homogenous, mainly concerned about political ramifications, or both.[37] Some former officials—Richard Clarke, Paul O'Neill, and John DiIulio—documented White House decision making in well-publicized accounts after leaving office. According to DiIulio, a political scientist and former director of the Office on Faith-Based and Community Initiatives,

> There is no precedent in any modern White House for what is going on in this one: a complete lack of a policy apparatus. What you've got is everything, and I mean everything, being run by the political arm. . . .

> And some staff members, senior and junior, are awed and cowed by [Karl Rove's] real or perceived powers. They self-censor lots for fear of upsetting him, and, in turn, few of the president's top people routinely tell the president what they really think if they think that Karl will be brought up short in the bargain.[38]

The insider accounts by Clarke, a former antiterrorism chief, and O'Neill, former Treasury secretary, make clear that most members of Bush's foreign policy and national security team—especially Vice President Dick Cheney, Secretary of Defense Donald Rumsfeld, and Assistant Secretary of Defense Paul Wolfowitz—began Bush's first term with a strong inclination to go to war with Iraq, a rare position at the time in the foreign policy community.[39] These advisers played a crucial role in persuading Bush—despite a lack of supporting evidence—that Iraq had assisted in the September 11 attacks and that it possessed weapons of mass destruction that were an imminent threat. In effect, they constructed a rationale for war that the president adopted but has been proven incorrect.

In some respects, the contrast between Bush and Kerry's decision-making approaches became evident throughout their three presidential debates. In the first debate, for instance, Bush repeatedly portrayed his steadfastness as a necessary quality of leadership in a time of war: "I understand everybody in this country doesn't agree with the decisions I've made. And I made some tough decisions. But people know where I stand. People out there listening know what I believe. And that's how best it is to keep the peace." [40] Kerry rejoined: "This president has made, I regret to say, a colossal error of judgment. And judgment is what we look for in the president of the United States of America." [41] Bush later countered,

> What is misleading is to say you can lead and succeed in Iraq if you keep changing your positions on this war. And he [Kerry] has. As the politics change, his positions change. And that's not how a commander in chief acts. . . . The only [thing] consistent about my opponent's position is that he's been inconsistent. He changes positions. And you cannot change positions in this war on terror if you expect to win.[42]

Kerry replied, "It's one thing to be certain, but you can be certain and be wrong." [43] During this exchange and throughout the campaign, however, Kerry never articulated the combination of traits that made Bush's habit of certainty dangerous: that he was personally disengaged; that he delegated decisions to a narrow, ideologically motivated group of advisers; and that he acted with undue certainty on their advice. Voters heard Kerry say that the war was "the wrong war, at the wrong place, at the wrong time." What they did not hear was a cogent and specific case that the mistake resulted from the president's general approach to making decisions, especially his reliance on a narrow group of conservative ideologues whose views were seldom subjected to effective criticism as part of the decision-making process.

Bush and Kerry presented the voters with important differences in decision-making styles, and the election was unusual for the attention given to "mistakes in judgment," "waffling," and indecision, among other attributes of decision making. In the end, the election became more about leadership than about policy. According to the exit polls, the voters preferred Bush as a leader, yet the campaign left much to be desired in how it explored this aspect of presidential qualification. The news media focused instead on irrelevancies about decades-old military service and failed even to treat these matters responsibly and accurately. The American public interpreted Kerry's discriminating yet generally consistent position on Iraq as mere waffling, and the central difficulties with Bush's approach to decision making were almost universally ignored.

Commitments

The president-elect's potential success in governing depends in part on whether the commitments he makes in the heat of the campaign will be substantively and politically viable after the election.

Varieties of Commitment

Cynics like to suggest that campaign promises are made to be broken. In fact, presidents work hard to fulfill most of the promises that they make during the campaign.[44] Looking at the presidencies from Kennedy through Reagan's first term, Jeff Fishel found that presidents, on average, submitted legislation or signed executive orders consistent with roughly two-thirds of their campaign promises. Even the lowest-scoring president, Reagan, acted on more than half of his 1980 promises, including some of the most important ones.[45]

Presidential candidates make explicit commitments by promising specific actions, such as Carter's 1976 pledge to create a Department of Education and Reagan's 1980 vow to cut income taxes by 30 percent. They also make implicit promises by attacking the proposals, past actions, and alleged intentions of the opposing candidate, as in Johnson's devastating attack in 1964 on Republican candidate Barry Goldwater's purported plan to abolish Social Security. In both such cases, it is politically costly for presidents to go back on their word, so they try to avoid doing so.

Promise making and promise keeping contribute to popular control of government, which is the whole point of democratic elections. They, in theory, provide voters with the assurance that what they see in a candidate is what they will get when they elect that candidate as president. Promises also sometimes have a broader effect: If a presidential candidate campaigns largely on issues and wins the election by a comfortable margin, his victory becomes his "mandate" to pursue promises made during the campaign.[46] For example, many viewed Johnson's landslide victory in 1964 as a mandate for his Great Society programs.

Often, however, the effect of campaign promises reflects the voters' lack of sophistication, the candidates' determination to win, and the superficiality of campaign debate. In pursuit of votes, a candidate may make promises that serve the needs of the campaign but ultimately are problematic, at best, from the standpoint of governing. Such promises may exploit voter ignorance or appeal to voters' emotions, stereotypes, or wishful thinking. A president-elect who has made such promises will nonetheless face pressure from one camp or another to fulfill them. He may fail to deliver, waste precious time and political support in pointless efforts to enact them, or, worse, deliver on the promises and harm the country.

Such problems do not arise from vague or obviously hyperbolic claims that lack specific implications. For example, Nixon's famous promise to "bring us together" and Clinton's vow to "build a bridge to the twenty-first century" created no constraints on presidential actions. Such puffery aside, candidates should ideally impose some discipline on their claims and promises and keep them reasonably connected to reality. The campaign debate and media coverage should provide enough scrutiny of the candidates' positions to induce discretion or, failing that, to help voters recognize and discount unsupportable claims.[47] Put simply, there should not be a vast gulf between the rhetoric of the campaign and the realities of governing.

Commitments and the 2004 Campaign

The issues debate in the 2004 presidential campaign focused mainly on Bush's policies and performance in his first term, rather than on what the two candidates would do during the next four years if elected. Nevertheless, both candidates made significant policy commitments. Predictably, some of these strained credibility and were likely to cause difficulties in governing for the victor. In particular, several of Bush's commitments will either be difficult to meet responsibly or impossible to meet at all.

His most important commitment was to continue his efforts in Iraq until they reached a successful conclusion. In this, Bush essentially defended his decision to go to war and his administration's subsequent handling of the occupation and administration of that country. In December 2003 in an address at the Council on Foreign Relations, Kerry charged,

> The Bush administration has pursued the most arrogant, inept, reckless and ideological foreign policy in modern history. In the wake of the September 11th terrorist attacks, the world rallied to the common cause of fighting terrorism. But President Bush has squandered that historic moment. The coalition is now in tatters, and the global war on terrorism has actually been set back [by the invasion of Iraq].[48]

In turn, Bush repeatedly attacked Kerry for his statement at a campaign rally in Cleveland that the Iraq War was the "wrong war, wrong place, wrong time."[49] He reminded audiences that Kerry had voted for the war and had considered Saddam Hussein a threat to the United States. Despite such rhetoric, Bush and Kerry said many of the same things about how they would deal with Iraq in the future. Neither advocated immediately pulling out and both supported "Iraqification" of the political and security structures and increased international support for dealing with the situation. Kerry even accused Bush of being less committed to success in Iraq than he was:

> I fear that in the run-up to the 2004 election, the administration is considering what is tantamount to a cut-and-run strategy. Their sudden embrace of accelerated Iraqification and American troop withdrawal dates, without adequate stability, is an invitation to failure. . . . [I]t would be a disaster and a disgraceful betrayal of principle to speed up the process simply to lay the groundwork for a politically expedient withdrawal of American troops.[50]

Kerry's criticism of Bush's plans for "accelerated Iraqification and troop withdrawal dates" was dubious, because Kerry too favored a rapid schedule for Iraqification and opposed postponing Iraqi national elections (scheduled for January 2005). However, both candidates' commitment to early elections and a rapid transfer of power, without an expanded U.S. effort to establish reasonable security, locked them into a risky strategy.

Although the main elements of the two candidates' Iraq policy were identical, Bush and Kerry differed in their general approaches to foreign affairs, with Bush following an essentially unilateral approach and Kerry urging a more multilateral one. In the first presidential debate Kerry asserted,

> No president, through all of American history, has ever ceded, and nor would I, the right to preempt in any way necessary to protect the United States of America. But if and when you do it . . . you have to do it in a way that passes . . . the global test where your countrymen, your people understand fully why you're doing what you're doing and you can prove to the world that you did it for legitimate reasons.[51]

Bush pounced on Kerry's choice of words, retorting, "I'm not exactly sure what you mean, 'passes the global test,' you take preemptive action if you 'pass a global test.' My attitude is you take preemptive action in order to protect the American people, that you act in order to make this country secure." [52] What Kerry meant was that a president should be able to prove the need for preemptive action to both domestic and international audiences, but Bush spun the phrase "global test" to mean that Kerry would act only if other countries agreed, a policy Kerry had rejected when he said he would never cede the right to preempt. Even though Bush managed to redefine Kerry's "global test" from its intended meaning, the phrase still indicated Kerry's greater willingness to seek multilateral cooperation in the face of security challenges. Kerry repeatedly promised renewed attention to "the fundamental tenets that have guided [U.S.] foreign policy for more than half a century: belief in collective security and alliances, respect for international institutions and international law, multilateral engagement, and the use of force not as a first option but truly as a last resort." [53]

In contrast, Bush promised to continue his assertive, unilateral approach to foreign policy. Not only was this approach markedly different from Kerry's, it also stood in contrast to Bush's campaign rhetoric in 2000. In his second debate against Democratic nominee Al Gore, Bush had warned, "If we're an arrogant nation, they'll resent us. If we're a humble nation, but strong, they'll welcome us. . . . [T]hey'll respect us." [54] By the time of his second debate with Kerry, Bush had changed his tune: "[S]ometimes in this world you make unpopular decisions because you think they're right. . . . People love America. Sometimes they don't like the decisions made by America, but I don't think you want a president who tries to become popular and does the wrong thing." [55]

To most voters, Bush's approach to foreign policy appealed more than Kerry's throughout the campaign. For instance, although declining in January 2004, polling numbers on the decision to go to war in Iraq stabilized between February and September, with between 50 and 60 percent of Americans believing that invading Iraq was the right thing to do. Furthermore, despite doubts about Bush's justification for the war and the course of the occupation, a majority of Americans still trusted him over Kerry to deal with the situation in Iraq (see Figure 7-1). Exit polls confirmed this tendency, with 51 percent of voters approving of the decision to go to war.[56]

The campaign success of Bush's unilateralism in foreign affairs—and of his distortion of Kerry's "global test"—are likely to reinforce his unilateral tendencies in his second term. In remarks following a postelection meeting with Canadian prime minister Paul Martin in Nova Scotia, Bush showed some inclination toward a change of approach, stating, "A new term in office is an important opportunity to reach out to our friends. . . . My country is determined to work as far as possible within the framework of international organizations, and we're hoping that other nations will work with us to make those institutions more relevant and more effective in meeting the unique threats of our time." [57] Bush's reshuffling of his foreign policy team, however, pointed toward a strong continuing commitment to U.S. unilateralism. The administration's most vocal multilateralists, Secretary of State Colin Powell and Deputy Secretary of State Richard Armitage, resigned on November 15. The next day Bush appointed Condoleezza Rice, his national security adviser, as Powell's replacement. In turn, Rice's deputy at the National Security Council—Stephen Hadley, one of the principal architects of postwar strategy in Iraq—replaced her as head of the NSC. Bush's decision to keep Donald Rumsfeld and Paul Wolfowitz in the two top positions at the Defense Department was equally telling. Within a month of the election, the Bush administration had visibly reinforced its commitment to a unilateralist foreign policy.

The most prominent policy commitment Bush made—and the most difficult to square with the federal government's fiscal condition—was to protect his first-term tax cuts. "Most of the tax cuts went to low- and middle-income

Figure 7-1 Pre-election Polling on Iraq, 2004

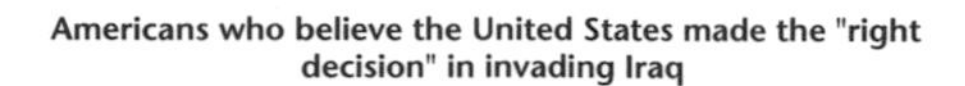

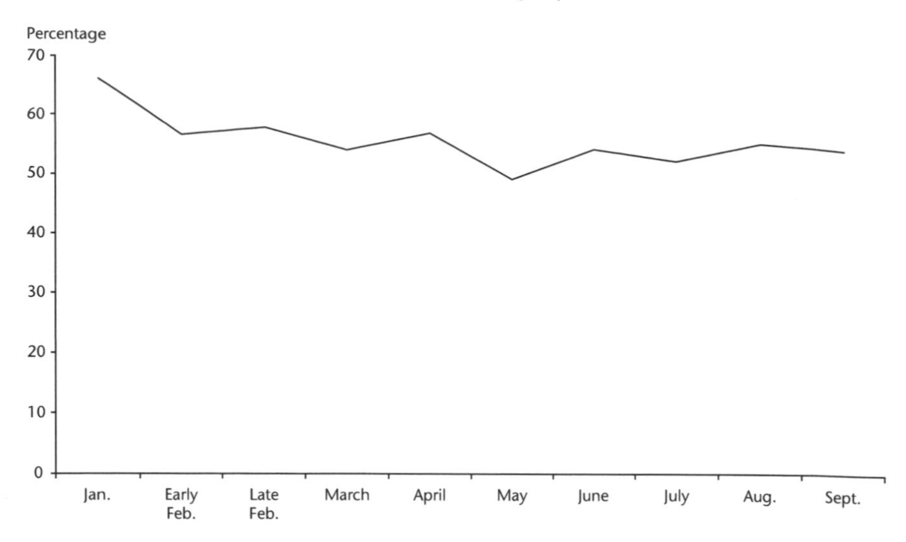

Who Americans trust more to handle the situation in Iraq

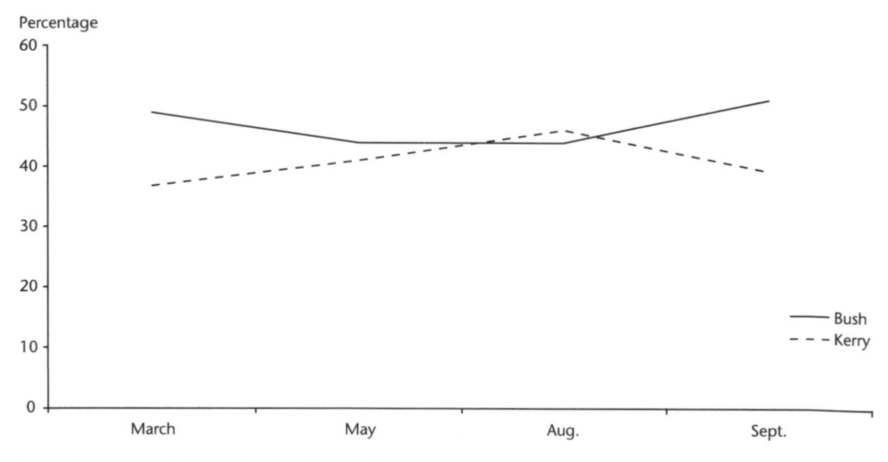

Source: Pew Research Center for People and the Press, October 2004, (top) http://people-press.org/reports/print.php3?Page ID=908 (question 14) and (bottom) http://people-press.org/reports/print.php3?PageID=899 (question 15).

Americans," he argued, "And now the tax code is more fair. Twenty percent of the upper-income people pay about 80 percent of the taxes in America today because of how we structured the tax cuts. If you have a child, you got tax relief. If you're married, you got tax relief. If you pay any tax at all, you got tax relief." Moreover, Bush claimed, the tax cuts had been vital economic stimulants: "The tax relief was important to spur consumption and investment to get us out of this recession. . . . The way to make sure our economy grows is not to raise taxes on small-business owners. It's not to increase the scope of the federal government. It's to make sure we have fiscal sanity and keep taxes low." [58]

Kerry countered that the tax cuts were giveaways to the wealthiest Americans: "Under President Bush," he argued, "the middle class has seen their tax burden go up and the wealthiests' tax burden has gone down. Now that's wrong. . . . One percent of America got $89 billion last year in a tax cut," enough over time, he continued, to protect Social Security until 2070.[59] Kerry's portrayal of the effects of the Bush tax cuts was misleading: the total federal tax burden on *all* groups declined, with the top 20 percent and bottom 40 percent of earners paying a smaller share of federal taxes, and the middle 20 percent a slightly greater share. His assertion, however, made for effective campaign rhetoric and set the stage for his own fiscal proposal.[60] In contrast, Kerry promised that he would repeal the tax cuts for the top 1 percent of Americans—those making more than $200,000 a year—while leaving the other Bush tax cuts, such as expansion of the child tax credit and elimination of the so-called marriage penalty, untouched. Bush promised not only to protect the tax cuts but to extend them beyond their 2011 expiration, a commitment that played well with voters but will make it extremely difficult to reduce the federal budget deficit.

In addition to preserving his tax cuts, Bush made repeated promises to reform the nation's tax code. In his acceptance speech at the Republican National Convention, he said,

> Another drag on our economy is the current tax code, which is a complicated mess—filled with special interest loopholes, saddling our people with more than six billion hours of paperwork and headache every year. The American people deserve—and our economic future demands—a simpler, fairer, pro-growth system. In a new term, I will lead a bipartisan effort to reform and simplify the federal tax code.[61]

In outlining his principles for tax reform after the election, Bush did not include reducing the budget deficit. Rather, he stated that any reform should be revenue neutral—that is, it should bring in neither more nor less revenue and, therefore, do nothing to shrink the deficit.[62]

Bush had company in his disregard for responsible fiscal policy. Throughout the campaign, neither candidate substantively addressed the exploding budget deficit. In just four years, the federal budget had undergone a $700 billion swing—from a surplus of $236 billion in fiscal year 2000 to a projected deficit of $475 billion in fiscal year 2004.[63] This dramatic turnaround in the federal government's bottom line had several causes, including the increased spending associated with the September 11 attacks, the wars in Afghanistan and Iraq, and the Medicare prescription drug benefit passed in 2004. The main culprit, however, was a huge decline in federal tax revenues caused by the collapse of the late-1990s stock market bubble, the 2000–2001 recession and subsequent weak recovery, and Bush's three tax cuts. As a result, federal revenue fell from an historic high of 20.8 percent of GDP in fiscal year 2000 to just 16 percent of GDP for fiscal year 2004.[64]

The gaping deficit poses serious challenges because of the future cost of baby boomers' retiring. Nevertheless, the only commitment Bush and Kerry made regarding the deficit was to cut it in half, in both cases by mostly unspecified means, Kerry in four years, Bush in five. The reality of their specific proposals was entirely different. The Concord Coalition, a nonpartisan group that advocates for balanced federal budgets, estimated that Kerry's economic plan would increase the national debt by $1.27 trillion over the next decade, while Bush's economic plan would increase it by $1.33 trillion.[65] In the end, both candidates' plans seemed to embrace Vice President Cheney's assurance that "Reagan proved deficits don't matter." [66] Although Cheney's analysis may be politically accurate, it is highly dubious economically. Federal Reserve Board chairman Alan Greenspan warned in the midst of the election campaign "that rising federal deficits may be the biggest threat to the nation's long-term economic stability." [67]

The other major domestic policy commitment that Bush made in the 2004 campaign revived a major issue from the 2000 election—reforming Social Security. Bush repeatedly promised to allow younger Americans to redirect a portion of their Social Security taxes into personal savings accounts—"a nest egg you can call your own, and government can never take away." [68] Although Bush never detailed how his plan would work, the President's Commission to Strengthen Social Security endorsed the concept of individually controlled personal savings accounts (PSA) in 2001. The commission also advanced three potential models for a new system, with workers in all three models diverting between 2 and 4 percent of their salary—as much as half of their payroll taxes—into a PSA. The difficulty will lie in making up for the estimated $400 billion to $1.1 trillion that would be diverted from the Social Security trust fund into private accounts.[69] Covering these transition costs is especially problematic, because the president ruled out increasing taxes to cover them. Instead, White House press secretary Scott McClellan hinted that the administration may simply add the transition costs to the already huge budget deficit.[70]

Presidential campaigns create powerful incentives for candidates to exaggerate promises and to ignore harsh realities, practices that in turn make governing difficult. The candidates in the 2004 campaign did just that. The winner, Bush, made especially daunting commitments for his second term. Of importance, he committed the United States to achieving enough stability in Iraq to allow for the transfer of most security responsibilities to a new, elected Iraqi government, but he did so without frankly acknowledging the difficulties and costs involved. He also committed to maintaining an assertive, unilateral foreign policy that is unlikely to win international support for the rebuilding of Iraq. Taken together, his domestic commitments—to reform the tax code, to partially privatize Social Security, and to cut the budget deficit in half, all without raising taxes—will prove to be impossible. Something must give. In all likelihood, the commitment with the weakest political constituency—reducing the budget deficit—is the one Bush will sacrifice. The nation may suffer the long-term economic consequences of Bush's campaign promises for many years to come.

Support

The results of presidential, and especially congressional, elections go far toward determining whether the president will have adequate political support for his policies. Congressional support can sometimes be crucial to a president's chances of policy success. In particular, a "presidency of achievement," such as those of Wilson, Franklin Roosevelt, Johnson, and Reagan, depends on a highly supportive political environment.[71] Support for a president's policies in Washington is not, however, necessary for boosting his popularity among the public. Clinton staged a political comeback in 1995 and 1996 largely by opposing ambitious Republican conservatives who controlled Congress. Strong political support is also not essential for presidential success in governing effectively.[72] The government often works fairly well when the president and Congress are controlled by different political parties.[73] Provided that the two parties are reasonably disposed to cooperate, a president may negotiate with an opposition-party Congress to deal effectively with national problems even if he cannot enact his first preferences.[74] Cooperation of this kind has become increasingly scarce as a result of the polarized partisan politics of the 1990s and 2000s.[75]

Sources of Support

Elections affect support for the president's policies in several ways. Most important, they determine the partisan and ideological balance in Congress. As considerable research demonstrates, presidential influence in Congress depends more on that balance than on personal presidential characteristics, such as popularity and leadership skills.[76] During Clinton's first term, the effects of the political composition of Congress on the president's influence were highly evident. In 1993 and 1994, when Clinton enjoyed Democratic majorities in the House and in the Senate, he got his way more than 85 percent of the time in each chamber on roll call votes in which he took a position. After losing both houses to the Republicans in the 1994 midterm elections, his success rate dropped precipitously, to 26 percent of the roll calls in the House—the lowest success rate of any president on record—and to 49 percent in the Senate.

In addition, congressional elections are an important barometer of national opinion regarding the president's policies and the proper role of government. The campaigns for 435 House seats and 33 or 34 Senate seats constitute a highly visible test of which issues and themes hold sway in the prevailing climate of opinion. If, for example, Republican congressional candidates stress their association with their party's presidential candidate, campaign for his or her policies, and are elected (along with that candidate) in large numbers, the results will be interpreted in Washington as powerful evidence of national support for the president's agenda.

The manner in which a president is elected also affects congressional support for his agenda. For example, whether a president campaigned primarily on issues may have consequences; a new Congress might hesitate to challenge a presidential initiative if he featured it prominently in his campaign. Another influence is the effect of the campaign on what Richard Neustadt calls the president's "professional reputation and prestige." [77] Presidents-elect who suffer effective attacks on their character or competence, endure embarrassing gaffes or scandals, or are viewed as the lesser of two evils will have a hard time rallying support. For example, questions that were raised in the 1992 campaign about Bill Clinton avoiding service in Vietnam undermined his credibility as commander in chief during his first term. This lack of credibility helped defeat his effort to end the ban on homosexuals in the armed forces.

The most important aspect of the president's manner of election is the margin of victory. Presidents who win in landslides are given credit for being popular and for their ability to rally public support. As a result, Congress tends to grant them longer or more generous honeymoons. In 1981 Reagan's economic program derived powerful momentum from his late surge to overtake Carter and win election by 10 percentage points in the national popular vote.

Elections also shape the disposition of the two parties to collaborate in effecting policy change. For example, ideologically divisive and brutally negative campaigns increase the possibility of the parties carrying over the spirit of partisan warfare into government. If centrist campaign strategies prevail, and negative attacks are restrained, the potential for bipartisan cooperation increases. In short, the parties draw lessons about the rewards for confrontation or cooperation from how the voters respond to these approaches. In 1995 congressional Republicans adopted an exceptionally aggressive partisan posture partly because their obstruction of Clinton during his first two years seemed to pay off in the 1994 elections.

The potential for bipartisan governance also depends on whether voters elect moderates or ideologues to Congress. Over a number of recent years, a gradual realignment of the party system has been weeding moderates—liberal Republicans and conservative Democrats—from Congress, especially in the House. This realignment has shrunk the base for bipartisan coalitions.[78]

Support and the 2004 Campaign

Unlike in 2000, in 2004 George W. Bush's victory was substantial and accompanied by congressional gains for the Republican Party, which now comfortably controls the House and the Senate. Bush's situation, however, is nonetheless ambiguous, though in a respect different from that in 2000. The 2004 election sent mixed signals about the direction and magnitude of policy change voters seek, with some evidence for a hard-line conservative mandate, especially on social issues, but other evidence, in the end stronger, against that. The elections also left intact in the Senate a pivotal moderate faction capable of blocking legislation. As a result, Bush faces pressure to satisfy his party's core constituencies with hard-line conservative policies, but will need to compromise on those policies to get bills through the Senate. There may be disappointed expectations on all sides.

Bush's 2004 win was much that his 2000 victory was not. It established his electoral bona fides in several respects. First, he captured 50.7 percent of the popular vote to Kerry's 48.3 percent, making him the first president to win a popular majority since his father, George Bush, defeated Michael Dukakis in 1988.[79] Second, though Bush's Electoral College victory of 286 votes to 251 was smaller than any other reelected president's since Woodrow Wilson's in 1916, it was decisive compared with his disputed, razor-thin victory of 271 votes to 266 in 2000. Third, Bush received nearly 11 million more votes in 2004 than in 2000, the largest increase for a president since Reagan in 1984. Fourth, Republicans increased their majorities in both chambers of Congress and made gains in state legislative and gubernatorial offices. Fifth, these gains occurred despite a unified and energetic effort by Democrats and independent groups dedicated to defeating Bush. Bush outspent Kerry, $361 million to $318 million, but the Kerry campaign more than doubled Al Gore's fundraising and narrowed the traditional Republican financial advantage; pro-Kerry independent groups actually outspent pro-Bush groups by a wide margin.[80] The Bush campaign's ability to overcome its highly motivated opposition invigorated conservatives and demoralized Bush's opponents.

Social conservatives trumpeted their role in Bush's victory and promised to cash in their IOU's during Bush's second term. Some early readings of exit poll data suggested that "moral values" had motivated an exceptionally large part of Bush's majority. Proposals to ban same-sex marriage appeared on the ballots in eleven states, drawing large numbers of socially conservative voters to the polls. All eleven measures were approved, and Bush carried nine of those states, including the key battleground state of Ohio. Media commentary proclaimed a "triumph of the right." Subsequent analyses, however, raised doubts about the influence of "moral values," a term that was not mentioned frequently in surveys in which respondents were asked to volunteer the reasons for their vote.[81] Furthermore, the same exit polls that supposedly demonstrated the importance of "moral values" also showed 60 percent of voters supporting some form of civil recognition of homosexual relationships (either marriage or civil unions), 55 percent saying that abortion should be always or mostly legal, and only one in six advocating that abortion should always be illegal.[82] Bush will be forced to temper the inflated ambitions of religious conservatives and deal with the fact that most Americans, including many Bush voters, do not support major elements of the conservative social agenda.

A harbinger of trouble on the Right rose immediately after the election, when Christian conservatives sought to deny moderate Republican Arlen Specter the chairmanship of the Senate Judiciary Committee. In a public statement after the election, Specter warned that judicial nominees clearly inclined to roll back abortion rights were unlikely to be confirmed by the Senate. His prediction was a reasonable inference from the basic arithmetic that any nominee would need the support of every Republican senator plus five Democrats to break a possible filibuster. Conservatives did not like hearing this: "He [Specter] either gets with the program or we shove him aside," warned Southern Baptist leader Richard Land.[83] In the end, Senate Republicans, including every Republican on the Judiciary Committee, rallied around Specter, but the incident served notice of social conservatives' intent to make demands that Bush and other Republicans will not be able to meet.

Whatever the trend of public sentiment, Bush gained a more Republican and somewhat more conservative Congress. Republicans increased their control of the Senate by four seats (resulting in a 55-44 margin of control, with 1 independent) and of the House by three seats (resulting in a 232-202 division). The effect of these gains on congressional support for Bush's policies, however, will be modest. Most of the gains, especially in the House, came at the expense of moderate Democrats who had supported much of Bush's first-term agenda. In the Senate, the loss of moderate Democrats may make it harder for Bush to build centrist coalitions when hard-line conservative measures are in jeopardy. At a minimum, the Republicans' increased control of the Senate protects them should there be defections in their ranks and allows them to control the agenda and prevail on some crucial measures, especially budget reconciliation bills, which are immune to filibuster.[84] Unfortunately for Bush, the opportunities to overcome a filibuster are limited, as Senate Republicans will not have the sixty votes needed to break one if Democrats remain unified.

In 2004 Senate majority leader Bill Frist began publicly testing the waters for a high-risk strategy to end the long-standing right of senators to filibuster judicial nominations.[85] To achieve this feat, a Republican senator would make a parliamentary objection, asserting that filibusters against judicial nominations are unconstitutional. As the presiding officer, the vice president would rule in favor of the objection, notwithstanding the long history seemingly to the contrary. The Democrats would appeal the ruling, but the Republican majority would vote to sustain it.[86] Such a maneuver would smooth the path for the president's judicial nominations, but it could trigger a costly escalation of partisan warfare in the Senate. Democrats, if they chose to do so, could retaliate by filibustering many or all of Bush's executive branch nominations and legislative proposals. Senate Democratic leader Harry Reid issued a threat to that effect in late 2004 in a statement to the *Washington Post:* "If they, for whatever reason, decide to do this, it's not only wrong, they will rue the day they did it, because we will do whatever we can do to strike back. I know procedures around here. And I know that there will still be Senate business conducted. But I will, for lack of a better word, screw things up." [87] From the standpoint of public support, to "screw things up" would be potentially costly for the Democrats. In all likelihood, neither party will want to test its ability to survive an all-out procedural war, but the Republicans' apparent readiness to consider launching one will induce Democrats to be more lenient with conservative judicial appointees than they were during Bush's first term.

Because Bush cannot force overly conservative bills through the Senate, he must rely on bipartisan, moderate support to advance the most ambitious elements of his second-term domestic agenda: reforming the tax code and partially privatizing Social Security. Judging from the record of his first term, he will seek such support. Bush's main legislative initiatives in his first year as president both required and received Democratic votes.[88] He followed a bipartisan strategy for education reform from the beginning of his administration, hiring a centrist Democrat as an education adviser and working closely with Democrats Ted Kennedy in the Senate and George Miller in the House. In the end, moderate Republicans and Democrats were generally pleased with the measure, while conservatives were disappointed. Bush also compromised with moderates to win passage of his tax cuts. With White House consent, Senate Finance Committee chairman Charles Grassley and ranking Democrat Max Baucus pared down the tax cuts from $1.6 trillion to $1.35 trillion, allowed poorer parents to claim part of the child tax credit, and expanded tax deductions for education. As a result, the bill avoided a filibuster and passed the Senate 62-38.[89]

To have a realistic chance of success on ambitious domestic initiatives such as Social Security privatization and tax reform, Bush will need to revive such bipartisan strategies. Doing so, of course, will constrain the outcomes. On Social Security, Bush will almost certainly have to back off from any plan to finance the new private savings accounts solely through increased deficit spending. Democrats (and some moderate Republicans) will unite against any attempt to replace the progressive income tax with a flat tax or national sales tax; in doing so, they will find strong support from business groups opposed to eliminating tax breaks crucial to their well-being. Instead, Bush will have to settle for simplifying the tax system, much as Ronald Reagan did in 1986. Congressional conservatives may well balk at these compromises, much as they balked at the compromises Bush made to secure adoption of his tax cuts and education reforms. Because it is unlikely that congressional leaders will allow Bush's major initiatives to die at the hands of conservatives, his real task remains to win the support of congressional moderates.

The prospects for needed support are much less favorable—indeed they are dire—for Bush's central objectives in the international arena: stabilizing Iraq, gaining international assistance for reconstruction efforts, withdrawing American forces, and fighting the war on terrorism. Around the world, Bush faces a breadth and intensity of antipathy unprecedented for a U.S. president. According to the Pew Research Center's 2004 Global Attitudes Survey, majorities in every country surveyed, except the United States, viewed Bush unfavorably. Sixty percent of Russians, 67 percent of Pakistanis and Turks, 85 percent of Germans and French, 90 percent of Moroccans, and 96 percent of Jordanians expressed negative opinions of him. Their views of Bush have also affected attitudes toward the United States in general. Roughly 59 percent of Germans and 62 percent of French view the United States unfavorably. Among Islamic countries, only 30 percent of Turks, 27 percent of Moroccans, 21 percent of Pakistanis, and 5 percent of Jordanians view the United States favorably.[90] Bush, from the outset of his presidency and especially in undertaking the war in Iraq, embarked on a grand experiment of largely ignoring world opinion. The Pew surveys highlight some of the consequences. Such negative attitudes toward Bush and the United States will make it extraordinarily difficult for him to gain foreign support for any controversial project in the international arena.

Bush will certainly not rest on his laurels in his second term. As he said after winning reelection, "I earned capital in the campaign, political capital, and now I intend to spend it. It is my style." [91] Even so, Bush confronts the political reality that achieving his primary ambitions depends on gaining support from moderate Republicans and centrist Democrats, not to mention leaders and nations abroad that are even less disposed to do his bidding. Considering the breadth and importance of his policy agenda—Iraq, terrorism, Supreme Court vacancies, and reform of Social Security and the tax code—Bush's second term offers possibilities for exceptional achievement or for failure on most fronts.

Implications for the Second Bush Term

The 2004 elections returned to office a president with a first term behind him that featured a sharp decline and slow rebound in the economy, and more important, the outbreak of a war on terrorism. The latter potentially will be the central issue of U.S. politics for years to come. In this environment, Bush experienced stellar successes in purely political terms: He helped his party recapture control of the Senate in the 2002 midterm congressional elections, and he induced Congress to enact his legislative priorities—three major tax cuts and the most significant changes to federal education policy since the 1960s. He then scored a solid victory with his 2004 reelection.

In dealing with the substantive issues of government, however, Bush's performance was mixed, at best. His economic policies—especially the tax cuts—helped produce long-term budget deficits of a magnitude that mainstream economics commentators regard with fear. They led the respected moderate-conservative *Economist,* which had supported Bush in 2000, to endorse his Democratic opponent in 2004. His foreign policies alienated the world and, above all, he took the United States into a war in Iraq that was justified (before the fact) on false premises and (after the fact) on incredible ones—namely, that the United States would go to war merely to remove a cruel dictator with long-term ambitions to develop weapons of mass destruction.

The 2004 elections affected Bush's prospects for success in his second term in three ways. First, because of the margin of his electoral victory and the gains of the Republican Party in Congress, the elections ensured that he will have considerable support for his ambitious second-term agenda. Second, because Republican and Democratic moderates remain in a position to block legislative action, the elections also left intact significant constraints on Bush's ability to enact conservative policies. Third, certain interpretations of the election created expectations on the part of Bush's core conservative constituencies that he will be unable to meet, a likely source of friction.

Motivated in part by the strategic needs of the presidential campaign, Bush complicated his situation by making commitments that he will not be able to keep but that may encourage him to make risky or irresponsible decisions in order to appear to keep them. The question in the near-term is what Bush will do concerning the transfer of authority to an elected Iraqi government and the continued U.S. presence in Iraq. The question for the long-term is what he will do if his plans for taxes, Social Security, and deficit reduction prove incompatible, a prospect that sheer arithmetic makes inevitable.

The 2004 elections appeared, if anything, to confirm the popularity of Bush's methods of decision making and leadership. The voters clearly approved the firmness and resolve that he repeatedly showed. To be sure, they did not hear effective criticisms from Kerry of Bush's disengaged, uninformed deference to senior advisers, who are dominated in foreign policy by a narrow, ideological faction and in the domestic arena by political operatives with minimal interest in public policy. Nothing about the election will, however, prompt Bush to reconsider the advisory and decision processes of his first term. Partly through Bush's doing, the circumstances facing the nation are far more perilous than when he became president. Judging from Bush's first four years in office, it is unclear whether he has the ability to make sound decisions in dealing with these circumstances.

Notes

1. The authors assume that the general category of U.S. presidents will some day include women. For simplicity of expression, the convention in this chapter is to use male pronouns for references to persons of either sex.
2. See Richard E. Neustadt, *Presidential Power: The Politics of Leadership* (New York: Wiley and Sons, 1960); James David Barber, *The Presidential Character* (Englewood Cliffs, N.J.: Prentice-Hall, 1972); Fred I. Greenstein, *The Presidential Difference: Leadership Style from FDR to Clinton* (New York: Free Press, 2000); and Marc Landy and Sidney M. Milkis, *Presidential Greatness* (Lawrence: University Press of Kansas, 2000).
3. Donald R. Kinder et al., "Presidential Prototypes," *Political Behavior* 2 (1980): 315–337. See also Stephen J. Wayne, "Great Expectations: What People Want from Presidents," in *Rethinking the Presidency,* ed. Thomas E. Cronin (Boston: Little, Brown, 1982). See also Stanley A. Renshon, *The Psychological Assessment of Presidential Candidates* (New York: New York University Press, 1996); and George C. Edwards and Stephen J. Wayne, *Presidential Leadership: Politics and Policy Making* (New York: St. Martin's Press, 1999), 105–107.

4. Fred Greenstein's analysis of the last eleven presidents using six qualities that influence presidential performance exemplifies this approach and largely mirrors our own list of relevant qualities. See Greenstein, *Presidential Difference.* See also Erwin C. Hargrove and Michael Nelson, *Presidents, Politics, and Policy* (Baltimore: Johns Hopkins University Press, 1984); and Paul J. Quirk, "Presidential Competence," in *The Presidency and the Political System,* 7th ed., ed. Michael Nelson (Washington, D.C.: CQ Press, 2002).
5. The discussion here follows closely the account in Paul J. Quirk and Sean C. Matheson, "The Presidency: Elections and Presidential Governance," in *The Elections of 1996,* ed. Michael Nelson (Washington, D.C.: CQ Press, 1997). It has been amended in modest ways to address issues that arose in the 2000 and 2004 elections. The argument is generally similar to that of Greenstein, *Presidential Difference.*
6. Barbara Kellerman, *The Political Presidency* (New York: Oxford University Press, 1984).
7. Samuel Kernell, *Going Public: New Strategies of Presidential Leadership,* 3rd ed. (Washington, D.C.: CQ Press, 1997).
8. We did not make this point in our previous discussion. Cf. "The Presidency: The Election and the Prospects for Leadership," in *The Elections of 2000,* ed. Michael Nelson (Washington, D.C.: CQ Press, 2001). We have been reminded of it by the case of George W. Bush, whose work habits are mentioned below.
9. Quirk, "Presidential Competence," 158–189.
10. Richard Rose, "Learning to Govern or Learning to Campaign?" in *Presidential Selection,* ed. Alexander Heard and Michael Nelson (Durham, N.C.: Duke University Press, 1987).
11. Michael Nelson, "Who Vies for President?" in Heard and Nelson, *Presidential Selection.*
12. See David Broder, "Al Gore: A Close Second," *Washington Post National Weekly Edition,* September 2–8, 1996, 6–7.
13. Barber, *Presidential Character.*
14. Jeffrey Tulis, "On Presidential Character," in *The Presidency in the Constitutional Order,* ed. Jeffrey Tulis and Joseph M. Bessette (Baton Rouge: Louisiana State University Press, 1977), 287.
15. Dean K. Simonton, *Why Presidents Succeed: A Political Psychology of Leadership* (New Haven: Yale University Press, 1987), 230–232. Although there is some evidence that a president's motivation—generally conceived as the desire for power, achievement, or affiliation—influences his behavior, no clearly preferable motivation has been established. David Winter and Abigail Stewart found, for example, that desire for power, a trait most Americans express concern about, strongly correlates with greater presidential success. They present open-mindedness and intellectual sophistication as the only two traits clearly viewed as desirable in a president. See David G. Winter and Abigail J. Stewart, "Content Analysis as a Technique for Assessing Political Leaders," in *A Psychological Examination of Political Leaders,* ed. Margaret G. Hermann (New York: Free Press, 1977), 28–62.
16. See Edmund Morris, *Dutch: A Memoir of Ronald Reagan* (New York: Random House, 1999), 662, 837. On Alzheimer's disease and its progression, see Napier University's Web site, www.lifesciences.napier.ac.uk/bws/courses/projects00/alzheimers/alzheime.htm (accessed December 18, 2004).
17. Elizabeth Drew, *On the Edge: The Clinton Presidency* (New York: Simon and Schuster, 1994).
18. Exit poll data from CNN.com, "America Votes 2004," www.cnn.com/ELECTION/2004/primaries/pages/epolls/IA/index.html (accessed December 22, 2004).

19. John F. Harris, "Kerry Stresses Military Past," *Washington Post,* February 1, 2004, A4.
20. Center for Responsive Politics, "527 Committee Activity: The Top 50 Federally Focused Organizations," www.opensecrets.org/527s/527cmtes.asp?level=C&cycle=2004 (accessed December 27, 2004).
21. An August survey conducted by CNN/Gallup found just 30 percent doubting Kerry's honesty about his service in Vietnam. A month later that number had more than doubled, with a September CBS News/*New York Times* survey reporting that 49 percent of respondents, including 41 percent of Democrats, said they thought Kerry was "hiding something" about his Vietnam record, and another 13 percent said he was "mostly lying" about his service. See CNN.com, "Poll: Presidential Race Remains Dead Heat," August 27, 2004, www.cnn.com/2004/ALLPOLITICS/08/26/prez.poll (accessed January 19, 2005); Adam Nagourney and Janet Elder, "Bush Opens Lead Despite Unease Voiced in Survey," *New York Times,* September 18, 2004, A1.
22. Cf. Kathleen Hall Jamieson, *Dirty Politics: Deception, Distraction, and Democracy* (Oxford: Oxford University Press, 1992).
23. Annenberg Public Policy Center of the University of Pennsylvania, "Bush a Military 'Deserter?' Calm Down, Michael," FactCheck.org, January 23, 2004 (modified February 11, 2004), www.factcheck.org/article131.html (accessed December 7, 2004).
24. CBSNews.com, "Text of John Kerry's DNC Speech," July 29, 2004, www.cbsnews.com/stories/2004/07/29/politics/main633010.shtml (accessed December 7, 2004).
25. House Joint Resolution 114, which became Public Law 107-243. The measure passed 296–133 in the House and 77–23 in the Senate.
26. S 1869, the Emergency Supplemental Appropriations for Iraq and Afghanistan Security and Reconstruction Act, which passed 87–12 on October 12, 2003.
27. Senate Amendment 1796, tabled on October 2, 2003, roll call vote 373.
28. Annenberg Public Policy Center of the University of Pennsylvania, "Did Kerry Vote 'No' on Body Armor for Troops?" FactCheck.org, March 16, 2004 (modified March 18, 2004), www.factcheck.org/article155.html (accessed December 7, 2004).
29. *Congressional Record,* 107th Cong., 2nd sess., October 9, 2002, S10174.
30. PBS, "The Choice 2004: Decision Making Style," *Frontline,* www.pbs.org/wgbh/pages/frontline/shows/choice2004/kerry/style.html (accessed December 7, 2004).
31. Philip Gourevich of the *New Yorker,* quoted in ibid.
32. Quirk and Matheson, "The Presidency," 177.
33. Cf. Bob Woodward, *Bush at War* (New York: Simon and Schuster, 2002).
34. Ron Suskind, *The Price of Loyalty: George W. Bush, the White House, and the Education of Paul O'Neill* (New York: Simon and Schuster, 2004); Richard A. Clarke, *Against All Enemies: Inside America's War on Terror* (New York: Free Press, 2004).
35. Richard L. Berke, "Bush Is Providing Corporate Model for White House," *New York Times,* March 11, 2001, A1.
36. See Quirk, "Presidential Competence," 158–189.
37. Ibid.
38. John DiIulio, quoted in Ron Suskind, "Why Are These Men Laughing," *Esquire,* January 2003, 98, also available at www.ronsuskind.com/newsite/articles/archives/000032.html (accessed January 19, 2005).
39. Suskind, *Price of Loyalty;* Clarke, *Against All Enemies.*
40. Commission on Presidential Debates, "Debate Transcript: The First Bush-Kerry Presidential Debate," September 30, 2004, www.debates.org/pages/trans2004a.html (accessed December 7, 2004).
41. Ibid.

42. Ibid.
43. Ibid
44. Jeff Fishel, *Presidents and Promises* (Washington, D.C.: CQ Press, 1985).
45. Ibid., 38–39.
46. John H. Aldrich, "Presidential Selection," in *Researching the Presidency: Vital Questions, New Approaches* (Pittsburgh: University of Pittsburgh Press, 1993), 23–68.
47. On the limitations of media coverage, see Thomas E. Patterson, *Out of Order* (New York: Random House, 1994).
48. John Kerry, "Making America Secure Again: Setting the Right Course for Foreign Policy" (address to the Council on Foreign Relations, New York, December 3, 2003), www.cfr.org.
49. David Halbinger and David E. Sanger, "Bush and Kerry Clash over Iraq and a Timetable," *New York Times,* September 7, 2004, A1.
50. Kerry, "Making America Secure Again."
51. Commission on Presidential Debates, "First Bush-Kerry Presidential Debate."
52. Ibid.
53. Kerry, "Making America Secure Again."
54. Commission on Presidential Debates, "Debate Transcript: The Second Gore-Bush Presidential Debate," October 11, 2000, www.debates.org/pages/trans2000b.html (accessed January 13, 2005).
55. Commission on Presidential Debates, "Debate Transcript: The Second Bush-Kerry Presidential Debate," October 8, 2004, www.debates.org/pages/trans2004c.html (accessed January 31, 2005).
56. CNN.com, "Election Results: U.S. President/National/Exit Polls," www.cnn.com/ELECTION/2004/pages/results/states/US/P/00/epolls.0.html (accessed December 27, 2004).
57. "President Discusses Strong Relationship with Canada," December 1, 2004, www.whitehouse.gov/news/releases/2004/12/20041201-4.html (accessed January 19, 2005).
58. Commission on Presidential Debates, "Debate Transcript: The Third Kerry-Bush Presidential Debate," October 13, 2004, www.debates.org/pages/trans2004d.html (accessed January 19, 2005).
59. Ibid.
60. Annenberg Public Policy Center of the University of Pennsylvania, "Kerry's Tax Ad: Literally Accurate, but Misleading," FactCheck.org, November 8, 2004, www.factcheck.org/article280.html (accessed January 19, 2005).
61. "President's Remarks at the 2004 Republican National Convention," September 2, 2004, www.whitehouse.gov/news/releases/2004/09/20040902-2.html (accessed January 19, 2005).
62. "President Holds Press Conference," November 4, 2004, www.whitehouse.gov/news/releases/2004/11/20041104-5.html (accessed January 19, 2005).
63. Andrew Taylor, "With Half-Trillion in Red Ink, U.S. Inc. Looks Bad on Paper," *CQ Weekly,* January 12, 2004, 132–137.
64. Jill Barshay, " 'Case of the Missing Revenue' Is Nation's Troubling Mystery," *CQ Weekly,* January 12, 2004, 144–147.
65. Concord Coalition, "Fiscal Policy in Campaign 2004: Electing the First President of the Senior Boom," issue brief, October 7, 2004, www.concordcoalition.org/federal_budget/041021issuebrief.pdf.
66. Suskind, *Price of Loyalty.*
67. Edmund L. Andrews, "Greenspan Warns of Deficit as Big Threat to Economy," *New York Times,* May 7, 2004, C7.
68. "President's Remarks at the 2004 Republican National Convention."

69. "Strengthening Social Security and Creating Personal Wealth for All Americans," report of the President's Commission to Strengthen Social Security, December 2001, http://csss.gov/reports/Final_report.pdf (accessed January 19, 2005).
70. Scott McClellan, White House press briefing, December 6, 2004, www.whitehouse.gov/news/releases/2004/12/20041206-6.html (accessed January 19, 2005).
71. The term is from Hargrove and Nelson, *Presidents, Politics, and Policy.*
72. Charles O. Jones, *The Presidency in a Separated System* (Washington, D.C.: Brookings Institution, 1994).
73. David Mayhew, *Divided We Govern* (New Haven: Yale University Press, 1992); Paul J. Quirk and Bruce Nesmith, "Divided Government and Policymaking: Negotiating the Laws," in Nelson, *Presidency and the Political System,* 570–594.
74. Jones, *Presidency in a Separated System.*
75. Sarah A. Binder, "Elections, Parties, and Governance," in *Congress and American Democracy: Institutions and Performance,* ed. Paul J. Quirk and Sarah A. Binder (New York: Oxford University, forthcoming).
76. Jon R. Bond and Richard Fleisher, *The President in the Legislative Arena* (Chicago: University of Chicago Press, 1990); George Edwards, *At the Margins: Presidential Leadership of Congress* (New Haven: Yale University Press, 1989); Mark Peterson, *Legislating Together* (Cambridge, Mass.: Harvard University Press, 1996).
77. See Neustadt, *Presidential Power;* Richard Neustadt, *Presidential Power and the Modern Presidents: The Politics of Leadership from Roosevelt to Reagan* (New York: Free Press, 1990). Neustadt's emphasis on the president's personal attributes has been seriously challenged since 1960, at least with respect to leadership of Congress. See the works cited in note 76.
78. Joseph Cooper and Garry Young, "Partisanship, Bipartisanship, and Crosspartisanship in Congress since the New Deal," in *Congress Reconsidered,* 6th ed., ed. Lawrence C. Dodd and Bruce I. Oppenheimer (Washington, D.C.: CQ Press, 1997), 246–273.
79. For 2004 figures, see Curtis Gans, Committee for the Study of the American Electorate, "Turnout Exceeds Optimistic Predictions," press release, January 14, 2005, http://election04.ssrc.org/research/csae_2004_final_report.pdf; and Michael P. McDonald, George Mason University, elections.gmu.edu/President_2004.htm (accessed January 19, 2005).
80. The Kerry campaign benefited from unprecedented spending by so-called 527 groups. Of the ten largest 527s, eight favored Kerry and other Democratic candidates. Combined, they raised more than $289 million. In contrast, the two Bush-leaning 527 groups in the top ten—Swift Vets and POWs for Truth and the Club for Growth—raised just $22 million. In addition to commissioning "issue advocacy" ads, these groups also sponsored aggressive voter registration and get-out-the-vote drives, efforts that succeeded in registering millions of new voters and bringing in 7 million more votes than Gore received in 2000. All financial data are from the October 1, 2004, Federal Election Commission reports, available through the Center for Responsive Politics, www.opensecrets.org/527s/527cmtes.asp?level=C&cycle=2004.
81. For a good overview of these problems, see "Effect of 'Moral Values' Voters Exaggerated, Say Analysts," *CQ Weekly,* November 12, 2004, 2688.
82. CNN.com, "Election Results: U.S. President/National/Exit Polls."
83. John Cochran, "Religious Right Lays Claim to Big Role in GOP Agenda," *CQ Weekly,* November 12, 2004, 2684.
84. Under Senate rules, reconciliation bills—in which Congress adjusts tax policy and appropriations to meet the annual budget resolution—cannot be filibustered.

As a result, they have become vehicles for adopting controversial legislation, such as Ronald Reagan's 1981 tax cuts. Senate rules also require that legislation in a reconciliation bill reduce the federal budget deficit, thus limiting the range of issues that Senate leaders can include in such a bill. They are, in effect, a means to circumvent possible filibusters, but their applicability is limited. Walter Oleszek, *Congressional Procedures and the Policy Process,* 6th ed. (Washington, D.C.: CQ Press, 2004).
85. John Crawford, "Minority's 'Tyranny' Necessitates GOP's 'Constitutional Option,' " *CQ Weekly,* November 19, 2004, 2721.
86. Oleszek, *Congressional Procedures and the Policy Process,* 246.
87. Helen Dewar and Mike Allen, "GOP May Target Use of Filibuster," *Washington Post,* December 13, 2004, A1.
88. Gary Mucciaroni and Paul J. Quirk, "Deliberations of a 'Compassionate Conservative': George W. Bush's Domestic Presidency," in *The George W. Bush Presidency: Appraisals and Prospects,* ed. Colin Campbell and Bert A. Rockman (Washington, D.C.: CQ Press, 2004).
89. "Senate Key Vote: Tax Cuts (Vote 165)," *CQ Weekly,* December 20, 2001, 3060.
90. Pew Research Center for the People and the Press, "A Year after Iraq War, Mistrust of America in Europe Ever Higher, Muslim Anger Persists," March 16, 2004, http://people-press.org/reports/display.php3?ReportID=206 (accessed December 27, 2004).
91. "President Holds Press Conference."

8

The Congress: The Structural Basis of Republican Success

Gary C. Jacobson

The outcome of 2004's fierce battle for the White House remained in doubt until election day, when a sharply polarized electorate delivered a narrow but decisive victory to President George W. Bush. In contrast, continued Republican control of the House of Representatives was never in question, regardless of what happened in the presidential race, and the Democrats had only a distant chance of winning the two additional seats they needed to take control of the Senate. In the end, the Republicans picked up three additional seats in the House and four in the Senate, leaving the GOP in firmer control of the federal government than at any time since the 1920s.

Why were the Democrats' prospects so much bleaker in their pursuit of Congress than in the race for the White House? What effect, if any, did Bush's victory have on the House and Senate results? What does the Republican victory portend for congressional politics in the 109th Congress? What are the prospects for continued Republican control beyond the 109th? These are the questions addressed in this chapter.

Table 8-1 summarizes the congressional results. The election brought little change to the House. Only seven of the 402 incumbents who sought reelection were defeated, and four of the seven were victims of a Republican gerrymander in Texas (discussed below), not of swings in voter sentiment. The party already in control held onto twenty-seven of the thirty-four open seats (those vacated by the incumbent), and two of the three that Democrats lost were also a legacy of the Texas redistricting, as was the Republican pickup of the state's new, open seat. Without the Texas remap, only eight House seats would have changed hands between the parties, an all-time low. The Senate elections saw considerably more action. Only one of the twenty-six incumbents seeking reelection lost, but he was the Democrats' Senate leader, Tom Daschle of South Dakota. Of the eight open seats, seven changed party control, and it was here that the Republicans enjoyed their greatest success.

The House: No Contest

Why was the hotly contested battle for the White House not accompanied by a similar battle for control of the House? After all, Democrats retain a small lead among the voters in party identifiers and were ahead in generic

Table 8-1 Membership Changes in the House and Senate in the 2004 Elections

	Republicans	Democrats	Independents
House of Representatives			
At the time of the 2004 elections	229	205	1
After the 2004 elections	232	202	1
Incumbents reelected	208	186	1
Incumbents defeated by challengers	2	3	
Incumbents defeated by incumbents		2	
Open seats retained	17	12	
Open seats lost	3	4	
New open seats	1		
Senate			
At the time of the 2004 elections	51	48	1
After the 2004 elections	55	44	1
Incumbents reelected	12	13	
Incumbents defeated		1	
Open seats retained	1		
Open seats lost	2	5	

Source: Compiled by the author.

House polls (those asking whether, if the election were held today, the respondent would vote for the Republican or the Democratic candidate, without mentioning the candidates' names) during the months leading up to the election.[1] The answer is simple: Republican voters are distributed more efficiently across House districts than are Democratic voters, giving the Republicans a major structural advantage in House elections. Without a strong national tide in their favor—and no national partisan tide ran in 2004—Democrats currently have no hope of winning control of the House.

The Republicans' structural advantage—their efficiency—is illustrated by the distribution of the major-party vote for president in 2000. Short-term political forces were evenly balanced that year, and party-line voting was the highest in decades, so both the national and district-level presidential votes reflected the electorate's underlying partisan balance with unusual accuracy. The Democrat, Al Gore, won the national popular vote by 540,000 of the 105 million votes cast. Yet the distribution of those votes across current House districts yields 240 in which Bush won a majority but only 195 with Gore majorities.

Part of the reason for this Republican advantage is demographic: Democrats win a disproportionate share of minority and other urban voters, who tend to be concentrated in districts with lopsided Democratic majorities.[2] But is it also the effect of a partisan gerrymander conducted by the Republicans in states where they controlled the redistricting process after the 2000 census, as Figure 8-1 indicates.[3] Although Gore received nearly 47 percent of the vote in states where Republicans were in charge of redrawing the district lines, Republican gerrymanders reduced the proportion of Gore-majority seats by twelve, from 39 percent of the total in 2000 to 30 percent in 2004. Demo-

Figure 8-1 Effects of Redistricting Control on District Partisanship, 2000–2004 (Measured by Presidential Vote)

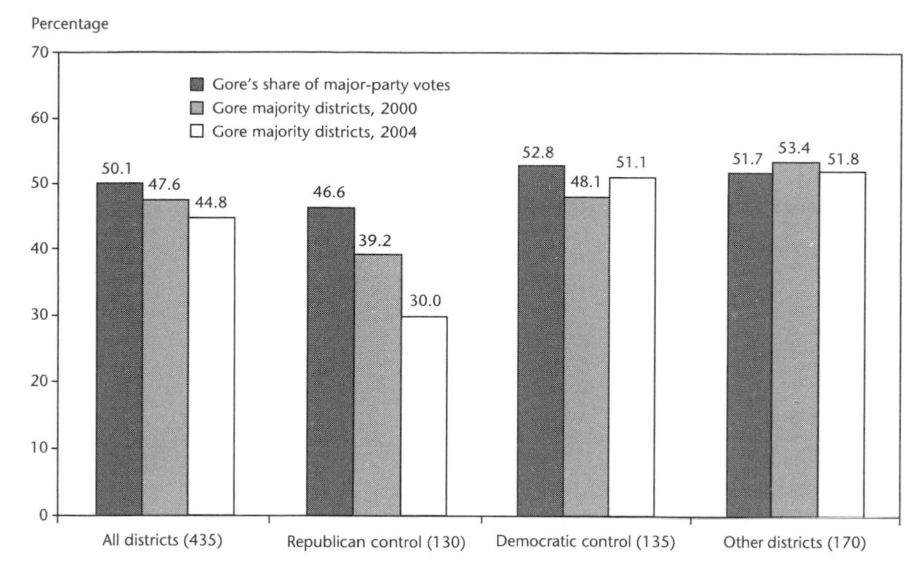

Source: Compiled by the author.

crats made small gains by this measure where they controlled the process, but they were completely offset by pro-Republican changes in states where neither party had full control. The Republican gerrymanders achieved their purpose, as Figure 8-2 demonstrates. The GOP added fifteen seats between 2000 and 2004 in states they redistricted, while losing only six elsewhere.[4]

Indeed, had it not been for the extraordinary second redistricting of Texas in 2003, Republicans would have lost House seats in 2004. Republicans won full control of the Texas state government in the 2002 elections, and at the behest of House majority leader Tom DeLay, they proposed new district lines that would thoroughly dismantle several House Democrats' districts. The effect would be to give those Democrats largely unfamiliar, more conservative constituencies; to force them to move by placing them in districts with other Democratic incumbents; or, in two cases, to pit them against incumbent Republicans in new, overwhelmingly Republican districts. With nothing in federal or Texas law standing in the Republicans' way, Democrats in the state legislature twice tried to thwart the remap by fleeing the state en masse (once to Oklahoma, once to New Mexico) to prevent action by denying legislative quorums, while avoiding arrest under a Texas statute aimed at preventing just this tactic.[5] It took five months and two special legislative sessions before the Democrats capitulated.

The Texas lawmakers did not overestimate the stakes. Prior to the 2003 redistricting, Republicans held fifteen of Texas's thirty-two House seats. After the new map was enacted, one House Democrat (Ralph T. Hall) defected to

Figure 8-2 Control of Redistricting and Change in the Distribution of House Seats, 2000–2004

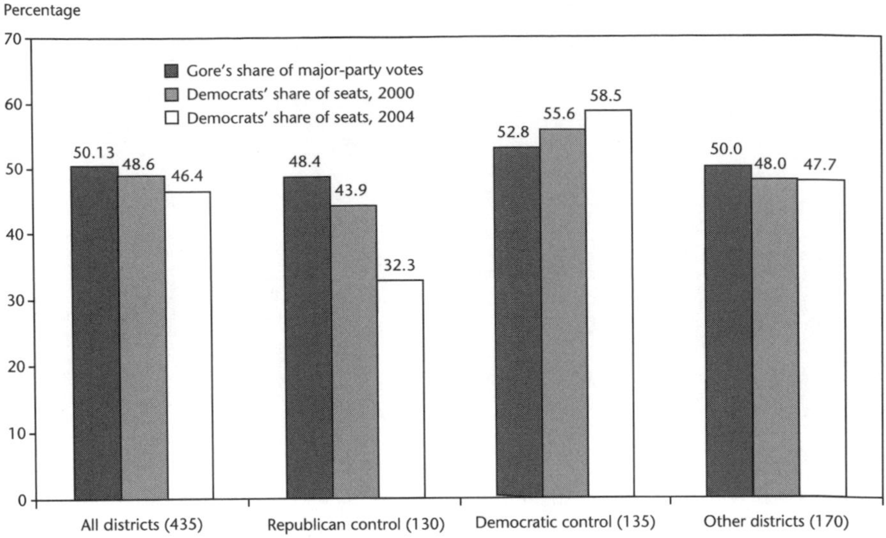

Source: Compiled by the author.

the Republican Party, another retired, another was defeated in a primary, and four were defeated in the general election. Only one targeted Democrat, Chet Edwards, managed to survive. After the 2004 election, Republicans held twenty-one of Texas's seats, their six-seat gain more than offsetting a net loss of three seats elsewhere in the country.

Aside from partisan gerrymandering, redistricting after the 2000 Census reduced the overall number of competitive House seats by strengthening marginal incumbents. Of the twenty-five districts Republicans won in 2000 with less than 55 percent of the major-party vote, eighteen were made more Republican by increasing the proportion of Bush voters; of the nineteen similarly marginal Democratic districts, fifteen were given a larger share of Gore voters. Thus three-quarters of the marginal districts in the country were made safer through redistricting, half of them by more than two percentage points (in the 2000 presidential vote share). Partly as a result, only four of the 382 incumbents seeking reelection in 2002 were defeated by challengers. (Four more lost to other incumbents in face-offs forced by redistricting.) The 2002 election also extended the long-term decline in the number of seats with a mismatch between the party of the incumbent representative and the partisan leanings of the district, as measured by its presidential vote.[6] Thus, approaching the elections of 2004, with no clear partisan tide in sight, neither party saw much opportunity to take many seats from the other, and the consequence was the lowest level of competition for House seats ever.

The dearth of competition is evident in Figure 8-3, which displays the percentage of competitive seats as defined by Congressional Quarterly in

Figure 8-3 Competitive House Elections, 1982–2004

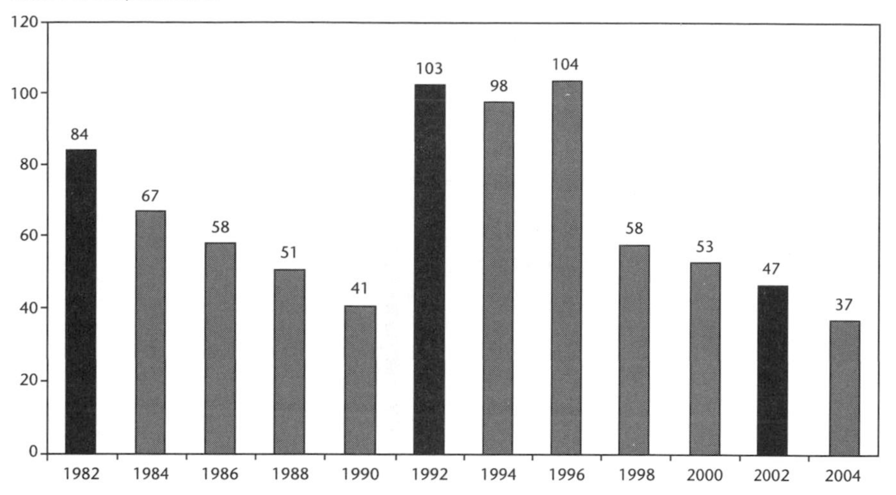

Source: Preelection issues of *CQ Weekly* for each election.

Notes: Competitive races are those classified by Congressional Quarterly as "tossups" or "leans Democrat (Republican)"; uncompetitive races are those classified as "safe" or "Democrat (Republican) favored." Black columns indicate elections following reapportionment.

October of each election year from 1982 to 2004.[7] Notice that in the 1980s and 1990s, elections that followed redistricting (1982, 1992) featured a relatively high number of competitive races, reflecting the opportunities and uncertainties created by the reshuffle of district lines. Competition then tended to diminish during the rest of the decade, as parties and candidates learned from experience where challenges were likely to be futile and gave up trying. The redistricting after the 2000 Census did not have this effect; instead, it reduced the number of competitive races. By 2004, the number of such races had fallen to the lowest in the period, thirty-seven, amounting to less than 9 percent of all House seats.

The narrow range of competition made it virtually impossible for Democrats to win the twelve seats they needed to take majority control. Their plight is illustrated by Table 8-2, based on Congressional Quarterly's late-October 2004 handicapping of the races. Republicans could keep their majority by winning all the seats where they were deemed "safe" or "favored" and just six of the eighteen seats "leaning" Republican. Democrats would have had to take all of the districts where they were favored in any way, all the "tossup" districts, and thirteen of the eighteen districts that leaned Republican in order to win a majority. As it was, the Republicans lost one and the Democrats lost two of the seats listed as "leaning" in their direction, and Democrats took six of the seven tossup races.

Congressional Quarterly bases its risk ratings on a district-by-district analysis of the candidates, the campaigns, and campaign finances. It found

Table 8-2 Competition in the 2004 House Elections

Congressional Quarterly rating	Number of seats	Cumulative total
Safe Democrat	176	176
Democrat favored	10	186
Leans Democrat	12	198
No clear favorite	7	205
Leans Republican	18	223
Republican favored	17	240
Safe Republican	195	435

Source: www.nytimes.com/packages/html/politics/2004_ELECTIONGUIDE_GRAPHIC/index_HOUSECQ.html, October 29, 2004.

Note: Of the House's 435 seats, 218 are needed for a majority; the preelection lineup was 229 Republicans, 205 Democrats, and one independent who votes with the Democrats on organizational matters.

that few districts were in play because the ingredients of a competitive race were missing in so many places, reflecting not only the scarcity of seats where local partisanship or missteps by the incumbent gave the out party hope, but also the absence of a national surge toward either party. Conditions traditionally thought to influence national electoral tides—namely, the state of the economy and the public's evaluation of the president's performance—were effectively neutral once the new, post–9/11 consideration, terrorism, was added to the mix. The economy's performance during the entire Bush administration was mediocre by historical standards, but growth accelerated in the year leading up to the election, and the economy's earlier weakness could be blamed in part on the damage done to markets by the attacks of 9/11. The net loss of jobs since Bush took office in 2001 gave Democrats something to talk about, but the modest improvements during 2004 took the edge off the issue.

President Bush's job approval ratings also fell into a politically neutral range. Although declining from the record high Bush enjoyed during the immediate post–9/11 rally, they generally remained above 50 percent until February 2004 and stayed close to that mark through the election. The relatively low performance ratings Americans gave the president on the economy were evidently offset by notably higher performance ratings on his handling of terrorism, raising the president's overall approval rating to a level that offered neither party's congressional candidates a discernible advantage, even after his handling of the Iraq war ceased to work in his favor (Figure 8-4).

More important, the *composition* of Bush's overall approval ratings promised neither party's congressional candidates any help. Bush enjoyed overwhelming support from Republicans, achieving the highest job approval ratings within his own party of any president in the more than fifty years that pollsters have been asking the question. But his approval ratings among Democratic identifiers fell steeply after the post–9/11 rally and by the beginning of 2004 had dipped below 20 percent (Figure 8-5). They fell further during the campaign, reaching the lowest point the Gallup Poll had ever

Figure 8-4 Approval of George W. Bush's Performance by Policy Domain, 2001–2004 (Monthly Averages)

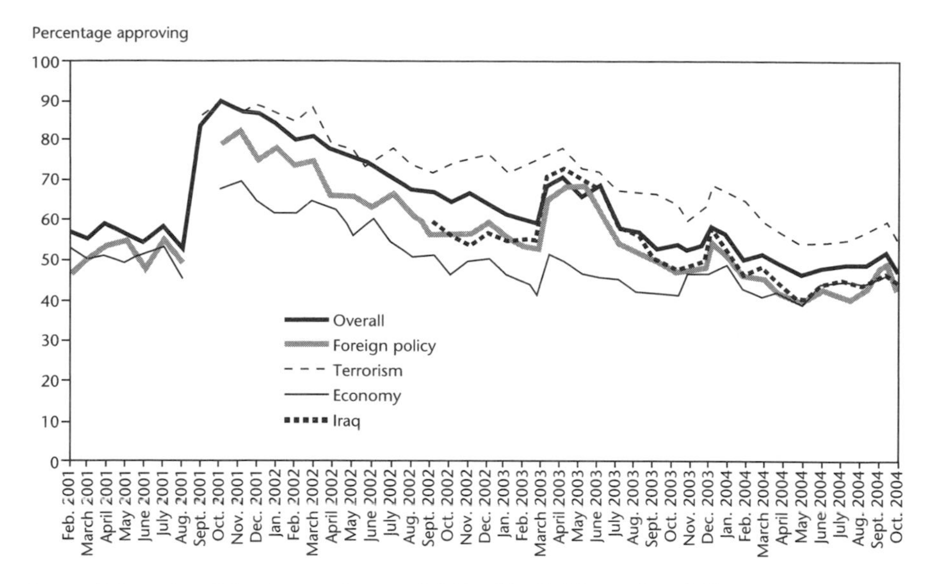

Sources: Gallup polls, available at www.gallup.com; CBS News/*New York Times* polls, available at www.cbsnews.com/sections/opinion/polls/main500160.shtml; ABC News/*Washington Post* polls, available at www.washingtonpost.com/wp-srv/politics/polls/polls.htm; and *Los Angeles Times* polls, available at www.latimes.com/news/custom/timespoll.

recorded among the rival party's identifiers—8 percent in one September 2004 poll. These partisan differences in approval of Bush were echoed in voters' responses to virtually all of the polling questions regarding which party would handle various policy issues better, as well as those about the state of the economy and the overall direction of the country.[8] In such a highly polarized atmosphere, neither party could anticipate attracting many partisan defectors on election day, further dampening prospects for taking House seats from the other side.

Without a national tide or exploitable issues, the best potential House challengers (typically, those wanting to climb to the next level in their pursuit of long-term political careers) were, as always under such conditions, reluctant to run. Their reluctance was reinforced by the knowledge that campaign contributors would be skeptical of their chances of winning and therefore unlikely to invest in their campaigns.[9] As a result, only the most vulnerable House incumbents—very few in number—attracted formidable challenges. Sixteen percent of each party's incumbents faced a challenger who had ever been elected to a public office, a number about average for Democratic incumbents but a third below the historical average for Republican incumbents. As usual, experienced challengers were heavily overrepresented in the few potential swing districts. For example, 49 percent of the incumbents in districts that were carried by the other party's presidential candidate in 2000 faced experienced challengers, compared with only 11 percent of other

Figure 8-5 Approval of George W. Bush's Performance, 2001–2004 (Monthly Averages)

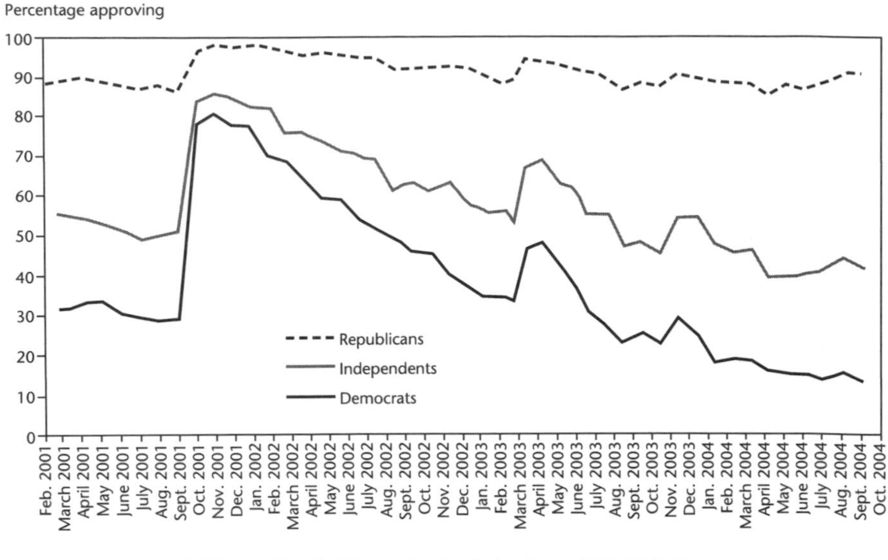

Sources: 219 Gallup and CBS News/*New York Times* polls taken during George W. Bush's first term.

incumbents. As discussed below, campaign money was also heavily concentrated in the small number of competitive districts.

In a departure from past elections, even open House seat contests were relatively quiet in 2004. Congressional Quarterly classified only eleven of the thirty-five as competitive. (In 2000 and 2002, more than half of the open seats were rated competitive.) One reason is that only nine of the open seats were in the "wrong" party's hands according to the district's 2000 presidential vote; in twenty-one open districts, the 2000 presidential vote for the candidate of the party already holding the seat exceeded 55 percent. In the end, five of the seven open seats that switched party control in 2004 went to the party with the 2000 presidential majority, as did the new, open seat in Texas, the two Texas seats where incumbents faced off, and four of the five other seats where challengers were successful. Thus, although the House elections produced relatively little change, they extended the long-term trend toward increasing district-level consistency in House and presidential voting that is documented in Figure 8-6.[10]

The Senate: The Southern Realignment Continues

The same trend toward greater consistency in voting for president and U.S. representative appeared in the 2004 Senate elections, resulting in a four-seat addition to the Republicans' Senate majority. Although Democrats had entertained some hope of adding the two seats they needed to become the majority party, their chances were slim. As Table 8-3 shows, to reach fifty-

Figure 8-6 Split House and Presidential Election Results, 1952–2004

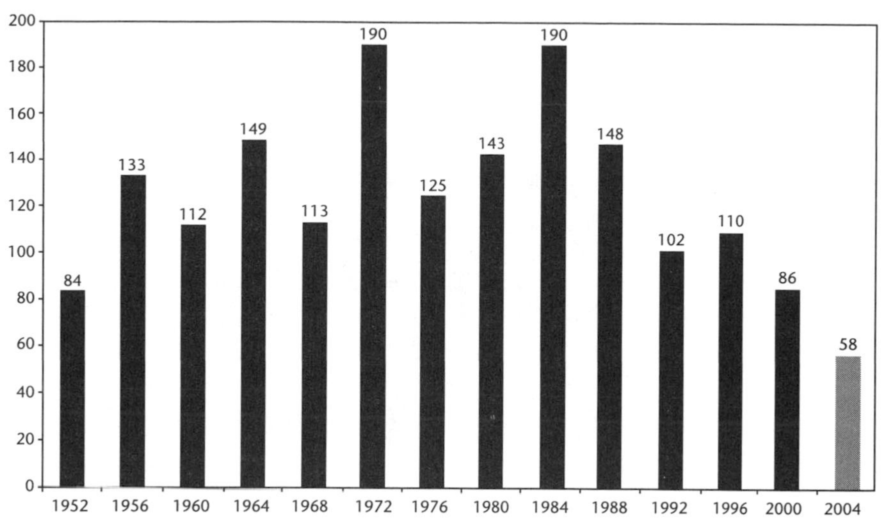

Source: Compiled by the author.

Note: The 2000 presidential vote is used for 2004 because the 2004 district-level presidential vote was not available at press time.

one seats, they would have had to win every seat where Congressional Quarterly gave them an edge and all of the seats rated tossups. Instead, Republicans won five of the six tossup races and another classified as leaning Democratic (Tom Daschle's seat). Table 8-4 shows what the Democrats were up against. Twenty-two of the thirty-four states with Senate contests in 2004 had been carried by Bush in 2000. Democrats had to defend ten seats in

Table 8-3 Competition in the 2004 Senate Elections

Congressional Quarterly rating	Number of seats	Cumulative total
Continuing Democrat	30	30
Safe Democrat	11	41
Democrat favored	3	44
Leans Democrat	1	45
No clear favorite	6	51
Leans Republican	2	53
Republican favored	3	56
Safe Republican	8	64
Continuing Republican	36	100

Source: www.nytimes.com/packages/html/politics/2004_ELECTIONGUIDE_GRAPHIC/index_SENATECQ.html, October 29, 2004.

Note: Of the Senate's 100 seats, 51 are needed for a majority; the preelection lineup was 51 Republicans, 48 Democrats, and one independent who votes with the Democrats on organizational matters.

Table 8-4 Senate Seats in Play, 2004

	States won by Bush in 2000			States won by Gore in 2000		
		Won in 2004 by			Won in 2004 by	
	Seats	Democrat	Republican	Seats	Democrat	Republican
Republican incumbent	10		10	2		2
Republican open seat	2	1	1	1	1	
Democratic open seat	5		5			
Democratic incumbent	5	4	1	9	9	
Totals	22	5	17	12	10	2

Source: Compiled by the author.

states that Bush had won, while Republicans were defending only three seats in states that Gore had won. Moreover, all five of the open Democratic seats were in the South, where support for Democrats has been ebbing for several decades.

The opportunities offered by the Senate seats up for election in 2004 attracted a much higher proportion of serious aspirants than did the House contests. Although most incumbents were spared serious challenges, at least ten faced experienced, reasonably well financed opponents, and eight ended up winning less than 60 percent of the vote. With one odd exception, the eight open seats produced heated, often lavishly financed contests between first-tier candidates. The principal contenders included eight current or former members of the House, three statewide officeholders, two former cabinet secretaries, and the heir to the Coors name and beer fortune. The exception was Illinois, where the Republican primary winner, Jack Ryan, withdrew after embarrassing revelations appeared about his first marriage. After weeks of futile searching for a viable and willing substitute, Illinois Republicans settled on Alan Keyes, a Maryland resident most noted for treating campaigns as an opportunity to rail against abortion, homosexuality, and other alleged social evils. Keyes was crushed by Barack Obama, a charismatic young Democratic state senator who won 70 percent of the vote to become the only African American in the Senate.

In the end, Republicans won all five of the open southern Democratic seats, plus Daschle's. Democrats picked up two open Republican seats with Obama's victory in Illinois and Ken Salazar's in Colorado. (Complete results for the 2004 Senate contests appear in Table 8-5.) Seven of the eight Senate seats that changed partisan hands in 2004 went to the party that won the state in the 2000 and 2004 presidential elections; Salazar's victory was the lone exception.

More generally, twenty-seven of the thirty-four Senate contests were won by the party whose presidential candidate won the state's electoral votes, tying 1964 for the highest level of congruence in president-Senate election results in the past half-century (Figure 8-7). When the 2004 winners are

Table 8-5 Senate Election Results, 2004

State	Vote total	Percentage of major-party vote
Alabama		
Wayne Sowell (D)	594,439	32.4
*Richard Shelby (R)	1,242,038	67.6
Alaska		
Tony Knowles (D)	110,699	47.8
*Lisa Murkowski (R)	121,027	52.2
Arizona		
Stuart Starky (D)	335,974	21.4
*John McCain (R)	1,234,558	78.6
Arkansas		
*Blanche Lincoln (D)	575,345	56.0
Jim Holt (R)	452,638	44.0
California		
*Barbara Boxer (D)	6,435,157	60.3
Bill Jones (R)	4,240,828	39.7
Colorado		
Ken Salazar (D)	1,041,018	52.2
Pete Coors (R)	953,677	47.8
Connecticut		
*Chris Dodd (D)	923,836	67.1
Jack Orchulli (R)	452,874	32.9
Florida		
Betty Castor (D)	3,582,280	49.4
Mel Martinez (R)	3,665,625	50.6
Georgia		
Denise Majette (D)	1,268,689	40.8
John Isakson (R)	1,839,385	59.2
Hawaii		
*Daniel Inouye (D)	313,269	78.2
Cam Cavasso (R)	87,119	21.8
Idaho		
Scott McClure (D-write in)	2,579	0.5
*Mike Crapo (R)	497,541	99.5
Illinois		
Barack Obama (D)	3,555,586	72.1
Alan Keyes (R)	1,376,044	27.9
Indiana		
*Evan Bayh (D)	1,495,808	62.3
Marvin Scott (R)	904,432	37.7
Iowa		
Arthur Small (D)	403,591	28.2
*Chuck Grassley (R)	1,026,356	71.8
Kansas		
Lee Jones (D)	307,968	28.4
*Sam Brownback (R)	777,198	71.6
Kentucky		
Daniel Mongiardo (D)	850,581	49.3
*Jim Bunning (R)	873,400	50.7
Louisiana		
(Four candidates) (D)	876,671	48.2
David Vitter (R)	942,755	51.8

(Continues)

Table 8-5 Senate Election Results, 2004 *(Continued)*

State	Vote total	Percentage of major-party vote
Maryland		
*Barbara Mikulski (D)	1,385,009	65.6
E. J. Pipkin (R)	725,898	34.4
Missouri		
Nancy Farmer (D)	1,153,422	43.2
*Kit Bond (R)	1,514,793	56.8
Nevada		
*Harry Reid (D)	490,232	63.5
Richard Ziser (R)	282,255	36.5
New Hampshire		
Doris Haddock (D)	221,011	33.7
*Judd Gregg (R)	434,392	66.3
New York		
*Charles Schumer (D)	4,423,892	74.2
Howard Mills (R)	1,539,279	25.8
North Carolina		
Erskine Bowles (D)	1,587,407	47.7
Richard Burr (R)	1,742,662	52.3
North Dakota		
*Byron Dorgan (D)	211,503	68.3
Mike Liffrig (R)	98,244	31.2
Ohio		
Eric Fingerhut (D)	1,907,852	36.1
*George Voinovich (R)	3,380,364	63.9
Oklahoma		
Brad Carson (D)	596,672	43.9
Tom Coburn (R)	763,332	56.1
Oregon		
*Ron Wyden (D)	1,072,079	66.6
Al King (R)	536,506	33.4
Pennsylvania		
Joseph Hoeffel (D)	2,296,379	44.3
*Arlen Specter (R)	2,890,791	55.7
South Carolina		
Inez Tenenbaum (D)	691,918	45.1
Jim DeMint (R)	843,884	54.9
South Dakota		
*Tom Daschle (D)	193,279	49.4
John Thune (R)	197,814	50.6
Utah		
Paul Van Dam (D)	237,415	29.6
*Bob Bennett (R)	564,260	70.4
Vermont		
*Pat Leahy (D)	212,850	74.0
John McMullen (R)	74,704	26.0
Washington		
*Patty Murray (D)	1,549,708	56.3
George Nethercutt (R)	1,204,584	43.7
Wisconsin		
*Russ Feingold (D)	1,632,562	55.6
Tim Michels (R)	1,301,305	44.4

Source: www.cnn.com/ELECTION/2004/pages/results/senate/full.list, December 8, 2004.

*Denotes incumbent.

Figure 8-7 States Won by the Same Party in Senate and Presidential Elections, 1952–2004

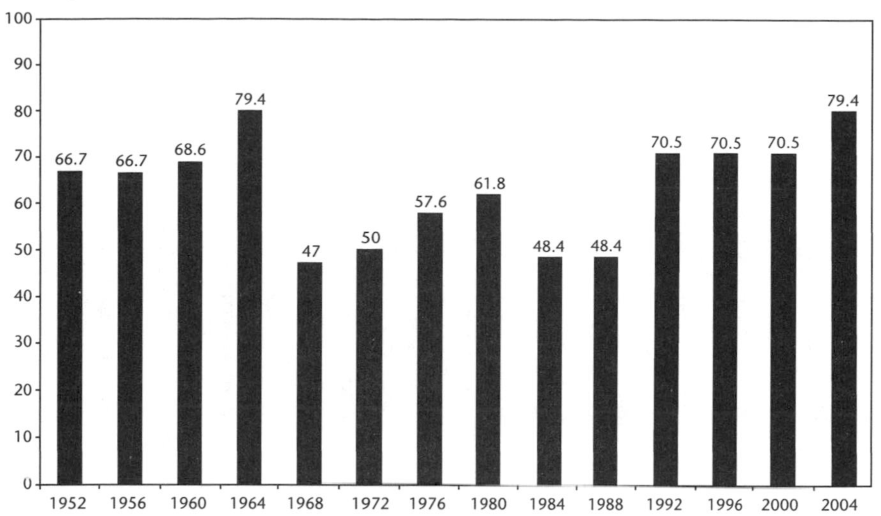

Source: Compiled by the author.

added to the continuing Senate membership, fully 75 percent of senators now represent states where their party's candidate won the most recent presidential election, the highest proportion in at least fifty years (Figure 8-8).

In both House and Senate elections, then, the trend toward increasing partisan consistency in election results continued in 2004. No doubt the national campaigns and the conditions that had shaped them had something to do with this result. With only minor exceptions, Bush spent his entire first term catering to his party's base in the corporate and small business sectors and among social conservatives and hard-line foreign policy nationalists, and he was rewarded with overwhelming support from Republican identifiers. His approach naturally alienated ordinary Democrats, who objected to the administration's policies on taxes, the environment, regulation, stem cell research, and most important, the war in Iraq. The consequences were a highly polarized electorate and high levels of party loyalty among presidential voters.[11] The 2004 congressional elections did not take place in an atmosphere conducive to heavy partisan defection or ticket splitting by voters, although the traditional incumbency advantage still produced its share. Senate incumbents typically ran well ahead of their party's presidential candidate (Republicans surpassed Bush by an average of seven percentage points; Democrats outpolled Kerry by an average of ten points). In contrast, the five Democrats defending open Senate seats in the South ran only slightly ahead of Kerry (three percentage points on average), dooming their candidacies in a region that has been moving toward the GOP.

Figure 8-8 Senate Seats Held by the Party Winning the State in the Most Recent Presidential Election, 83rd–109th Congresses

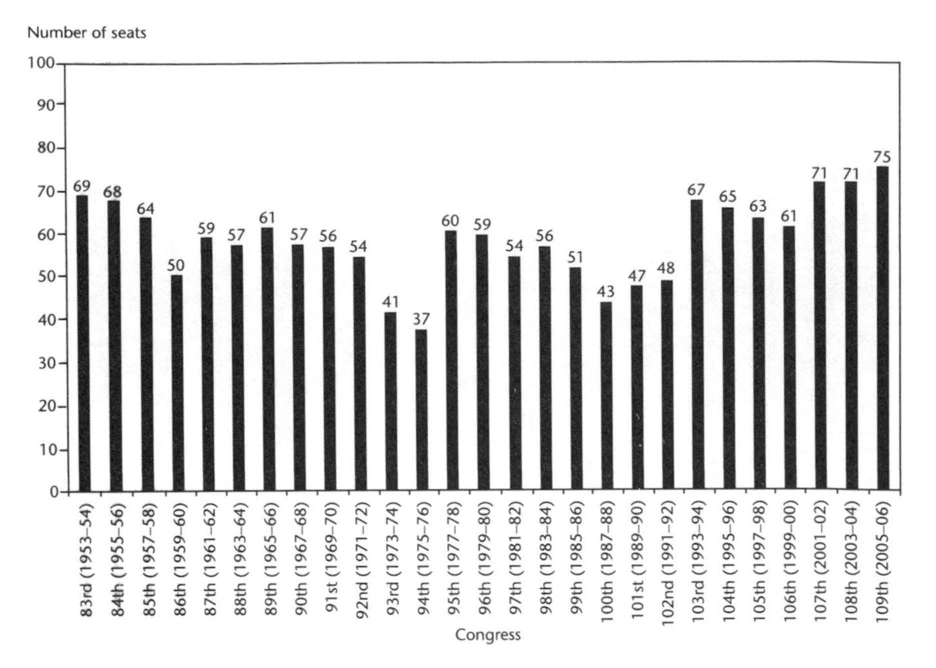

Source: Compiled by the author.

The Regional Realignment Continues

The 2004 congressional elections extended the historic reversal of the parties' areas of regional strength. Fifty years ago, the Republican Party was strongest in the Northeast, Midwest, and West Coast; Democrats dominated in the South, Plains, and Mountain West.[12] Since then, the parties have exchanged regions of dominance in contests for the presidency and both chambers of Congress (Figures 8-9 and 8-10), with the congressional results in 2004 matching the red state–blue state division of the electoral vote for president with considerable accuracy. The most extensive regional changes in party alignment have taken place in the South. As recently as 1960, all twenty-two senators from the eleven states of the old Confederacy were Democrats; after 2004, eighteen were Republicans.

Partisan Polarization Continues

Partly, but by no means entirely, because of the southern realignment in recent decades, both the House and the Senate have become increasingly polarized along partisan and ideological lines. This trend is displayed in Figures 8-11 and 8-12, which show the mean scores of House and Senate

Figure 8-9 Republicans' Share of House Seats, by Region, 1946–2004

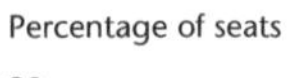

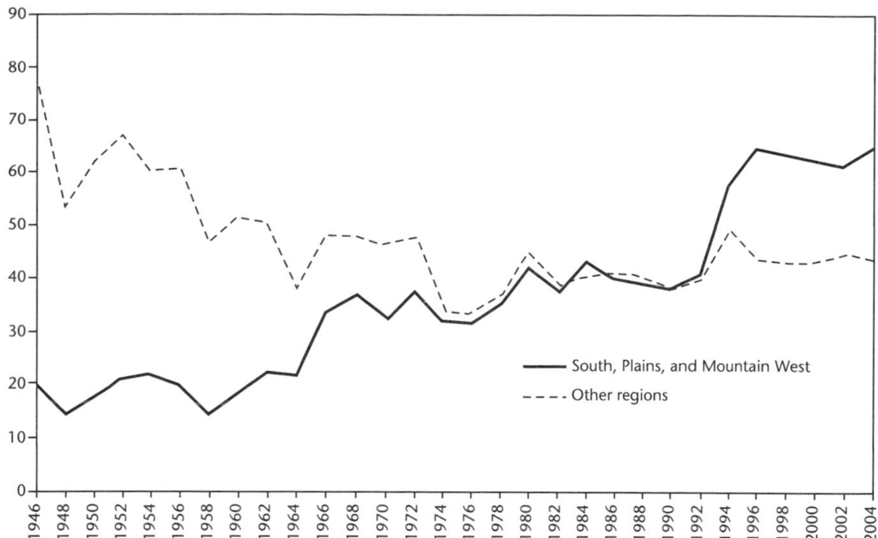

Source: Compiled by the author.

Figure 8-10 Republicans' Share of Senate Seats, by Region, 1946–2004

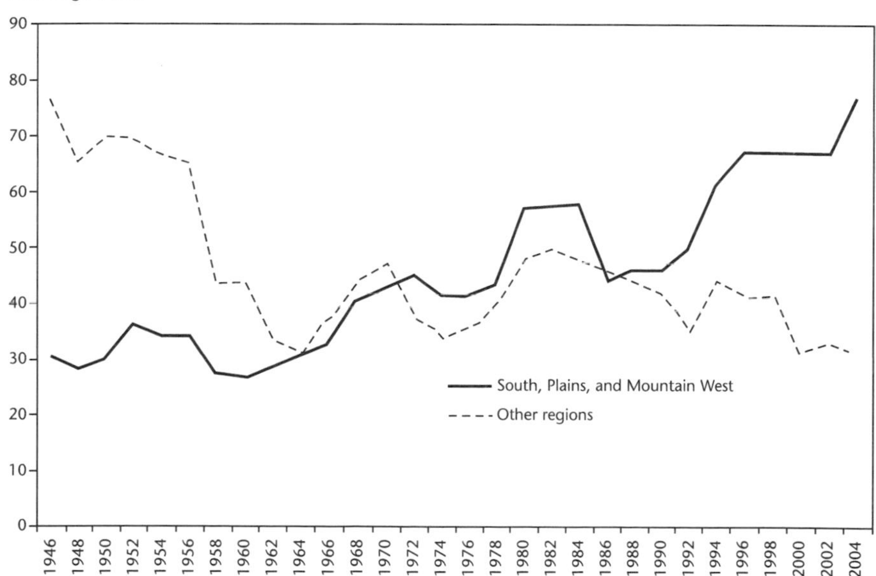

Source: Compiled by the author.

Figure 8-11 Partisan Polarization in the House of Representatives, 92nd–107th Congresses

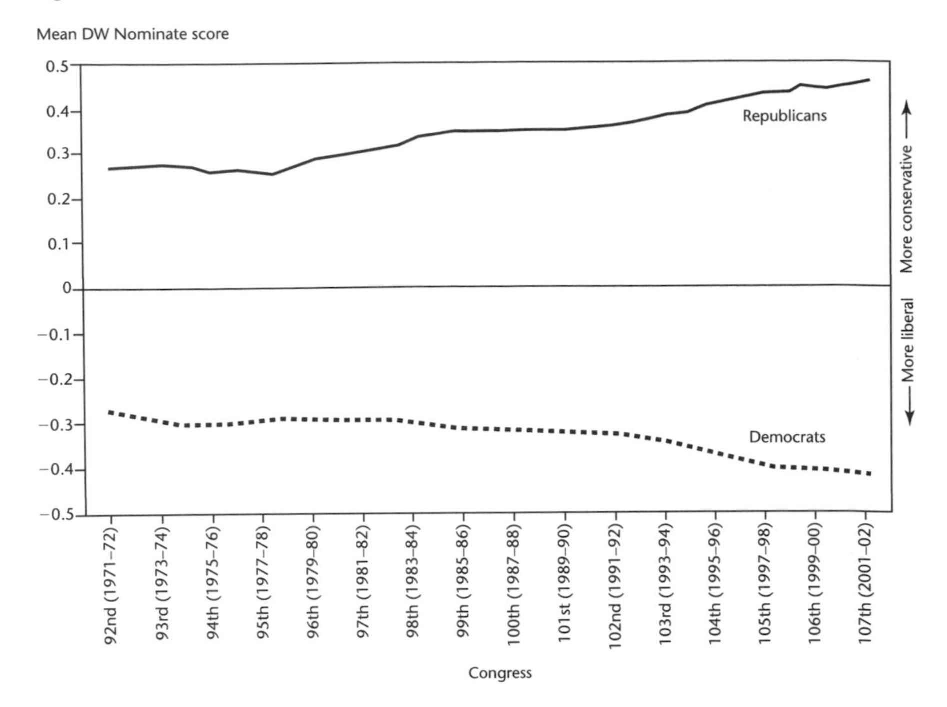

Source: Data provided by Keith T. Poole, available at http://voteview.uh.edu/dwnomin.htm, October 8, 2003.

Democrats and Republicans on Poole and Rosenthal's DW Nominate scale, a standard measure of where legislators fit ideologically. The DW Nominate scale is calculated from all the non-unanimous roll call votes cast in all congresses since the 80th (1947–1948). Because each member's pattern of roll call votes locates him or her on a liberal-conservative scale ranging from −1.0 (most liberal) to 1.0 (most conservative), we can compare the average ideological locations of Republicans and Democrats from congress to congress.[13] The parties in both chambers have, by this measure, become increasingly polarized since the 1970s. The gap between the two parties' ideological means has grown by 61 percent in the House and by 74 percent in the Senate since the 92nd Congress (1971–1972).

The turnover in congressional seats in 2004 is likely to polarize both houses even further. All six of the Senate Democrats who were replaced by Republicans were more moderate than the Democratic average, with mean DW Nominate scores for the 107th Congress (2001–2002) of −.229, compared with −.427 for the other Senate Democrats (the difference is significant at $p < .01$). Six of the newly elected Republicans, including four of the five who replaced southern Democrats, had served in the House. Four of the six had more conservative DW Nominate scores than their party's average in that body (.466); their scores were even further to the right of the Republican

Figure 8-12 Partisan Polarization in the Senate, 92nd–107th Congresses

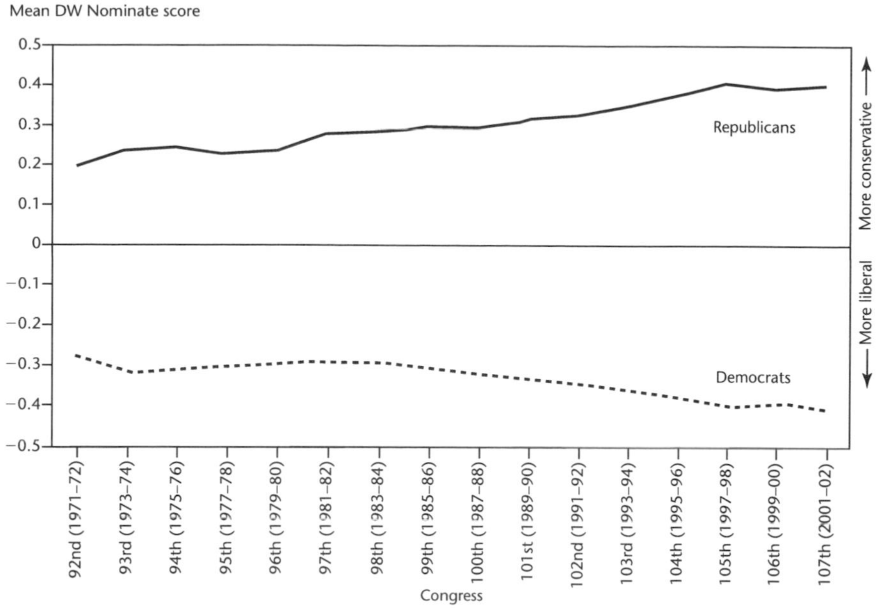

Mean DW Nominate score
0.5
0.4
0.3
0.2
0.1
0
−0.1
−0.2
−0.3
−0.4
−0.5
Republicans
Democrats
More conservative
More liberal
92nd (1971–72)
93rd (1973–74)
94th (1975–76)
95th (1977–78)
96th (1979–80)
97th (1981–82)
98th (1983–84)
99th (1985–86)
100th (1987–88)
101st (1989–90)
102nd (1991–92)
103rd (1993–94)
104th (1995–96)
105th (1997–98)
106th (1999–00)
107th (2001–02)
Congress

Source: Data provided by Keith T. Poole, available at http://voteview.uh.edu/dwnomin.htm, October 8, 2003.

Senate average (.393). Moreover, the two retiring Republican senators whose seats were won by Democrats (Peter Fitzgerald of Illinois and Ben Nighthorse Campbell of Colorado) were both to the left of their party's mean (.235 and .248, respectively, compared to .393). Thus in the Senate both parties lost moderates, and the Republican side gained strong ideologues.

The changes brought about by the House elections were similar, though the effect will be smaller because a much smaller proportion of House seats changed party hands. All five of the Texas Democrats who were pushed out by redistricting and replaced by Republicans were more moderate than their party's House mean; if we include Hall, the party switcher, the average DW Nominate score for the six departing Democrats is −.181, compared to −.410 for all other House Democrats (the difference is significant at $p < .01$). The net ideological effect of the other six party turnovers in the House, however, is likely to be neutral.

In general, then, the changes in Congress that the 2004 elections wrought are likely to further the polarizing trends documented in Figures 8-11 and 8-12. Not only did the changes in membership reinforce the trends, but the electoral bases of the parties also continued to grow more disparate. This is evident in Figure 8-13, which displays the difference in the mean presidential vote between districts represented in the House by Republicans and Democrats since 1952, and Figure 8-14, which provides comparable data for the Senate. As Figure 8-13 shows, the presidential vote gap between Republican

Figure 8-13 The Polarization of House Districts, 1952–2004

Difference in presidential vote between Republican and Democratic districts (percentage)

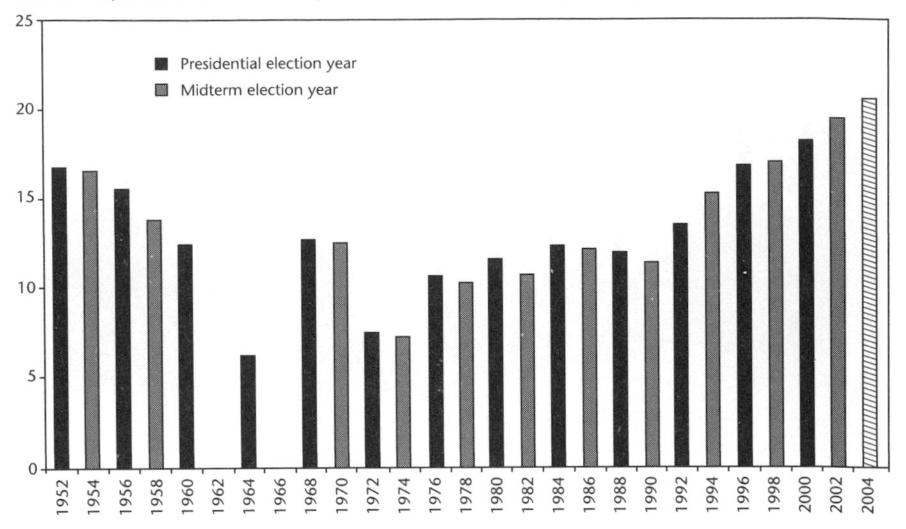

Source: Compiled by the author.

Note: Entries for midterms are from the previous presidential election; 1962 and 1966 are omitted because data for those years are not available. The entry for 2004 is based on the 2000 presidential results pending the release of district-level presidential vote data for 2004.

and Democratic House districts has more than tripled since its low point in 1964; after the 2004 election (using the 2000 presidential vote in lieu of the 2004 vote, not yet available) the gap exceeded twenty percentage points, the widest on record. The same trend appears in Figure 8-14, though the gap is of course smaller because statewide electorates tend to be considerably more heterogeneous than House district electorates. Increasingly divergent constituencies have contributed to the widening partisan divide in both the House and the Senate since the 1970s and should continue to do so in the next Congress.[14]

Money Was No Object

The 2004 elections were the first to take place under the revisions in campaign finance rules embodied in the Bipartisan Campaign Reform Act of 2002 (BCRA). Although BCRA was intended mainly to close the "soft money" loophole in party fund raising and rein in advocacy groups that had been spending unlimited and unreported sums on independent campaigns under the guise of "voter education," the act also contained provisions that had a more direct effect on congressional campaign finance. Most notably, it raised the individual contribution limit to $2,000 per candidate, per campaign (primary and general election campaigns are treated separately), doubling the limit that had been in place since 1974. BCRA also provided even higher contribution limits for donors contributing to candidates who were running against self-financed millionaires.[15]

Figure 8-14 The Polarization of States, 1952–2004 (Presidential Vote)

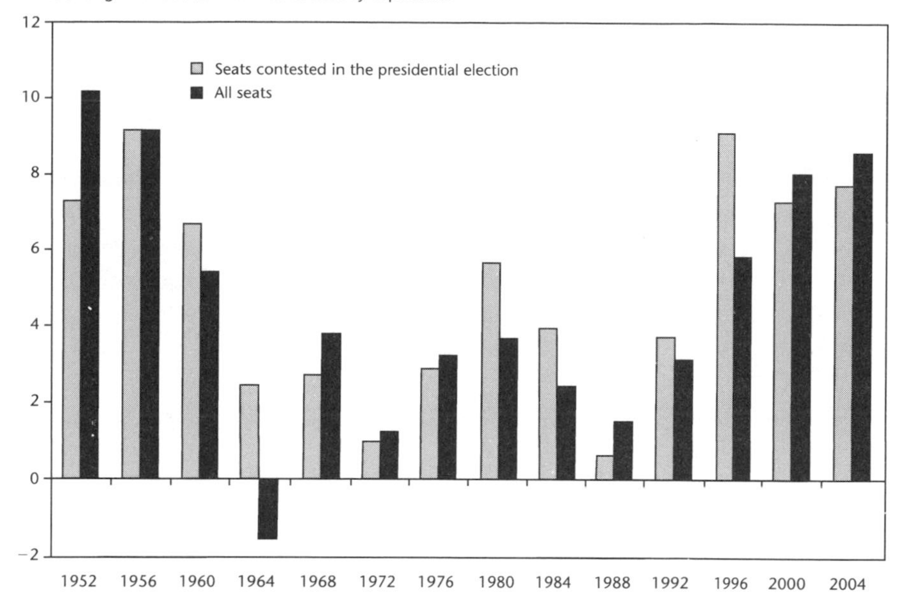

Source: Compiled by the author.

Although the final tally is not yet available, it is already clear that nothing in the BCRA inhibited the flow of money into the 2004 House and Senate campaigns. Indeed, money surged into federal elections at record rates throughout the campaign season, reflecting not only the close, intensely fought presidential election and hot contests for Senate seats but also the explosion of Internet fund raising, which sharply increased the number of individual donors. The higher individual contribution limit also evidently had an effect; by one account, nearly 12,000 donors had given the maximum ($4,000) by October 13, not far below the 15,135 who had given the maximum (then $2,000) by mid-October in 2000.[16]

As of November 22, 2004, overall contributions to House candidates were up about 13 percent over 2000 and 2002 (inflation-adjusted dollars); with so few competitive races, the candidates who did end up in tight contests were very generously financed. In thirty-one of the thirty-seven races that Congressional Quarterly identified as competitive (see Figure 8-3), both candidates spent more than $1 million, and in all but three, both spent more than $650,000. The twenty-four challengers in competitive races spent an average of more than $1.48 million, more than eight times as much as the average for the 310 challengers in less-competitive contests. As always, incumbents typically outraised their opponents by a wide margin (the ratio was about 3.8:1), but in the tightest races the balance was much more even. Most of the defeated incumbents spent more money than their opponents, but all of the successful challengers had more than enough funds to wage a full-scale campaign, none less than $1.4 million.

The tight Senate contests generated the highest totals (and biggest increases) in funding. The amount of money raised through the November reporting period in 2004 was 32 percent higher (in inflation-adjusted dollars) than it had been for the same seats in 1998 and almost as high as it was in 2000, when two abnormally expensive races distorted the average upward.[17] Candidates for open Senate seats raised a disproportionate share of the money, but plenty was also raised by safe incumbents. The most remarkable financial story took place in South Dakota. Republicans across the country targeted Senate minority leader Tom Daschle, to punish him for obstructing Bush's agenda, and Democrats nationwide rallied to his defense. Daschle's challenger, John Thune ended up spending more than $14 million, while Daschle spent more than $19 million, astonishing amounts for a state with only 502,000 registered voters. At more than $67 per voter (through the November 22 reporting date), the South Dakota Senate campaign was the most expensive in history by far. Outside groups—the national parties and ideological organizations—were also heavily involved in this contest, contributing to a level of saturation campaigning difficult to imagine unless one lived in the state. The Alaska campaigns of popular former governor Tony Knowles and Republican senator Lisa Murkowski, who had been appointed to the Senate by her father when he became governor in 2003, were also remarkably well financed on a per voter basis, with more than $11 million spent to reach an electorate of fewer than 480,000 registered voters.

A good deal of the money that flowed into these two lightly populated states, as well as into the eight states with open Senate seats, came from out of state, underlining the national significance of competitive Senate races in an era when highly polarized parties fight to control the Senate. With the national stakes so high, politically active Americans have more reason than ever to care about, and try to influence, elections far from home.

Although BCRA adjusted its contribution limits to accommodate the incumbent's nightmare of facing a multimillionaire opponent unconstrained by campaign finance laws, the track record of self-financed candidates in 2004 suggests that the fears were, at least in this election, wildly overblown. Only one of the twenty-two House and Senate candidates who spent more than $1 million of their own money won (Michael McCaul, a Texas Republican, who won an open seat without an opponent in the general election); two-thirds of them did not even win the primary and make it onto the general election ballot.[18]

Looking Forward to 2006

With firm control of Congress and the White House, Republicans are in their strongest position in Washington since 1928, when Herbert Hoover was elected president. Does this portend an era of Republican dominance of national politics? From one perspective, it does not. By several measures, the country is as evenly divided between the parties as it was in 2000. Recent Republican gains in the House have been entirely the product of redistricting, not of changes in voters' sentiments. Similarly, Republican gains in the Senate have been a consequence more of Democratic retirements and the mix of seats that happened to be up for election in 2002 and 2004 than of any general move by the electorate into the Republican camp. If there has been any shift in the distribution of party identifiers toward the Republicans during the first Bush administration, it has been small, no more than a percentage point or so.[19]

On the other hand, Republicans will continue to benefit from the structural advantage conferred by the more efficient distribution of their voters—reinforced in the House after 2000 through judicious redistricting—so that even with an edge in party identification, Democrats have little hope of retaking either chamber without the help of a strong pro-Democratic national tide. Such a tide could, however, be enough to break the Republican hold on the House. Figure 8-15, which shows the frequency distribution of Republican and Democratic House seats according to the size of Gore's share of the major-party vote in 2000, raises this possibility. The Democratic seats at the far right of the figure outnumber the Republican seats at the far left, evidence of the larger number of "wasted" Democratic voters in House elections. But the Republican seats just to the left of the fifty-fifty line outnumber the Democratic seats just to its right, indicating that, at least in theory, more Republi-

Figure 8-15 Partisan Makeup of Districts and Party Control of House Seats after the 2004 Elections

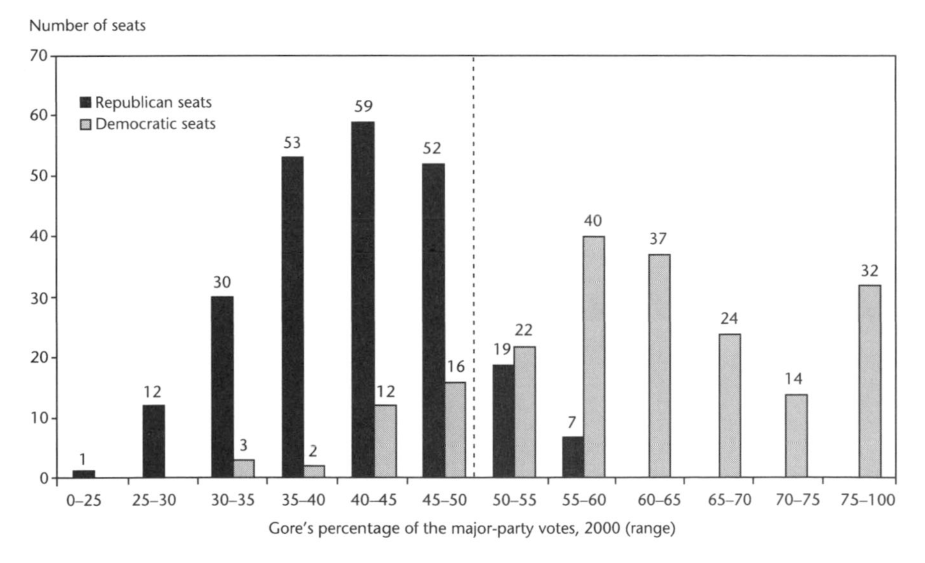

Source: Compiled by the author.

can than Democratic House seats would be vulnerable to an unfavorable national swing. Thus if national conditions—the economy's performance, Bush's standing with the public, perhaps deteriorating conditions in Iraq—were to favor the Democrats at the time of the 2006 midterm elections, they might be able to retake the House—assuming that the party recruited enough high-quality candidates with the skill and resources to take advantage of the electoral opportunities such conditions would offer.

The configuration of Senate seats that will be on the ballot in 2006 is also more favorable to the Democrats than it was in 2002 or 2004, although not sufficiently so to make a Democratic Senate majority more than a long shot, even with favorable national conditions. Sixteen of the thirty-three seats that are up in 2006 are in states that Gore and Kerry won, but only three of them are currently held by Republicans, two of whom are popular moderates, Olympia Snowe of Maine and Lincoln Chaffee of Rhode Island. Only the third, Rick Santorum of Pennsylvania, a hard-line social conservative in a state that leans Democratic, seems potentially vulnerable. Moreover, five of the seventeen seats that Democrats will be defending in 2006 are in states that Bush won in 2004 (Florida, Nebraska, New Mexico, North Dakota, and West Virginia). The Republicans' structural advantage in Senate elections will continue to stand in the way of Democrats' dreams of majority status. Again, only a strong and pro-Democratic national tide could put them in a position to retake control.

More generally, a continuation of the current era of relatively high partisan loyalty and sharp partisan polarization would appear to serve congressional Republicans well. If voters in the evenly divided electorate stick to their parties, the Republicans' structural advantage will keep them in control of Congress. The Bush administration's strategy of serving the party's base while in office and putting most of its energies into mobilizing core supporters during the campaign is, in this sense, even more productive for congressional Republicans than for the president. A partisan standoff, with both sides highly motivated and loyal to their party, assures continued Republican control of Congress.

Notes

1. For example, in the sixteen CBS News/*New York Times* Polls taken between January 2004 and the election, the Democrats' share of party identifiers averaged 53 percent; in thirty generic House polls taken between August 1 and the election, an average of 51.4 percent said they would vote for the Democrat. See www.pollingreport.com.
2. For example, according to the CBS News/*New York Times* Poll of August 20–25, 2004, Democratic identifiers outnumbered Republicans nearly five to one in New York City. See "New York City and the Republican Convention," at www.cbsnews.com/htdocs/CBSNews_polls/nyc.pdf (accessed November 6, 2004).
3. The most important of these states were Florida, Michigan, Ohio, Pennsylvania, and after 2002, Texas.

4. In 2004 in Republican-controlled states, Republicans won 90 percent of the Bush-majority districts, while Democrats won 85 percent of the Gore-majority districts; the figures for the other states are 84 percent and 88 percent, respectively.
5. DeLay sought help from federal agencies to track the missing Democrats, a move that earned him a formal admonishment from the House Ethics Committee.
6. Gary C. Jacobson, "Terror, Terrain, and Turnout: Explaining the 2002 Midterm Election," *Political Science Quarterly* 118 (Spring 2003): 1–22.
7. Congressional Quarterly classifies seats as safe Republican, Republican favored, leaning Republican, no clear favorite, leaning Democratic, Democrat favored, or safe Democratic. These classifications are usually quite accurate; in 2004, all of the seats classified as safe or favored went to the party so designated; only three of the thirty classified as leaning to a party were won by the other party. For Figure 8-3, I count seats classified as leaning to a party or tossup as competitive. For 2004, the data are from www.nytimes.com/packages/html/politics/2004_ELECTIONGUIDE_GRAPHIC/index_HOUSECQ.html; for earlier years, they are from the October election previews in the *Congressional Quarterly Weekly Report* and *CQ Weekly.*
8. See, for example, "One Year Away: The 2004 Presidential Election," CBS News Poll of November 13–20, 2003, www.cbsnews.com/sections/opinion/polls/main500160.shtml (accessed December 10, 2003).
9. Gary C. Jacobson and Samuel Kernell, *Strategy and Choice in Congressional Elections,* 2nd ed. (New Haven: Yale University Press, 1983).
10. The 2000 presidential vote is used for the 2004 observation because the 2004 district-level vote for president was not yet available.
11. According to Gallup, Bush's support among Republicans rose from 92 percent to 95 percent between his first and second elections, while his support among Democrats dropped from 10 percent to 7 percent. See Jeffrey M. Jones, "How Americans Voted," Gallup News Service, November 5, 2004, http://gallup.com/poll/content/print.aspx?ci=13957 (accessed November 7, 2004).
12. The South includes Alabama, Arkansas, Florida, Georgia, Kentucky, Louisiana, Mississippi, North Carolina, Oklahoma, South Carolina, Tennessee, Texas, and Virginia; the Plains include Kansas, Nebraska, North Dakota, and South Dakota; the Mountain West includes Alaska, Arizona, Colorado, Idaho, Montana, Nevada, New Mexico, Utah, and Wyoming. The Northeast includes Connecticut, Delaware, Maine, Maryland, Massachusetts, New Hampshire, New Jersey, New York, Pennsylvania, Rhode Island, and Vermont; the Midwest includes Illinois, Indiana, Iowa, Michigan, Minnesota, Missouri, Ohio, West Virginia, and Wisconsin; the West Coast includes California, Hawaii, Oregon, and Washington. I have placed Alaska in the Mountain West because it has far more in common—geographically, culturally, and politically—with the mountain states than with the West Coast states.
13. Nolan M. McCarty, Keith T. Poole, and Howard Rosenthal, *Income Redistribution and the Realignment of American Politics* (Washington, D.C.: American Enterprise Institute, 1997); DW Nominate is an updated version of their D-Nominate measure; I am obliged to Keith Poole for providing these data, which may be found at http://voteview.uh.edu/dwnomin.htm (accessed October 8, 2003).
14. Gary C. Jacobson, "Partisan Polarization in Presidential Support: The Electoral Connection," *Congress and the Presidency* 30 (Spring 2003): 1:36.
15. For a summary of BCRA, see /www.cfinst.org/eguide/update/bcra.html (accessed March 9, 2004).
16. Center for Responsive Politics, " '04 Elections Expected to Cost $4 Billion," press release, October 21, 2004, at www.opensecrets.org/pressreleases/2004/04spending.asp (accessed December 9, 2004).

17. In 2000, self-financed Democrat Jon Corzine had put $63 million into his New Jersey campaign, and the combined receipts for New York candidates Hillary Rodham Clinton and Rick Lazio approached $70 million.
18. Center for Responsive Politics, "2004 Election Outcome: Money Wins," at www.opensecrets.org/pressreleases/04results.asp (accessed November 20, 2004).
19. The National Annenberg Election Study's huge samples of registered voters (44,877 in 2000 and 67,777 in 2004) showed the Democrats with 53.0 percent of major-party identifiers in 2000 and 52.1 percent in 2004; see Adam Clymer, "Party Identification Shifts toward Republicans, but Democrats Still Lead, Annenberg Data Show," www.annenbergpublicpolicycenter.org/naes/2004_03_party-id_11-19_pr.pdf (accessed November 20, 2004). The sixteen CBS News/*New York Times* Polls for January–October 2004 put the Democrats' share at 52.8 percent, compared to 54.8 percent in 2000; but in those polls the Democrats' share of identifiers had been even smaller in 1989 and 1995.

9

The Meaning of the Election: Ownership and Citizenship in American Life

Wilson Carey McWilliams

Once again, as John Zogby recognized, there were intimations of Armageddon in American politics.[1] Interest ran high in 2004, with a high percentage of voters saying the election mattered "a great deal" to them. Voters were also intensely partisan, most having settled on their choice by July.[2] In 2000, George W. Bush offered himself as a "uniter, not a divider." Yet as president, Bush—presented after 9/11 with a remarkably unified country, with patriotism grandly ascendant—pursued an ideological and partisan agenda. When he appealed to the memory of 2001 during the campaign, E. J. Dionne observed, "Bush only underscored how divided we have become." [3]

David Brooks thought the "presidency wars" could be attributed to "hatred" of Bush, but hatred was evident on both sides.[4] Rhetoric turned startlingly apocalyptic, with many conservative Christians speaking of the country as "on the verge of self-destruction" or likening the election to the eve of the Civil War, while on the left, Michael Moore's *Fahrenheit 911* stopped just short of accusing the president of being an agent of Saudi Arabia.[5]

Of course, much of this thunder can be discounted as the routine excess of democratic politics. Taken literally, for example, Theodore Roosevelt's assertion that his followers in 1912 were standing "at Armageddon" implied the unlikely proposition that William Howard Taft was the Antichrist. As Samuel Popkin observes, polarization—notable enough among political elites—is not so great among the people at large.[6] Compared with the election of 2000, moreover, American institutions worked fairly well in 2004. There were grumbles, more or less well founded, about unreliable voting machines and Republican efforts to suppress minority voting, but the election produced a clear majority (although the shift of about 60,000 votes in Ohio would have had the deliciously ironic result of handing the Democrats a victory in the Electoral College).

After the election, most voters were optimistic, and it would be possible to say that the system "worked." In another sense, however, it did not work at all: most postelection respondents were also sure that George W. Bush would divide America.[7] As Harry Boyte commented, "If you think of democracy as elections and voting, then this is a great moment. If you think of democracy as a way of life, it's very uncertain what the result is going to be." [8]

G. K. Chesterton claimed that American idealism was caught up in the "romance" of the citizen. In that sense, the election of 2004 was a lovers' quarrel, marked not only by a clash of interests and ideals between citizens, but by a struggle for citizenship itself, an effort to preserve the romance—fumbling, to be sure, halfhearted and less than half articulate, but often edged with a not-so-quiet desperation and worry for democracy's future.[9]

Flawed Politics: The Candidates

In many ways the election results were simply a replay of 2000, with Ohio replacing Florida as the pivotal state. There was a small but decisive shift to Bush across the country, with the president making notable gains in the "blue" states and among women and Hispanics, while Democrats took cold comfort in their gains among young voters and Asian Americans.[10] It was probably decisive that, with relatively high levels of voting, the GOP won the turnout war in the trenches, as it had at midterm in 2002. Democrats did well, but not well enough to overcome the Republicans' "grass roots army." [11]

Democrats were shocked by the outcome, astonished at the showing of a president whose approval ratings were remarkably low and whom, his dealing with terrorism aside, voters faulted on almost every issue.[12] Even Bush's friendly critics, after all, were apt to concede his limitations in the executive office. Richard Brookhiser noted his inability to theorize and his relative lack of imagination and curiosity: "Bush thinks in prose," Brookhiser wrote. "Can he hear music?" [13] Others questioned the president's attention to detail and his disposition to work or, noting his distaste for conflict or dissent, commented on the extent to which Bush works in a "bubble." Still others voiced persistent doubts—fueled by the president's insistence that Dick Cheney join him when he testified to the 9/11 Commission—that Bush is really in charge of his administration.[14]

As a candidate, however, Bush has many virtues. He enjoys campaigning and the encounters with crowds, with whom he is oddly artful, with what William Kristol calls "a certain understanding of what arguments will work with the American people." [15] In his campaign mode, Bush tends to embrace the center, often rather emphatically. His practice as president is quite another thing, especially when policies involve costs. (Marvin Olasky, the architect of "compassionate conservatism," gave Bush an A for "message" but an F for "follow through," a charge also leveled with respect to the limited funding of Bush's No Child Left Behind Act.)[16] But this approach has its own shrewdness, since it allows Bush to suggest that voters can have "values" without paying for them. And in any case, Bush's appeal does not lie in his policies, which have often, even regularly, been disapproved by popular majorities.[17]

In fact, at least one of Bush's weaknesses as a policymaker—his tendency to prefer boldness to the point of being rash and perseverance to the point of being pigheaded—contributes to the perception that he is a strong leader, very likely his greatest political asset.[18] Bush often falls short as a political educator; convinced of the rightness of his goal, he seems to believe that the reasons for his policy are less important than the ends it is intended to serve, as in the ever-changing rationales for his tax cuts.[19] Although Bush's policies show a great many changes of front, the administration tries hard to protect its politically invaluable appearance of unswerving moral determination.[20]

For millions of Americans, Bush's oratorical faults—his labored delivery, his petulant demeanor, his near-whine—give his performances, all highly scripted, a presumptive sincerity, leaving the impression that the president is a straight shooter, a regular, stand-up guy.[21] In all likelihood, Bush is just as sincere as he is thought to be. In Robert Dallek's judgment, Bush spins and exaggerates but does not literally lie; rather, he has the gift for talking himself into believing whatever will persuade. For example, he was almost surely convinced that Iraq had weapons of mass destruction.[22]

Conservative Christians were not alone in admiring Bush's personal story, his triumph over alcohol, his life sustained by God.[23] Probably a decisive number of Americans were attracted by Bush as Everyman, the champion of "common sense" as opposed to experts and baffling data, a man who is game and self-reliant, tenacious in defending his dignity and the country's.[24] "No president," Frank Rich wrote, "has worked harder than George W. Bush to tell his story as a spectacle, much of it fictional, to rivet his constituents while casting himself in an unfailingly heroic light." [25]

By contrast, John Kerry's weaknesses as a candidate were almost all evident from the beginning. He has little charm, less humor, and virtually no common touch (among other things, he even managed to mangle the names of players on the Boston Red Sox—for a Massachusetts politician, almost the unforgivable sin). His rhetoric is somber and stentorian, and in the presidential debates even one of Kerry's virtues, his ramrod posture, seemed to emphasize his stiffness.

On the eve of the primaries, Kerry's candidacy seemed a lost cause.[26] His nomination resulted from the zeal of Democratic voters to beat Bush and the flaws of Kerry's Democratic rivals, not from any devotion to Kerry himself. The belief that Kerry was "electable" was rooted in the perception of voters in Iowa—correct, but just barely—that Kerry was more likely to win than Howard Dean.[27] It more or less epitomized the Kerry campaign that a group called "Kerry Haters for Kerry" urged us, on the Web, to "vote for him before you vote against him." [28]

Kerry's campaign, moreover, was sadly flawed, partly because his staff was a work in progress until late in the season.[29] Through the convention, Kerry's theme was overwhelmingly "positive," apparently relying on survey data that show popular distaste for "attack ads" and other forms of "negative" campaigning. But such responses reflect the voters in their public-spirited mood, in which they dislike negative campaigning and think it bad for the country. As private individuals, however, they are apt to remember and respond to it.[30] To the end the Kerry campaign ran relatively few attack ads; meanwhile, Bush's advertising was almost entirely devoted to a largely successful effort to define Kerry in an unflattering way.[31]

It didn't help that so much of Kerry's positive message, especially at the Democratic Convention, was a monotone on his decades-ago service in Vietnam. In the primaries, this approach had been more-or-less effective; it let Kerry showcase his leadership and courage, and because he had eventually become a leader in the antiwar movement, it did not alienate Democratic doves. But it underrated the perennial ambivalence of democratic peoples toward heroes, who make us look bad by comparison—consider Shakespeare's *Coriolanus,* in which the Roman people insist that the hero show his wounds as an implicit mark of their own supremacy—a sentiment that is especially true of those who served in the Vietnam era, when so many Americans sought to avoid service altogether. Bush's modest and ambiguous term in the National Guard was a more comfortable expression of patriotism. In any case, the Kerry campaign ruinously underestimated the damage done by—and the ready audience for—the almost entirely false attacks on his war record by the Swift Boat Veterans for Truth.[32]

The upshot of the Republican attacks and Kerry's own deficiencies was that he did not seem strong or trustworthy. Republicans successfully portrayed Kerry as a "flip-flopper" who tells voters what they want to hear, drawing on the labyrinthine complexities of Kerry's record in the Senate and his gift for the unfortunate phrase, most notoriously his comment that he had "voted for" funding for the wars in Iraq and Afghanistan "before I voted against it." [33] Kerry did well in the debates, winning all three by the public's reckoning, but that success underscored his intelligence, not his moral qualities, and it was the latter that the Republicans had made the issue.[34] In fact, as devoted a Republican as Lyn Nofziger concluded that the election was not so much an endorsement of Bush as an expression of distrust in Kerry.[35]

It did not help that Kerry was relentlessly cautious, or that his campaign had no signature issue.[36] In many cases, his trimming played into the portrait of him that Republicans were painting. For example, Kerry did not own up to the costs of his promised programs much more than Bush did his, and his effort to speak to popular anxieties about globalization—pretty much limited to an attack on "unfair trading practices"—sounded hollow, especially coming from a devoted internationalist who had voted to give "fast track" negotiating authority to every president and to extend trading rights to China.[37] Like many politicians, Kerry construed appealing to the center as positioning himself somewhere between more coherent alternatives, a stance that is almost certain to seem unprincipled and uninspiring.[38] By contrast, Sen. John McCain (and Bill Clinton, from time to time) claimed a place in the center by alternately adopting fairly strong positions from left and right, a stance that seems to suggest both independence of mind and "large ideas." [39] And, less eloquently, that was the voice that President Bush adopted on the campaign trail; his conduct in the White House is quite another matter.

Flawed Politics: Parties and Public

In the aftermath of the election, Karl Rove had every reason to think that the results signaled the success of his design to make Bush the analogue of William McKinley, who—at least in Rove's reading—broke the partisan deadlock at the end of the nineteenth century and built a durable Republican majority.[40] Some obvious parallels exist between the two presidents: McKinley and Bush are alike in their personal piety and reliance on divine guidance, the sort of "virgin innocence" that attracted Marc Hanna to McKinley. Both, too, lean heavily on the support of the upper class; both became involved in an easily won imperial war, followed by a prolonged and messy insurrection.[41] Democrats in 2004 were left complaining, like Ignatius Donnelly in 1896, that "the bankrupt millions voted to keep the yoke on their own necks." [42]

On the other hand, McKinley had a real war record. Moreover, apart from McKinley's home state, Ohio, Bush's coalition in 2004 rested on precisely the base—the South and the prairie and mountain states—that were the home turf of the Democratic candidate, William Jennings Bryan, in 1896 and 1900. Most important, it was Bryan, not the mainstream McKinley, who stirred evangelical fervor. At the turn of the last century militant Protestants were apt to see the connections between Christ's suffering and the pain of working Americans, or between Roman power and economic oligarchy, a fact which points to at least one educational opportunity for Democrats.[43]

Democrats, however, may be tempted to play a waiting game instead. The Republicans, triumphant, are sure to pursue an ambitious agenda, hoping to advance "market-based policies," and they may easily overreach, inasmuch as a good many items on the party's wish list are not popular with the broader public.[44] Moreover, Bush will have to deal with the tension between a small-government tax strategy and big-government ambitions, mirrored in the intraparty conflict among libertarians, social conservatives, and neoconservatives devoted to the ideal of "national greatness." These conflicts can be expected to be especially sharp because the administration will be an increasingly lame duck, with no clear heir apparent.[45]

Fundamentally, however, Democrats will have to come to terms with the fact that the New Deal coalition, as a majority, has finally played itself out. Donald Green and Eric Schickler argued, after the election of 2002, that the old coalition was still in place outside the South and that the Republicans had won only because national security issues so dominated public thinking. But those two exceptions tower: there are a lot of congressional seats and electoral votes in the South, and national security issues are not likely to subside any time soon.[46] More important still, as Paul Krugman describes, is the unraveling, in economic life, of the political culture of equality, the New Deal's grandest legacy.[47] Memories thin rapidly in America: In 2004, ads calling Kerry a "McGovern liberal" fell relatively flat, as did ads proclaiming that Bush had the worst employment record since Hoover, because too few voters felt any strong association with those names.

It has been sixty years since Franklin Roosevelt died, and a whole generation has grown up since Ronald Reagan left office: Democrats need to look beyond the shelter of "the shadow of FDR." [48]

The Democratic need to rebuild a partisan majority touches a larger lesson: the liberal-left is facing Tocqueville's grand truth, that majorities really are sovereign in American democracy and that any successful politics must, in the not-very-long run, be majoritarian. "Politics by other means," as described by Benjamin Ginsberg and Martin Shefter, is showing its limits, especially with the courts increasingly in conservative hands, and it soon will be not just desirable, but necessary, to return to a broader, deliberative and electoral, understanding of citizenship.[49]

As Robert Putnam argues, America urgently needs to rebuild citizenship's foundations in voice and association.[50] Democratic politics is an acquired taste, a habit and art learned largely in the context of community, through the pleasures of civic friendship and the gratifications of having a say, however small, in how one is governed. Less and less in our national life cultivates those sensibilities: in the schools, for example, civic education has been on the decline since the 1970s.[51] By itself, cyberspace isolates, and volunteering, always sporadic and episodic, has been tending downward since 1989.[52]

The public more and more resembles Walter Lippmann's "phantom." [53] With the proliferation of cable television channels and alternative media, "audience segmentation" is increasingly the rule.[54] An increased number of Americans watch little or no news, widening the "knowledge gap." Moreover, the highly informed are likely to follow specialized and partisan sources, engaging in what James Gimpel calls "voluntary political segregation." [55] It is one of the more benign developments that so many young Americans get their news from *The Daily Show;* that they are also more inclined to rely on the Internet may be less encouraging.[56] Reporting the news, Anne Applebaum writes, is reverting to a "more combative, pre-television norm" of partisanship, especially because the Internet (witness the *Drudge Report*) is not governed by the minimal norms of civility that govern the broadcast networks.[57]

Citizenship as an encounter with different views is yielding to an echo chamber of the like-minded, with a resulting decline in appreciation for—or even, awareness of—the attitudes of others.[58] As Robin Toner observes, among viewers of the 2004 Super Bowl, about as close to a civic event as we have, the display of Janet Jackson's breast evoked outrage and controversy, whereas it might have gone unnoticed on *Sex and the City.*[59] And the increasing fragmentation of the audience leaves public opinion disorganized and incoherent, uncertain about the connections between values and policy, and more than ever dependent on the way issues are framed by the media.[60]

It is no surprise that most citizens tend to find democratic debate by turns boring, infuriating, and incomprehensible.[61] This is true much of the time even for aficionados and for democratic deliberation at its best, and contemporary political speech, shaped to audiences schooled by the media, is predictably scripted, repetitive, and opaque, a prescription for disinterest.[62]

As both parties recognized in 2004, this election reaffirmed the effectiveness of personal contact or face-to-face association: apart from mobilizing voters, door-to-door campaigning, with "the opportunity to have a conversation" had a chance of changing a few minds, even with the campaign's partisan temper.[63] Despite declining membership, labor unions worked effectively for the Democrats, especially through the "Working America" initiative, which sought to educate three-quarters of a million "associate members" on economic issues, while Republicans made powerful use of conservative churches and the pseudoassociation of talk radio.[64]

Needing as they do to change the direction the political wind blows, Democrats have a special need to reconnect to the grass roots, ideally in living rooms and neighborhood gathering places where discussion can be fuller, and preferably in the less-suspect and more open-ended periods between elections.[65] As Howard Dean's campaign recognized, the Internet can be a first step toward association. People make connections over the Internet, Robert Putnam comments, "but what they really want is not just the cyberfriend but a real connection." [66] But the Internet, by itself, bids to increase the influence of the middle-class, liberal whites who use it most, rather than to broaden the party's base.[67]

Thomas Jefferson's encounter with the associational strength of the New England towns—"I felt the foundations of government shaken under my feet"—helped make him an evangelist for local political organization.[68] Breath-holding would be ill-advised, but perhaps the elections of 2004 will be earthquake enough to send Democrats back to the trenches to refurbish their credentials as "the party of the people who have been left out." [69]

Vulnerabilities, Foreign and Domestic

"The fact is that if you think we are safer," David Brooks wrote, "you probably voted for Bush. If you think we are less safe, you probably voted for Kerry." [70] Just as Brooks suggests, the desire to be safe from terrorism was a major, even the decisive, source of support for Bush. Yet for all their horrors, memories of the 2001 attacks and the dread of new assaults in the future were only symptomatic: in contemporary America, vulnerability is protean and pervasive. The United States is an intricately interdependent society, where minor failures or small applications of force at critical points can do vastly disproportionate damage. Moreover, terrorism itself simply gives dramatic, lethal focus to America's long evolution from autarchy to interdependence, the now-precipitate decline of the local and the private, and with it, the attenuation of voice and democratic self-government.[71] Shocking as they were, the September 11 attacks were in another way oddly familiar, the realization of a decade and more of films built around terrorist plots and alien invasions. The growing sense that we are penetrated by alien forces has become, as Paul Cantor demonstrates in his book *Gilligan Unbound*, a motif of American popular culture, reflecting the feelings of "disordering powerlessness" that the late

Michael Rogin described in 1992 as the "paranoid position" of an alarming number of Americans.[72]

Despite the president's improved showing in the "blue" states, much of it probably born of concerns about terrorism, one is bound to be struck by the fact that in the places that have suffered, or are more likely to experience, Al Qaeda attacks, majorities went for Kerry. By contrast, Dale Maharidge found anxiety and anger running high in rust belt cities that are very unlikely to be targets of international terrorism: The danger those citizens feel and resent is general and subtle, woven in the fabric of American life.[73]

Immigrants and products come into the United States, while jobs (and increasingly, middle-class jobs) go out; whole industries disappear; and localities and cultures are shaken and reordered by technology and the information revolution. International terrorists are not our only worry: the first great terrorist attack was inflicted on Oklahoma City in 1995 by people who look like most of us.[74] Political space has become ambiguous, with boundaries less secure and less reliable in demarcating friends and enemies. This is true not only of the nation but of the home, where television, that old invader, seems relatively benign compared to the Internet, with its cargo of pornographers and pedophiles and the risk that identity itself may be stolen. It makes matters worse that most of these developments also bring benefits that we enjoy, for that makes us accomplices in the threats that trouble us.

Evidently, great numbers of voters in 2004—probably a plurality and perhaps all of us to some degree—were looking for leaders who radiate strength and the old "masculine" virtues. (After all, California, among the bluest of the blue states, made Arnold Schwarzenegger its governor in 2003.) The desire for someone who can take charge has obvious dangers, but it also reflects the hope that human virtue can sway events, an expression, however elemental, of the aspiration for self-government.

In one way or another, the international aspects of security preoccupied us during the election. For Bush's presidency, 9/11 was a transforming event.[75] Previously the administration's hand in foreign policy had been anything but sure.[76] In 2000, candidate Bush had criticized "nation-building" and insisted that any such ventures by the United States must include a clear "exit strategy." This hesitant disposition also showed early in 2001, when the administration took an accommodating, even apologetic, stance toward China, which was detaining the flight crew of a crashed American spy plane.[77] After the 9/11 terrorist attacks on the United States, however, the president's splendid use of the symbolic aspects of the presidency established his continuing image as a strong leader, just as the attacks moved or enabled Bush to pursue an aggressive, even imperial policy.[78]

There are any number of critics of Bush's embrace of preventive war and his Wilsonian desire to spread democracy, but the fundamental defects of Bush's leadership are clear on the president's own terms.[79] He combines bold initiatives and a grand vision with a persistent tendency to underestimate their costs in money and troops—"cut-price colonization," Niall

Ferguson called it.[80] American policy, consequently, seems founded on a kind of wishful thinking.[81]

This pattern is certainly clear in Iraq, where the administration—discerning a grand opportunity for a regime change that might reshape politics in the Middle East—was overeager to credit any supposed justification for war (from weapons of mass destruction to the virtually manufactured link between Saddam Hussein and Al Qaeda), exaggerated Iraqis' support for a U.S. invasion, minimized the need for postwar planning, and pursued a "war on the cheap" that left a dangerous amount of room for a recovering insurgency.[82]

Foreign policy professionals were increasingly outraged by this approach, including a surprising amount of dissent in the military and something close to open hostility in the CIA.[83] But criticism from these circles was, in its own way, an element of political strength for Bush, reinforcing his image as the vindicator of common sense against the experts, the voice of the "second tier" of American politics.[84]

Moreover, despite the obvious differences between the neoisolationist Bush of 2000 and the post–9/11 "war president," an element of consistency united the two positions, the emphasis on unilateralism. In both campaigns Bush stressed America's right to decline supposed international obligations. In 2004, for example, the president and his party were quick to seize on Kerry's unfortunate reference to a "global test," suggesting that it implied giving other nations a veto over American policy. In other words, Bush championed the efficacy of political will, or at least juridical sovereignty—resistance to being ruled by others or by events—which was politically potent, whatever its deficiencies as policy. It allowed Bush to stand against globalization in relation to government while embracing its transformations of economic and social life, a position that an opponent less internationalist than John Kerry might have described as defending the form and surrendering the substance of self-rule.

At any rate, a considerable majority of Americans were initially convinced that the war in Iraq—for most, a distant, cinematic event—would make the United States safer.[85] By mid-2004, however, some 50 percent were saying that the war was "not worth fighting." Yet for decisive elements of the electorate the problem of Iraq was defined by the fear that to withdraw—or simply not to win—would leave us more exposed to terror; they were moved, in other words, by a fear of defeat more than a hope of victory.[86] The president's stubborn resolve was more optimistic, but it suited that mood, at least long enough to help the Republicans attain their victory in 2004.

Democrats, by contrast, still suffered from the image, acquired with the McGovern campaign of 1972, of being soft on national security. John Kerry made considerable efforts to take a position stronger than Bush's on military issues, and although his party's antiwar wing extracted a certain amount of politically damaging rhetoric from him (i.e., "the wrong war, in the wrong place, at the wrong time") it largely tolerated Kerry's bows to hawkish sentiment. But Kerry never found a credible voice, partly because he was no more willing than Bush to call for sacrifice.[87]

Democrats need to rearticulate their version of internationalism, which is, after all, the tradition that steered American policy to victory in the cold war. But they also need to understand the political advantages—at least in the short term—of Bush's stance. Most Americans know that America can't "go it alone," which is the reason Bush never forgot to mention the support of a "coalition of the willing" and why he was so delighted, in the first presidential debate, when Kerry left Poland, with its special resonances in American politics, off the list of significant coalition participants.[88] At the same time, they want to be sure that in international councils America speaks with a strong and authentic voice.

Paradoxically, Democrats may have found elements of that new voice in an old antagonist. To a surprising extent, Democrats in 2004 found themselves appreciating and invoking Ronald Reagan, another "war president" but also an "archpragmatist" whose sometimes ferocious talk was balanced by an instinct for conciliation and who was capable of exiting, artfully, from any involvement that seemed too costly.[89]

Domestic life also felt unsettled and invaded in 2004, not least because the American economy speaks with an increasingly international accent. Economic globalization gives us access to lower-priced products assembled by lower wage labor, and foreign capital—at least as long as our creditors are willing to finance our enormous trade deficit—helps to fund American consumerism.[90] Part of the political price we pay, of course, is increased dependence on foreign markets and lenders. A more important cost is that globalization privileges capital and consumption at the expense of work.[91] Capital moves easily across borders to take advantage of market opportunities; labor, relatively tied to place, is left with a weaker hand.[92] Arguments can be made on both sides, but retiring Sen. Ernest Hollings, D-S.C., has made a good case that globalized economics supports the American standard of living by exporting jobs and lowering the quality of work at home.[93]

What is unarguable, however, is that employment felt increasingly uncertain in 2004. During much of Bush's first term, the economy was in recession, and Democrats eagerly reminded voters that Bush was the first president since Hoover to preside over a net loss of jobs. The modest recovery that ran through much of the election season featured rising corporate profits but no gain in real wages.[94] New jobs were relatively few and generally of lower quality than those that had been lost.[95] In the new economy, there are as many temporary or on-call workers as members of unions, and growing insecurity marks the work life even of middle-level managers. Increasingly competitive and tinged with anxiety, workplaces, as Robert Frank remarks, are "meaner and more unpleasant." [96]

It is no secret, moreover, that economic inequality in America is radical and rising, a dynamic accelerated by Bush's policies but already evident in the Clinton years.[97] The division between winners and losers may be more rigid and unforgiving than it was in the Gilded Age: James Heckman, a libertarian economist, notes that the "accident of birth" has never been more important in determining life outcomes than it is today.[98]

To a number of observers—to a great many Americans, for that matter—this inequality is not particularly alarming. The rich may get richer, they argue, but if the rest of us are at least a little better off there is little cause for complaint. But as a justification for the Bush tax cuts this notion can be challenged on economic grounds. It is even more suspect politically.[99]

In a country that has so emphatically promised opportunity, people are likely to chafe at the restrictions of egalitarian policy. But, as Ronald Inglehart observes, they also resent elite privilege and the crushing aspects of economic power.[100] Symptoms of that indignation are evident in the increased risk of employee sabotage and "layoff rage" (notably celebrated in the movie *Office Space*).[101] It does not discourage such resentment that too many employers follow a "two-tiered morality," breaking the rules themselves but exhorting their employees to abide by a rigid, even self-sacrificial, code of ethics.[102] About half of Americans now see the country as divided between haves and have-nots. Even before Bush took office, 45 percent of Americans said that they saw a fundamental conflict between employers and employees, nearly double the 25 percent who said so during the Great Depression.[103]

Not that these sentiments are readily translated into political terms, as the Democrats discovered in 2004. Most Americans are inclined to interpret a great part of their economic fortunes in personal terms and are apt to accept market outcomes as authoritative, or at least inevitable.[104] Class politics has never come easily in America, and classes today are, if anything, less coherent than usual, with the old ethnic divisions giving way to differences of culture and style.[105] In the Clinton era, considerable numbers of Reagan Democrats returned to their party, but even then their economic loyalties were strained by what Andrew Levison calls their "undiminished hostility" to liberal cultural elites.[106] Millions of working Americans suspect that government—itself constrained by the dynamics of globalization and technology—is either "responsible for the economic conditions that dominate their private lives" or "of little use for remedying them," or both.[107] If there is a lesson to be learned from recent economic crises, however, it is that markets are neither omniscient nor omnipotent and that frequently government intervention is needed to make things right.[108] In 2004 Sen. Barack Obama moved a broad national audience by gracefully articulating the message that "government can help." It takes more than one playing to teach a song, however, and Senator Kerry rarely sounded so clear a trumpet.[109]

Culture: Worried Warriors

"Moral values" was the concern cited as decisive by the largest number of voters (about 22 percent) in election day polls, and because about 80 percent of these "values voters" went for Bush they became the media's consensus explanation of the outcome.[110] Inevitably, as David Brooks noted, this "story line" of the "commentariat" was overblown: among other things, the percentage of voters listing moral values was pretty much the same as in 2000.[111] But Karl Rove was right to think that worries about morality, while part of the "broader fabric" of the election, were a crucial asset to Bush and his party.[112]

Although the great majority of Americans agree broadly on moral questions, most of them tend to see morals as private preferences, more or less a matter of personal "rights." In popular moral discourse, tolerance holds almost all the trumps.[113] By and large, moreover, Americans have become radically indifferent to questions of theology, switching denominations, if not faiths, with remarkable ease.[114]

Yet the morality of tolerance, while it disdains any desire or willingness to hurt others, also involves no great willingness to help them.[115] Principally, tolerance involves forbearance where the private lives of others are concerned (as in, "the privacy of your own bedroom") but not necessarily when those we tolerate make claims on us or in public life.

The difficulty is especially great when the moral challenges intrude into what Americans regard as their own space, either by disrupting civic rituals and routines—the singing of Christmas songs in public schools, for example—or, even more intimately, through the media and the Internet, especially since the Web virtually destroys privacy as a social fact.[116] Because these electronic penetrations of our homes are ubiquitous, it is not surprising that concern about morality is general rather than ideologically specific: In May 2004, a Gallup poll found that 82 percent of Republicans and 78 percent of Democrats rated the state of morals in America as only fair or poor.[117] Gary Bauer was speaking for more than his own right-wing constituency when he observed that "Joe Six-Pack doesn't understand why his world and his culture are changing and why he doesn't have any say in it." [118] Across a very wide spectrum, Americans are troubled by changes imposed through means other than democratic voice and politics: The right blames the media, elite opinion, or the courts, while the left points to corporate power. Americans in general worry that science and technology are moving "faster than moral understanding" and political control and increasingly feel a need for moral landmarks.[119]

Social conservatives, however, are more than just uneasy or ambivalent: they recognize that the drift of the culture has been running against them. If nothing else, majority opposition to the impeachment of Bill Clinton taught that lesson. Especially among evangelical Protestants, the talk is millenarian, featuring images of a "Warrior Jesus," vindicator as well as Savior, and they were correspondingly ready to treat the election of 2004 as a line in the moral sand.[120]

For both the desperate right and the ambivalent center, gay marriage was a sensitive issue because it pointed to the unsettled state of marriage itself—an institution that has been reordered and redefined by the routinization of divorce and remarriage, with families more and more likely to be characterized by complex overlappings, on one hand, and single parents on the other.[121] The shrewdest defenders of gay marriage, in fact, presented it as an endorsement of long-term commitment and union against the individualizing tendencies of American culture.[122] Most conservatives, by contrast, see gay marriage as an assault on the last defenses of marriage, one that threatens to redefine marriage as purely a matter of personal choice, with polygamy not far down the road.[123]

Most Americans don't accept the extreme version of the conservative position on gay marriage, but they have some sympathy for it. They are reluctant to tamper with a fundamental social institution, especially one that the Supreme Court, speaking through one of its staunchest liberals, William O. Douglas, accorded a sanctity deeper than law.[124]

In fact, public sentiment on the issue was decidedly mixed. In March, a considerable majority of survey respondents favored a measure banning gay marriage, but a comparable majority thought such an amendment not important enough to be included in the Constitution. By November, some 60 percent were at least in favor of legally sanctioned civil unions.[125] For Democrats, however, the warning signs were clear: At the time of the party's convention, 33 percent of Democratic voters (as opposed to 5 percent of convention delegates) opposed any legal recognition of gay unions.[126]

Politically, it was probably crucial that the issue of gay marriage was precipitated by a Massachusetts court decision, then amplified by the decisions of local officials (most visibly, the mayors of San Francisco and New Palz, N.Y.) to grant marriage licenses in violation of existing statutes, so that gay marriage could be portrayed as yet another challenge to democratic debate and majority rule.[127] That the enthusiasm of the moment resulted in mass weddings, Rep. Barney Frank, D-Mass., observed, "created a sense there was chaos"; by playing into the worst public fears, Mayor Gavin Newsom of San Francisco may have contributed to Bush's victory.[128] (Asked about the Republican debt to Newsom, Karl Rove was observed to "stifle a grin."[129]) Paul Starr, understandably irked, was largely accurate in writing that the gay marriage question, as it manifested itself in 2004, was—like Ralph Nader's independent candidacy—the product of "groups on the left that have little interest in majoritarian politics." [130]

By contrast, their very desperation moved social conservatives toward electoral pragmatism.[131] Despite grumbles, they bore with Republican efforts to conciliate the center. The GOP convention adopted a right-wing platform, but its public face showcased the party's pro-choice leaders—Rudolph Giuliani, George Pataki, and Arnold Schwarzenegger—along with Sen. John McCain, pro-life but otherwise anathema to conservative evangelicals. Sen. Sam Brownback, R-Kan., a militant conservative in the "culture war," was not even allowed on the convention podium.[132] Bush himself never explicitly opposed the basic right to an abortion, limiting himself to a rejection of the "partial birth" procedure. As early as March, Bush endorsed the right of states to provide for civil unions between gay and lesbian couples, and even more startlingly, he used a late-October appearance on *Good Morning, America* to disown the Republican platform's opposition to such unions.[133]

Conservatives relied on the president's inward sympathies, especially as manifested in rhetoric that artfully included evangelical and more broadly religious turns of phrase such as "a culture of life." [134] Effectively, they treated Bush's concessions to the center as guile, a religious form of Machiavellianism, and they were encouraged in this view by aggressive—but largely off-media—Republican efforts to appeal more directly to their fears and sensibilities.[135] However, as Steven Waldman observed, conservatives know that they "have a history of being taken advantage of when they focus on symbolism." Confident of their contributions to the Republican victory, they are not likely to be so accommodating in Bush's second term.[136]

Democrats in 2004 found themselves in a much worse position on social and moral issues. To be sure, the liberal-left, passionately anti-Bush, demonstrated a measure of democratic pragmatism: liberals did not wince much at Kerry's pledges to continue the war in Iraq, his downplaying of gun control, or his rejection of gay marriage in favor of civil unions. At the polls, Nader was a non-factor. Yet these concessions were guarded and limited. The liberal-left sees itself, with some reason, as the wave of the cultural future, but it is not half so confident about that future as it is about the rightness of its positions. In fact, it tends to be anxious, fearful of a "slippery slope" in which any concession leads to disaster, a position that contributes to what Cynthia Gorney identified as an all-or-nothing strategy.[137]

The Democratic Convention took a low-key approach to social issues (with the exception of federal funding for embryonic stem cell research, exploiting a division among Republicans), but it opened no doors to pro-life Democrats comparable to the Republicans' showy gestures in the other direction. Indeed, in speech Democratic support for abortion rights was "cheerful," Sarah Blustain wrote, rarely suggesting that abortion is always a "sad," if sometimes preferable option.[138] John Kerry said that he could not impose his religious convictions on others, but he never said, in any articulate way, that he regards abortion as wrong. Even Bill Clinton's doctrine—that abortion should be "safe, legal, and rare"—got little emphasis, and too many Democrats were maneuvered into the politically perilous position of opposing legislation making it a second felony to kill a pregnant woman.[139] In general, Democrats conformed too closely to the depiction of liberals as too eager to reshape social life, without any consideration for broadly held values and traditions, and too willing to show a disdain for rural, religious, and especially southern Americans that they would never show for any other group.[140] Large sections of America—whether defined by geography or class—were left with the feeling that even if Republicans might violate their economic interests, the GOP at least would not treat them with contempt.[141]

Evangelical voters were so prominent among Bush's supporters that they caught most of the media attention. Catholics, however, played a much more pivotal role in the election. A vital element of the New Deal coalition, most Catholic voters are now torn between their church's position on issues such as abortion and homosexuality and its egalitarian teachings on economic and social justice. American Catholics, E. J. Dionne has observed, are almost guaranteed to feel guilty no matter how they cast their votes.[142] In 2004 some conservative bishops, emboldened by the pope's teaching and by signs of growing rank-and-file support, proclaimed that candidates—or even voters—who support abortion rights might be denied communion.[143] Even modernists, still probably a majority of Catholics, were unmoved by Kerry, whose references to religion were awkward at best, especially since pro-life Democrats found it so difficult "to gain traction or much respect."[144] In any case, Catholics returned to the pattern of the Reagan years, voting for Bush by about the same margin as voters generally (52 percent to 47 percent), and Democrats almost certainly will have to reverse that result to have a chance of winning in 2008.

At the very least, Democrats need to acknowledge the power of religious experience and yearning in American life and find a way of speaking that great second language of American culture.[145] Religious sensibilities may need to be educated, but they first need to be addressed, ideally by someone who not only knows the words but also feels the music.[146] Bill Clinton did and does; as David Brooks reminded Democrats, to reach religious Americans, "their president doesn't have to be a saint, but he does have to be a pilgrim."[147]

There is potential support for Democrats among Bush's religious supporters. Many of them are broadly liberal—or faithful to the Gospel—in their dedication to equality or to economic and social welfare.[148] Bush's compassionate conservatism was designed to speak to those sentiments. For similar reasons, the president argued in 2002 against a "culture of selfishness," or lives devoted to profit, in a speech that properly struck Frank Rich as surreal.[149] So far, Bush's pronouncements have proved almost entirely empty. He embraced "faith-based" programs in theory, for example, but as E. J. Dionne observed, "in practice, his priorities are always somewhere else."[150] Cardinal Mahoney, of the Los Angeles archdiocese, remarked that the administration's programs seem to come down to "more competition over the same or fewer resources."[151]

Many people of faith, moreover, are deeply troubled by the war in Iraq and Bush's aggressive foreign policy, by his treatment of religion as a partisan base, or by the association of religion with an individualism and nationalism incompatible with biblical teaching. "God," Jim Wallis reminds believers, "is always personal, but never private."[152] With some modest but heartfelt changes of language and position, Democrats might make inroads among conservative believers.

Beyond electoral calculations, an effort to appeal to "red" America might bring Democrats back to their own roots.[153] The great Democratic voices, from Bryan to FDR and beyond, have spoken in religious metaphors, from Bryan's Cross of Gold speech to Roosevelt's invocation of Jesus driving the money changers from the temple. But the Democratic tradition also includes the Progressive movement's reliance on relativism and the language of interest-based politics to debunk the pretensions of established power, a habit of mind and speech that gradually undermined the combination of moral indignation and hope that was Progressivism's raison d'être.[154]

Interest narrowly construed does not comprehend politics. A great many—and possibly most—liberals do not vote their economic interests, and there is an element of condescension when they assume that appeals to interest will move other voters not driven by necessity. Economic issues are fundamental, but loyalty, faith, and dignity are also dimensions of "class politics." Voting, and especially partisanship, is an expression of civic identity, a location of the self in the community and in the continuing story of national life.[155] With communities of memory declining, Democrats—and Republicans for that matter—are obliged to develop a narrative that connects the present of Americans with their past and future.[156]

Regime Change at Home?

Great stakes and a grand story permeate contemporary American politics. The voters know all too well that their government must be strong enough to deal with the powers and principalities of the time. The 9/11 terrorist attacks acutely intensified Americans' recognition of their collective dependence on government, and various corporate scandals (Enron being only the most visible) and a long list of crises and problems—all going to prove that markets, particularly when it comes to essential public services, cannot regulate themselves—only underlined the lesson.[157]

"Big government," the era of which Bill Clinton pronounced at an end, is back in style; on the eve of the election, Anne Applebaum wrote that small-scale government is "so 1990s." [158] Republicans, or so David Brooks claimed, had come to recognize that most Americans may want their government reformed, but they do not want it sharply reduced.[159] And even though plenty of Republicans dissented from that view, the GOP hijacked much of the Democrats' agenda. (Even so, it wasn't hard to discern the Republican Party's continued allegiance to corporate America.)[160]

To be sure, American trust in government is limited. The very power that government needs to address the world's abounding threats makes it overwhelming and arcane in relation to the individuals it is defending. Experience, to say nothing of anxiety, has led Americans to doubt the moral intentions of government, as well as its competence and efficacy, so that most of us are not disposed to commit ourselves too deeply to public institutions and causes.

A great deal might have been possible in the wave of patriotism that followed 9/11—Senators McCain and Evan Bayh, D-Ind., revived talk of national service, for example[161]—but the president preferred not to ask for heroic measures, telling Americans, in effect, to devote themselves to private life and consumption. As Frank Rich wrote, "we are told to go shopping, take in a show, go to Disneyland. On this war's home front, 'sacrifice' is easy-to-crack code for 'vacation.' " [162] Predictably, the high levels of trust in government fell by the next spring.[163] We were moved by 9/11, Thomas de Zengotita observed, but we have also moved on. Our resilience, but also our indisposition to sacrifice, reflects the ways our culture schools us in the "numbness of busyness," superficial relations built on the premise of transience.[164]

The American view of reality, in fact, is increasingly fabricated and cinematic, epitomized by the "reality" show that is television's latest vogue. "Reality," in this genre, is something staged, with at least a family resemblance to the political style exemplified by the Bush campaign, which treated us to a performance of leadership that was reassuring but not very demanding.[165] Citizenship, in this mode, is at best spectatorial, like the banners and signs proclaiming, "We support our troops," displayed by a public apparently resistant to higher taxes, let alone conscription.

That tendency in American life and politics, however, highlights the 2004 election as a scene in the ongoing American drama, the uneasy and contested compromise that is commercial democracy. Aristotle taught that a political regime is more than its form and hence that majority rule is an incomplete guarantee of democracy. Ultimately, the quality of a regime turns on its ideas of justice and the good life, its weighing of contributions to the common good.[166]

In these terms, commerce is essentially oligarchic, since it holds implicitly that the greatest good is economic prosperity and that the greatest contribution to the common good is wealth and invested capital. And that oligarchic idea pretty much captures the one "big idea" of 2004, the Republican vision of an "ownership society." [167] Morally, this vision is defined by its goal of enabling people to take responsibility for their lives by rewarding—or at least radically reducing the burdens on—savings and invested capital. Politically, the ownership society rests on the calculation that when people enter the equities market (and counting small and indirect owners, that figure topped 50 percent in 2000), they become more likely to vote Republican.[168]

In fairness, the tilt toward oligarchy in American culture, and the increased deference toward wealth associated with it, began before Bush took office.[169] Still, E. J. Dionne was accurate in describing Bush's policy as an "effort to shift taxes from wealth to work," an embrace of oligarchic principle that overrode the traditional democratic feeling that, in time of war, the rich ought to pay more, rather than less.[170] (Frank Rich called the tax cuts "as obscene as war profiteering.")[171] Ben Stein was half serious in arguing that, since the country is "already an aristocracy," the government ought to sell titles to raise revenue.[172]

Stein was playful but on the mark in indicating the political consequences of the inequality of income that the Bush tax policy accentuates. Even Alan Greenspan has been heard to say that "increased concentration of incomes" is "not a very desirable thing to allow to happen" in a democratic society.[173] Kevin Phillips was more pointed in contending that the result of the new inequality promises to be a kind of regime change at home: just as Aristotle might have warned, "plutocracy by some other name." [174]

In contrast to the oligarchic ideal, democratic justice holds that the greatest good is self-rule, so much so that self-government in poverty is preferable to affluence without it. The greatest contribution one can make to political society, in democratic terms, is a life freely given to the common good—through the risk or sacrifice of life itself in war or crisis, and in peace, through work. It is something we can all give equally. Democratic justice presumes that wealth and commerce are subordinate goods, subject to the measure of democratic politics.[175]

For much of their party's history, Democrats have taught that doctrine (if the Bank of the United States had been rechartered, Andrew Jackson declared, "the forms of your Government might for a time have remained, but its living spirit would have departed from it"),[176] and it is a heritage worth reclaiming. Strong evidence exists that beyond a certain point, affluence is associated with a loss of happiness rather than a gain.[177] Private ownership, as James Skillen writes, is only half the story, although it is a half that deserves its Republican champions; the "other half . . . is that we, as citizens, share in the joint ownership of the commonwealth." [178] If the Democrats are to rebuild a majority, they will need to make the case for government as the custodian of the common good and for their party as the defender of the frontiers of democratic self-government.

Making that case will be difficult, given the public's limited taste for the slow rhythms of democratic politics in this cinematic time. For most of us, democracy is always likely to be "fugitive," in Sheldon Wolin's term—a thing of moments and not a way of living—but not less worth cherishing for that.[179] Yet perhaps Chesterton's old romance is stronger than we think. Among younger Americans, the phenomenal readership of the Harry Potter series developed in a largely autonomous way, initially with little hype and to the astonishment of its publishers, at least in part an expression of nature as opposed to convention.[180] The books give us magic, to be sure, but the grander side of the story is the friendship and loyalty among children who are willing to run great risks to help defend their way of life against an evil whose doctrine is elitism and mastery. Harry Potter reminds us that we are, in fact, political animals by nature. In their cold season, Democrats have at least that much reason to hope that democratic citizenship will find a new rendezvous with destiny.

Notes

1. John Zogby, "Armageddon Election," http://moneycentral.msn.com/content/CNBCTV/Articles/TV Reports/P77448.asp.
2. Robin Toner, "Voters Are Very Settled, Intense and Partisan, and It's Only July," *New York Times,* July 25, 2004, 1; Ford Fessenden, "A Big Increase of New Voters in Swing States," *New York Times,* September 26, 2004, 11.

3. E. J. Dionne Jr., "The Preemptive President," *Washington Post National Weekly* July 7–13, 2004, 21.
4. David Brooks, "The Presidency Wars," *New York Times,* September 30, 2003, A29.
5. The quotation is from James Dobson, cited by David Kirkpatrick, "Some Backers of Bush Say They Anticipate a 'Revolution'," *New York Times,* November 4, 2004, P1; for the comparison to the Civil War, see Kirkpatrick's "Battle Cry of the Faithful Pits Believers against Unbelievers," *New York Times,* October 31, 2004, 24.
6. Popkin is cited by Todd Purdom, "The Year of Passion," *New York Times,* October 31, 2004, WK1.
7. See the *New York Times*/CBS Poll cited in Adam Nagourney and Janet Elder, "Americans Show Clear Concerns on Bush Agenda," *New York Times,* November 23, 2004, A1.
8. Boyte is cited by Purdom, "The Year of Passion."
9. G. K. Chesterton, *What I Saw in America,* (New York: Dodd Mead, 1922), 16; Matthew Crenson and Benjamin Ginsberg, *Downsizing Democracy: How America Sidelined Its Citizens and Privatized Its Public* (Baltimore: Johns Hopkins University Press, 2002); Theda Skocpol, *Diminished Democracy: From Membership to Management in American Civic Life* (Norman: University of Oklahoma Press, 2003).
10. See Philip Klinker's observations, as reported by Dean Murphy, "Can History Save the Democrats?" *New York Times,* November 7, 2004, WK1. The comments on voting data depend on Marjorie Connelly, "How Americans Voted: A Political Portrait," *New York Times,* November 7, 2004, WK4.
11. Elizabeth Bumiller, et al., "Turnout Effort and Kerry, Too, Were G.O.P.'s Keys to Victory," *New York Times,* November 4, 2004, A1. The phrase "grass roots army" is from Mike Cox, the attorney general of Michigan, cited by Adam Clymer, "Buoyed by Resurgence, G.O.P. Strives for an Era of Dominance," *New York Times,* May 25, 2003, 1.
12. See the *New York Times*/CBS News Poll cited by Adam Nagourney and Janet Elder, "Polls Show Tie: Concern on Both Rivals Cited," *New York Times,* October 19, 2004, A1.
13. Richard Brookhiser, "The Mind of George W. Bush," *Atlantic Monthly,* April 2003, 68.
14. Brookhiser, "The Mind of George W. Bush," 61; Harold Meyerson, "One Guy in a Bubble," *Washington Post National Weekly,* October 25–31, 2004, 26.
15. Kristol is cited by David Von Drehle, "Misunderestimating the GOP," *Washington Post National Weekly,* November 18–24, 2002, 12; John Nichols, "Campaigner in Chief," *The Nation,* November 1, 2004, 4–5.
16. Frank Rich, "Joe Millionaire for President," *New York Times,* January 18, 2003, A17.
17. For example, see Richard Morin and Claudia Deane, "Corporate Scandals? No Problem," *Washington Post National Weekly,* July 22–28, 2003, 34.
18. Bush's style, Fred Greenstein remarked, "might not keep him from driving off a cliff. But he would be a very good race-car driver." Cited in Mike Allen, " 'This Is a Man Who Is in Control'," *Washington Post National Weekly,* May 5–11, 2003, 10; David Broder, "Bush's Leadership Pinnacle," *Washington Post National Weekly,* May 5–11, 2003, 4.
19. Paul Krugman, "A Credibility Problem," *New York Times,* January 28, 2003, A21.
20. Richard Cohen, "The Buck Doesn't Stop," *Washington Post National Weekly,* April 12–18, 2004, 27; David Broder, "Wobbly Words," *Washington Post National Weekly,* July 22–28, 2002, 4.

21. Von Drehle, "Misunderestimating the GOP."
22. Dallek is cited by David Sanger, "Bush May Have Exaggerated, but Did He Lie?" *New York Times,* June 22, 2003, WK1; see also Dionne, "The Preeemptive President."
23. Brookhiser, "The Mind of George W. Bush," 59, 63; Steven Waldman, "On a Word and a Prayer," *New York Times,* November 6, 2004, A19.
24. William Gamson, *Talking Politics* (Cambridge: Cambridge University Press, 1992); David Kirkpatrick, "A Call to Win the Culture War," *New York Times,* September 1, 2004, P1.
25. Frank Rich, "Decision 2004: Fear Fatigue vs. Sheer Fatigue," *New York Times,* October 31, 2004, AE1; weirdly, some admirers saw Bush as a "self-made man." David Finkel, "Full Tanks and Empty Wallets," *Washington Post National Weekly,* May 31–June 6, 2004, 19–20.
26. For example, see Jim VandeHei and Dan Balz, "Howard Dean, the Inevitable Nominee?" *Washington Post National Weekly,* December 15–21, 2003, 10.
27. E. J. Dionne Jr., ". . . Or a Rational Response?" *Washington Post National Weekly,* January 5–11, 2004, 26; David Broder, "Dean: Denominator or Detonator?" *Washington Post National Weekly,* January 12–18, 2004, 4. One conservative analyst, William Kristol, thought Dean just might win, but that seems to have been chiefly a measure of his distaste for Bush. "How Dean Could Win," *Washington Post National Weekly,* December 15–21, 2003, 27. It did not help, of course, that the primaries were in practice decided by a handful of voters in Iowa and New Hampshire; nominally "inclusive," the primaries made the mass of Democratic voters irrelevant. Rhodes Cook, "The Illusion of Inclusion," *Washington Post National Weekly,* February 2–8, 2004, 21.
28. Cited in Rich, "Decision 2004."
29. David B. Halbfinger, "Familiar Democratic Faces, but New Duties in Kerry Camp," *New York Times,* September 16, 2004, A24.
30. Speaking of the Democrats' attack mode in the Louisiana gubernatorial election of 2003, Susan Howell remarked, "It's negative campaigning. But it works." Jeffrey Gettleman, "In Louisiana Election, a First and a Near First," *New York Times,* November 17, 2003, A18.
31. "The Great Ad Wars of 2004," *New York Times,* November 1, 2004, A19; John M. Broder, "Republicans Pack Punch, Democrats Take It (for Now)," *New York Times,* September 12, 2004, WK3.
32. David Broder, "Swift Boats and Old Wounds," *Washington Post National Weekly,* August 30–September 5, 2004, 4; Frank Rich, "You Can't Skip Vietnam Twice," *New York Times,* February 22, 2004, AR1.
33. Bumiller et al., "Turnout Effort and Kerry, Too, Were G.O.P.'s Keys to Victory"; Alan Brinkley, "What's Next?" *American Prospect,* December 2004, 18–23; the charge that Kerry panders to his audiences was first raised in the Democratic primaries, notably by Howard Dean, and was fairly well planted in the public's mind by March. "Presidential Candidates," *New York Times,* March 16, 2004, A24. On Kerry's Senate record, see Jim VandeHei, "Haunted by His Past Votes," *Washington Post National Weekly,* March 1–7, 2004, 13.
34. Katharine Q. Seelye, "Moral Values Cited as a Defining Issue of the Election," *New York Times,* November 4, 2004, P4.
35. Lyn Nofziger, "Bush's Troubles Ahead," *New York Times,* November 7, 2004, WK11.
36. Adam Nagourney, "Kerry Struggling to Find a Theme, Democrats Fear," *New York Times,* May 2, 2004, 1; Leon Panetta, "Pick a Message, Any Message," *New York Times,* September 19, 2004, WK11.
37. "Missed Opportunity," *Washington Post National Weekly,* August 9–15, 2004, 24; VandeHei, "Haunted by His Past Votes"; James Skillen, "Bush's Deeds,

Kerry's Words," *Capital Commentary* (Center for Public Justice), September 6, 2004.
38. Robert Reich, "The Political Center Is Bogus," *New York Times,* April 14, 2001, A13.
39. The concept of "large ideas" is drawn from Thomas Patterson, *The Vanishing Voter: Public Involvement in an Age of Uncertainty* (New York: Knopf, 2002).
40. Stephen K. Tootle, "The Return of William McKinley," *Claremont Review of Books* 4 (Summer 2004): 60–61; Todd Purdom and David Kirkpatrick, "Campaign Strategists in Position to Consolidate Republican Majority," *New York Times,* November 5, 2004, A22.
41. Another parallel is the problem that McKinley's imperial venture in the Philippines caused for Democrats: William Jennings Bryan persuaded his followers to vote for a peace treaty with Spain in order to confront the issue of imperialism separately, so that he and his party could be said to have "voted for" the acquisition of the Philippines before they "voted against it." Louis Koenig, *Bryan* (New York: Putnam's, 1971), 288–291.
42. Cited in Koenig, *Bryan,* 253.
43. Ibid., 252–253; Geoffrey Nunberg, "The Curious Fate of Populism: How Politics Turned into Pose," *New York Times,* August 15, 2004, WK7.
44. Richard W. Stevenson, "Confident Bush Outlines Ambitious Plan for 2nd Term," *New York Times,* November 5, 2004, A1; Adam Nagourney and Janet Elder, "Americans Show Clear Concerns on Bush Agenda," *New York Times,* November 23, 2004, A1.
45. Nofziger, "Bush's Troubles Ahead"; E. J. Dionne Jr., "Iraq and the Conservative Crackup," *Washington Post National Weekly,* June 7–13, 2004, 27.
46. Donald Green and Eric Schickler, "Winning a Battle, Not a War," *New York Times,* November 12, 2002, A2.
47. Paul Krugman, "For Richer," *New York Times Magazine,* October 20, 2002, 66.
48. William Leuchtenberg, *In the Shadow of FDR* (Ithaca: Cornell University Press, 1983).
49. Benjamin Ginsberg and Martin Shefter, *Politics by Other Means: The Declining Importance of Elections in America* (New York: Basic Books, 1990); Paul Starr, "Morals of the Election," *American Prospect,* December 2004, 4.
50. Robert Putnam, *Bowling Alone* (New York: Simon and Schuster, 2000); see also Crenson and Ginsberg, *Downsizing Democracy.*
51. Jane Eisner, "No Kidding on November 2," *Washington Post National Weekly,* October 11–17, 2004, 22.
52. Fred Andrews, "Learning to Celebrate Water-Cooler Gossip," *New York Times,* January 25, 2001, BU6; Alan Krueger, "Economic Scene," *New York Times,* February 7, 2002, C2.
53. Walter Lippmann, *The Phantom Public* (New York: Harcourt Brace, 1925).
54. Paul Fahrl, "More Media, Less Message," *Washington Post National Weekly,* June 21–27, 2004, 11.
55. Markus Prior, "Liberated Viewers, Polarized Viewers—The Implications of Increased Media Choice for Democratic Politics," *The Good Society* 11 (3): 10–16 (2002); Gimpel is cited by David Von Drehle, "Culture Clash," *Washington Post National Weekly,* May 24–30, 2004, 6–7.
56. "Internet Said to Gain as Source for News," *New York Times,* January 11, 2004, C4.
57. Anne Applebaum, "Rather Irrelevant," *Washington Post National Weekly,* September 27–October 3, 2004, 27; Jim Rutenberg, "In Politics, Web Is a Parallel World with Its Own Rules," *New York Times,* February 22, 2004, WK3.
58. Cass Sunstein, *Republic.com* (Princeton: Princeton University Press, 2001).

59. Robin Toner, "The Culture Wars, Part II," *New York Times,* February 29, 2004, WK1.
60. Larry Bartels, "Is 'Popular Rule' Possible?" *Brookings Review,* Summer 2003, 12–15; Alan Krueger, "Economic Scene," *New York Times,* October 16, 2003, C2.
61. This finding, by John Hibbing and Elizabeth Theiss-Morse, is reported by Richard Morin, "Leave-Us-Alone Democracy," *Washington Post National Weekly,* February 3–9, 2003, 34.
62. See David Brooks's splendid satire of the presidential debates, "Debate, Declaim, Debacle," *New York Times,* October 16, 2004, A17. On the problem of democratic deliberation, see my essay, "Toward Genuine Self-Government," *Academic Questions* 15 (1): 53 (2001–2002).
63. Joyce Purnick, "One-Doorbell-One-Vote Tactic Reemerges in Bush-Kerry Race," *New York Times,* April 6, 2004, P2; Sarah Wildman, "Wedding Bell Blues," *American Prospect,* December 2004, 39.
64. Robert Borosage and Katrina vanden Heuvel, "Progressives: Get Ready to Fight," *The Nation,* November 29, 2004, 11–14.
65. Jeff Faux, "All Action, No Talk," *American Prospect,* December 2004, 45–46; Andrei Cherny, "Why We Lost," *New York Times,* November 5, 2004, A31.
66. Cited in Purdom, "The Year of Passion."
67. Richard L. Berke, "A New Movement Logs On to the Democratic Party and May Reshape It," *New York Times,* December 28, 2003, WK5. With his characteristic flair, Rev. Al Sharpton referred to Internet voting as a "high-tech poll tax." Adam Liptak, "Is Internet Voting a 'High-Tech Poll Tax'?" *New York Times,* January 18, 2004, WK3.
68. Thomas Jefferson, letter to Joseph Cabell, February 2, 1816, in *The Life and Selected Writings of Thomas Jefferson,* ed. Adrienne Koch and William Peden (New York: Modern Library, 1944), 660–662.
69. Robert Reich, "What Kind of Party for the Democrats?" *New York Times,* February 25, 2001, WK15.
70. David Brooks, "The Values-Vote Myth," *New York Times,* November 6, 2004, A19.
71. Theodore J. Lowi, "Think Globally, Lose Locally," *Boston Review,* April/May 1998, 4–10.
72. Paul Cantor, *Gilligan Unbound: Popular Culture in an Age of Globalization* (Lanham, Md.: Rowman and Littlefield, 2001); Michael Paul Rogin, "JFK: The Movie," *American Historical Review* 97 (1992): 502.
73. Dale Maharidge, "Rust and Rage in the Heartland," *The Nation,* September 20, 2004, 11–14.
74. When the FBI discovered a major weapons cache—including a chemical bomb—in Noonday, Texas, in April 2003, the attorney general—so eager to trumpet the arrest of suspected Al Qaeda operatives—did not even call a press conference, possibly thinking that unveiling a white, right-wing terrorist would have made Americans feel less, rather than more, secure. Paul Krugman, "Noonday in the Shade," *New York Times,* June 22, 2004, A19.
75. Gary L. Gregg II, "Crisis Leadership: The Symbolic Transformation of the Bush Presidency," *Perspectives on Political Science* 32 (3): 143–148 (Summer 2003).
76. Most saliently, although not all the responsibility lies with the administration, it failed to react adequately to warnings of an impending terrorist attack. Thomas Kean et al., *The 9/11 Commission Report* (New York: Norton, 2004), 254–277.
77. Gerald M. Pomper et al., *The Election of 2000* (New York: Chatham House, 2001), 189–190; William Kristol and Richard Kagan called the administration's response to the crisis with China a "national humiliation." Frank Rich, "What Big Test?" *New York Times,* April 13, 2001, A13.

78. Marc J. Hetherington and Michael Nelson, "Anatomy of a Rally 'Round the Flag Effect: George W. Bush and the War on Terrorism," *PS: Political Science and Politics* 36 (2003): 37–42.
79. For one criticism of Bush's position, see Benjamin R. Barber, *Fear's Empire: War, Terrorism and Democracy* (New York: Norton, 2003).
80. Niall Ferguson, "The Administration Can't Build an Empire on a Shoestring," *Washington Post National Weekly,* July 28–August 3, 2003, 21; Paul Krugman, "What Went Wrong?" *New York Times,* April 23, 2004, A23, refers to a "pattern of conquest followed by malign neglect."
81. Richard Hart Sinnreich, "Wishful Thinking," *Washington Post National Weekly,* June 7–13, 2004, 23.
82. Steven V. Monsma, "Lessons from Iraq," *Capital Commentary* (Center for Public Justice), June 30, 2003; David Ignatius, "Bush's Confusion, Baghdad's Mess," *Washington Post,* April 23, 2003, A35; David Brooks, "The Uncertainty Factor," *New York Times,* April 13, 2004, A23.
83. Harold Meyerson, "The Professionals' Revolt," *Washington Post National Weekly,* March 29–April 4, 2004, 26.
84. See my essay, "Two-Tier Politics Revisited," in *Seeking the Center: Politics and Policymaking at the New Century,* ed. Martin Levin, Marc K. Landy, and Martin Shapiro (Washington: Georgetown University Press, 2001), 381–400.
85. James Lindsey, "Rally Round the Flag," *Brookings Review* 21 (Summer 2003): 20–23.
86. Dana Priest and Thomas E. Ricks, "Yes, It's Getting Worse," *Washington Post National Weekly,* October 4–10, 2004, 15.
87. Matthew Yglesias, "Insecurity Blanket," *American Prospect,* December 2004, 37–38.
88. Poland has played an even bigger role in the past. In 1976, Gerald Ford may have lost the election when, in a debate with Jimmy Carter, he appeared to suggest that he thought Poland was free from Soviet domination.
89. The term "archpragmatist" is taken from Strobe Talbott's review of Jack F. Matlock Jr., *Reagan and Gorbachev: How the Cold War Ended* (New York: Random House, 2004), in the *New York Times Book Review,* August 1, 2004, 7.
90. Jeff Madrick, "Economic Scene," *New York Times,* March 18, 2004, C2.
91. Jeffrey Frankel, "It's a Tough Job to Create Jobs," *Washington Post National Weekly,* April 19–25, 2004, 23; Louis Uchitelle, "As Factories Move Abroad, So Does U.S. Power," *New York Times,* August 17, 2003, BU4.
92. G. M. Tamàs, "On Post-Fascism," *Boston Review,* Summer 2000, 46.
93. Ernest F. Hollings, "Protectionism," *Washington Post National Weekly,* March 29–April 4, 2004, 23; Steve Lohr, "Questioning the Age of Wal-Mart," *New York Times,* December 28, 2003, WK5.
94. Frankel, "It's a Tough Job to Create Jobs."
95. Steven Roach, "More Jobs, Worse Work," *New York Times,* July 22, 2004, A21.
96. Frank is cited by Griff Witte, "The Vanishing Middle Class," *Washington Post National Weekly,* September 27–October 3, 2004, 6–7; see also Louis Uchitelle, "It's Not New Jobs, It's All the Jobs," *New York Times,* August 29, 2004, BU6.
97. Krugman, "For Richer," 62ff; James K. Galbraith, *Created Unequal* (Chicago: University of Chicago Press, 2000).
98. Robert Perrucci and Earl Wysong, *The New Class Society* (Lanham, Md.: Rowman and Littlefield, 2002); Heckman is cited by Alexander Stille, "Grounded by an Income Gap," *New York Times,* December 15, 2001, A17.
99. Paul Krugman, "A Touch of Class," *New York Times,* January 21, 2003, A23.
100. Inglehart is cited by Stille, "Grounded by an Income Gap."
101. Eve Tahmincioglu, "Vigilance in the Face of Layoff Rage," *New York Times,* August 1, 2001, C1.

102. Barbara Ehrenreich, "Two-Tiered Morality," *New York Times,* June 30, 2002, WK10.
103. Pomper et al., *The Election of 2000,* 186–187; David Callahan, *The Cheating Culture: Why More Americans Are Doing Wrong to Get Ahead* (New York: Harcourt, 2003).
104. See the discussion of middle managers in Paul Osterman, "Middle Managers in the Class War," *Washington Post National Weekly,* September 13–19, 2004, 26.
105. Paul Kingston, *The Classless Society* (Stanford: Stanford University Press, 2000).
106. Andrew Levison, "Who Lost the Working Class?" *The Nation,* May 14, 2001, 30. It illustrates both the virtues and the limits of the liberal imagination that *The Nation*'s postelection verdict that, "the economic cards simply weren't dealt" was right enough, but its claim that "morals didn't trump economics" seems to accept that the two really can be separated. Borosage and vanden Heuvel, "Progressives: Get Ready to Fight," 13.
107. W. Lance Bennett, "The Uncivil Culture: Community, Identity and the Rise of Lifestyle Politics," *PS: Political Science and Politics* 31 (1998): 758; David Finkel, "Full Tanks and Empty Wallets," *Washington Post National Weekly,* May 31–June 6, 2004, 19–20.
108. Kurt Eichenwald, "Could Capitalists Bring Down Capitalism?" *New York Times,* June 30, 2002, WK1; Joseph Kahn, "Losing Faith," *New York Times* March 21, 2002, A8.
109. Rick Perlstein, "Conviction Politics," *American Prospect,* December 2004, 26–27.
110. Todd Purdom, "An Electoral Affirmation of Shared Values," *New York Times,* November 4, 2004, A1.
111. Brooks, "The Values-Vote Myth."
112. Adam Nagourney, " 'Moral Values' Carried Bush, Rove Says," *New York Times,* November 10, 2004, A20.
113. Morris Fiorina et al., *Culture War? The Myth of a Polarized America* (New York: Longman, 2004); Alan Wolfe, *One Nation after All* (New York: Viking, 1998).
114. Alan Wolfe, *The Transformation of American Religion* (New York: Free Press, 2003). David Brooks called attention to the "peripatetic" religious history of a number of the candidates in 2004, perhaps most striking, that of Gen. Wesley Clark, who has by turns been a Methodist, a Baptist, and now, a Catholic, though he often attends Presbyterian services. "The National Creed," *New York Times,* December 30, 2003, A21.
115. James Davison Hunter refers to it as the "thin fabric of consumer-oriented individualism." "Bowling with Social Scientists," *Weekly Standard,* August 29–September 4, 2000, 31.
116. On the challenge of television's "hidden curriculum," see Uri Bronfenbrenner, "Contexts of Child Rearing," *American Psychologist* 34 (1979): 844–850.
117. "A Nation Seeks Its Moral Compass," *New York Times,* May 23, 2004, WK2.
118. Bauer is cited by Timothy Egan, "Democrats in Red States: Just Regular Guys," *New York Times,* August 22, 2004, WK3.
119. The quotation is from Michael Sandel's admirable "The Case against Perfection," *Atlantic Monthly,* April 2004, 51–62. Even in intellectual circles, especially after 9/11, relativism and postmodernism, still reigning orthodoxies, found themselves on the defensive. Edward Rothstein, "Moral Relativity Is a Hot Topic? Yes, Absolutely," *New York Times,* July 13, 2002, B7.
120. David Kirkpatrick, "The Return of the Warrior Jesus," *New York Times,* April 4, 2004, 1.
121. David Machacek, "Same-Sex Culture War," *Religion in the News* 7 (Spring 2004): 5–6.

122. This position was considerably weakened by the insistence of advocacy groups on appealing to the language of individual rights. See the critique in Timothy Sherratt, "The Myth of Essential Privateness," *Capital Commentary* (Center for Public Justice), November 3, 2003.
123. Joel Achenbach, "Whose Values Won the Election?" *Washington Post National Weekly,* November 8–14, 2004, 10–11.
124. *Griswold v. Connecticut,* 381 U.S. 479, 1965. Implicitly most voters sense that the legal recognition of marriage is a delicate point of overlap between the "spirit of religion" rooted in the culture and the "spirit of liberty" embodied in the laws, the two forces that Tocqueville thought framed the balance of American democracy; *Democracy in America* (New York: Knopf, 1980), 1:43. Notably, not long after *Griswold,* a more conservative Court, in *Eisenstadt v. Baird,* 405 U.S. 438, 1972, defined marriage as simply a contract between individuals.
125. "Presidential Contenders," *New York Times,* March 16, 2004, A24; Wildman, "Wedding Bell Blues."
126. E. J. Dionne Jr., "Democrats Drop the Lunch Pail," *Washington Post National Weekly,* October 20–26, 2004, 27.
127. David von Drehle and Alan Cooperman, "A Fast-Moving Movement," *Washington Post National Weekly,* March 15–21, 2004, 10–11.
128. Dean Murphy, "Some Democrats Blame One of Their Own," *New York Times,* November 5, 2004, A18.
129. Nagourney, " 'Moral Values' Carried Bush, Rove Says."
130. Starr, "Morals of the Election."
131. Waldman, "On a Word and a Prayer."
132. David Kirkpatrick, "A Call to Win the Culture War," *New York Times,* September 1, 2004, P1.
133. Steven Waldman, "Bush Advances Gay Rights," *Washington Post National Weekly,* March 8–14, 2004, 27; Alan Cooperman, "A Faith-Based President," *Washington Post National Weekly,* September 20–26, 2004, 6–7.
134. Bush, Stanley Carlson-Thies wrote, made little effort to show just how his faith related to "the goals and limits, the hopes and concerns of his policy"; "Partisan Religion," *Capital Commentary* (Center for Public Justice), November 1, 2004. See also David Kirkpatrick, "Some Democrats Believe the Party Should Get Religion," *New York Times,* November 17, 2004, A20.
135. David Kirkpatrick, "Battle Cry of Faithful Pits Believers against Unbelievers," *New York Times,* October 31, 2004, 24.
136. Waldman, "Bush Advances Gay Rights"; see also his "On a Word and a Prayer."
137. Cynthia Gorney, "Gambling with Abortion: Why Both Sides Think They Have Everything to Lose," *Harper's,* November 2004, 33–46; Adam Clymer, "Democrats Seek a Stronger Focus, and Money," *New York Times,* May 26, 2003, A1.
138. Sarah Blustain, "Choice Language," *American Prospect,* December 2004, 36–37.
139. David Kirkpatrick, "Some Democrats Believe the Party Should Get Religion." The political difficulty is evident in the prosecution and conviction of Scott Peterson—in California, that blue bastion—for the killing of his unborn son as well as that of his wife.
140. Thomas Frank, "Why They Won," *New York Times,* November 5, 2004, A31. On *The Simpsons,* for example, Apu's name and accent are the objects of good-natured fun, but he is intelligent, hardworking, and respectable, very different from "Cletus, the slack-jawed yokel," who is ignorant, slothful, dubiously moral, and of course, southern.
141. Dionne, "Democrats Drop the Lunch Pail."
142. E. J. Dionne Jr., "Courting the Catholic Vote," *Washington Post National Weekly,* June 26, 2000, 22.

143. Laurie Goldstein, "Bishop Would Deny Rite for Defiant Catholic Voters," *New York Times,* May 14, 2004, A16.
144. E. J. Dionne Jr., "Kerry and His Church," *Washington Post National Weekly,* May 10–16, 2004, 26.
145. It is a bit of an exaggeration for Michael Sandel to argue that "Democrats have ceded to Republicans a monopoly on the moral and spiritual sources of American politics," but he is right that Democrats will need to speak to those yearnings if they are to recover. Cited in Thomas L. Friedman, "Two Nations under God," *New York Times,* November 4, 2004, A25.
146. See James Skillen's characteristically shrewd argument in "An American Covenant with God?" *Capital Commentary* (Center for Public Justice), December 15, 2003.
147. David Brooks, "A Matter of Faith," *New York Times,* June 22, 2004, A19.
148. For example, see the argument of Richard Land, cited in Edmund L. Andrews and David Kirkpatrick, "G.O.P. Constituencies Split on Tax Change," *New York Times,* November 22, 2004, D1.
149. Frank Rich, "Sacrifice Is for Losers," *New York Times,* June 22, 2002, A11.
150. E. J. Dionne Jr., "Faith-Based Talk—Where's the Action?" *Washington Post National Weekly,* June 16–22, 2003, 27.
151. Dennis Hoover, "Faith-Based Update: Bipartisan Breakdown," *Religion in the News* 4 (Summer 2001): 14–17.
152. Jim Wallis, "Putting God Back in Politics," *New York Times,* December 28, 2003, WK9; James Skillen, "Religiously Political Conservatism," *Capital Commentary* (Center for Public Justice), October 18, 2004.
153. Ruy Teixeira, "As the Left Turns," *American Prospect,* May 21, 2001, 46.
154. Eric Goldman, *Rendezvous with Destiny* (New York: Knopf, 1953), 199–200, 203, 310–313, 330, 450–452; Theodore J. Lowi, *The End of Liberalism* (New York: Norton, 1969), 3–97.
155. Sidney Verba and Gary Oren, *Equality in America* (Cambridge: Harvard University Press, 1985), 248–249; Gerald M. Pomper and Loretta Sernekos, "Bake Sales and Voting," *Society,* July/August 1991, 10–16.
156. Sheldon S. Wolin, *The Presence of the Past* (Baltimore: Johns Hopkins University Press, 1989), 140–141; Joel Kotkin and Thomas Tseng, "All Mixed Up," *Washington Post National Weekly,* June 16–22, 2003, 22.
157. Robert Putnam, "Bowling Together," *American Prospect,* February 12, 2002, 20–22; Robert Kuttner, "Enron: A Powerful Blow to Market Fundamentalists," *Business Week,* February 4, 2002, 20; and "An Industry Trapped by a Theory," *New York Times,* August 16, 2003, A25.
158. Anne Applebaum, "Small Government Is So 1990s," *Washington Post National Weekly,* October 11–17, 2004, 26.
159. David Brooks, "Running on Reform," *New York Times,* January 3, 2004, A15.
160. "The New Republicans," *New York Times,* December 28, 2003, WK8.
161. John McCain and Evan Bayh, "A New Start for National Service," *New York Times,* November 6, 2001, A21.
162. Frank Rich, "War Is Heck," *New York Times,* November 10, 2001, A23.
163. Richard Morin, "A Jittery Nation," *Washington Post National Weekly,* May 6–12, 2002, 34.
164. Thomas de Zengotita, "The Numbing of the American Mind," *Harper's,* April 2002, 33–40.
165. It certainly says something about American public life—it's probably better not to ask what—that in December 2003, President Bush's interview with Diane Sawyer drew a smaller viewing audience than an episode of *The Simple Life,* starring the egregious Paris Hilton. "Paris Hilton Outdraws Bush," *New York Times,* December 19, 2003, E32.

166. Aristotle, *Politics,* Loeb Classical Library edition, trans. H. Rackham (Cambridge: Harvard University Press, 1977), 207–221.
167. Steven Weisman, " 'Sort of a Deafening Silence'," *Washington Post National Weekly,* August 30–September 5, 2004, 20; Robin Toner and Richard Stevenson, "Bush Pledges a Broad Push toward Market-Based Policies," *New York Times,* November 4, 2004, P1.
168. Claudia Deane and Dan Balz, "The GOP Banks on Investors," *Washington Post National Weekly,* November 3–9, 2003, 12.
169. Krugman, "For Richer," 66, 76.
170. E. J. Dionne Jr., "A Test of Toughness," *Washington Post National Weekly,* August 23–29, 2004, 26.
171. Rich, "Sacrifice Is for Losers."
172. Ben Stein, "For Sale: The Ultimate Status Symbol," August 15, 2001, *New York Times,* August 15, 2004, BU3.
173. Greenspan is cited by Witte, "The Vanishing Middle Class."
174. Kevin Phillips, *Wealth and Democracy* (New York: Broadway Books, 2003); see also Paul Krugman, "Plutocracy and Politics," *New York Times,* June 14, 2002, A37.
175. Sheldon S. Wolin, *Tocqueville between Worlds* (Princeton: Princeton University Press, 2002), 564, 571; Samuel Bowles and Herbert Gintis, *Recasting Egalitarianism: New Rules for Markets, States and Communities* (London: Verso, 1999).
176. Andrew Jackson, Farewell Address, March 4, 1837, in *Messages and Papers of the Presidents,* ed. James D. Richardson (Washington, D.C.: Bureau of National Literature and Art, 1917), 3:308.
177. Robert Lane, *The Loss of Happiness in Market Democracies* (New Haven: Yale University Press, 2000).
178. James Skillen, " 'Ownership Society' Misconceived," *Capital Commentary* (Center for Public Justice), December 27, 2004.
179. Sheldon S. Wolin, *Politics and Vision: Continuity and Innovation in Western Political Thought* (Princeton: Princeton University Press, 2004), 601–606.
180. Frank Rich, "Harry Crushes the Hulk," *New York Times,* June 29, 2003, AR1.